"Powerful prose, honest and humble. Only a Marine could write this. I'd be proud to have Kacy in my gun-team. Semper Fi."
–Johnnie Clark, author of the bestselling military classic *Guns Up!*

"As introspective as he is entertaining, Tellessen uses a captivating blend of muscular and minimalistic prose to give us an uncomfortably honest look at where courage and nature diverge. *Freaks of a Feather* immediately separates itself from the litany of exploitative military accounts by avoiding political grandstanding or vicarious violence in favor of a remarkably intimate and often heart-pounding narrative. Despite this being his debut, Tellessen is able to use the deft touch of a seasoned writer to relay his story in a way that feels universal and yet wholly personal. This book will stay at the front of my mind and my shelf for years to come."
–James Wade, Spur Award-winning author of *All Things Left Wild* and *River, Sing Out*

"Kacy Tellessen joined the Marines and went to war because he read *The Iliad* in high school. A writer of great heart and mind, Tellessen, in rich, crisp prose, provides both gripping war stories and the deep insights of a person who knows that literature helps us to live."
–Rachel Toor, author and professor of creative writing

"Author Tim O'Brien's discussion of "happening truth" and "story truth" is an incredibly important concept in the telling of war. But for me, even more valuable than O'Brien's binary validation of "story truth" arising from the ashes of accuracy, is that built upon a foundation of brutal, honest, "happening truth." That is what Kacy Tellessen accomplishes with *Freaks of a Feather: A Marine Grunt's Memoir* and, if there is such a thing as literary justice, you will find his beautiful, brutal truth shelved alongside Sledge and Leckie and O'Brien."
–Lieutenant Colonel Russell Worth Parker, USMC, retired

"A marine's journey, honestly and eloquently depicted, realizing and accepting who he is through the means of the written word, the heroes within, tradition and expectations."

–Tyler James Carroll, combat veteran and co-founder of Dead Reckoning Collective

"Tellessen's memoir opens at the cyclic rate and never lets up. Freaks of a Feather is a book that you'll stick in your cargo pocket and never leave it more than one arm's distance until you've read it cover-to-cover."

–Major Thomas Schueman, USMC infantry officer and English instructor at the Naval Academy

"Powerful. Poetic. Honest. You will not find a victim or a hero in these pages. Instead, you get a regular grunt's view of the dangerous, tedious Iraq war without fanfare or histrionics. This is how you write a war memoir. A must read for military and civilian alike."

–Michael Ramos, Iraq vet, writer, and former editor at *OAF Nation*

FREAKS OF A FEATHER

FREAKS

OF A

FEATHER

A Marine Grunt's Memoir

Kacy Tellessen

Two chapters from this book ("Death Comes" and "Alonzo") were derived from
pieces the author previously published in *The New York Times* and *0-Dark-Thirty*
respectively.

Book and cover design by Kevin Breen
Cover image used with permission from RMI gear

ISBN: 978-1-7360127-3-4
Cataloging-in-Publication Data is available upon request

Manufactured in the United States of America

Published by
Latah Books, Spokane, Washington
www.latahbooks.com

Dedication

For Melissa, my wife and constant reader, and for the fallen, who stood in my place so that I can watch my babies grow.

1. Book Clubbing for Grunts

When we weren't walking the streets of Haqlaniyah with machine guns, we read. Books passed through our hands like contraband. We were often too tired to hold a conversation, but we still had energy to pass off paperbacks like dime bags.

We never called it a book club. But looking back, that time in Iraq was the closest I've come to being in one. Maybe it would be better to call us a roving band of savages with bookish tendencies, but that makes us sound a lot cooler than we were. In reality, we were just a pack of nerds who signed up to hold machine guns but never put down our books.

Our grunt book club didn't have a formal meeting time. We never gathered every second Thursday to drink rosé and talk smack. We had no structure. One of us would read something worth a shit, and it would pass hands until most of us had read it. I remember titles like *The Old Man and the Sea, The Shining, Helmet for My Pillow, With the Old Breed,* and The Wheel of Time series. This led to conversations about how much we loved or hated a given book, whenever a lull in operations was long enough to stand beside each other for more than a passing moment. We read quite a bit of junk, given that we were at the mercy of whatever books were sent or left behind at the Forward Operating Base. Fantasy and horror were common, and I suspect some of us may have been sneaking romance novels when no one was looking. We also read the classics, but only those we thought extolled our masculine and violent virtues, virtues we were desperately trying to adopt. Hemingway was stuffed into our packs, McCarthy atop an MRE box-turned-nightstand, Homer snuck onto post in flak jackets and gas mask bags.

Our little book club was central to my identity, my way of separating myself from a world where everyone dressed the same and had the same crappy haircut. Books gave me something to talk about other than killing, chasing women, and getting drunk. Most of us only partook in the last, so stimulating conversations were hard to come by, but when you found a fellow grunt that could not only read, but enjoyed it, there was a different kind of bond. A comfort in knowing you weren't alone.

One of the many pitfalls of signing your life away to the Marine Corps is that it whittles away your personal vocabulary. I was the jerk in high school who would learn a fancy-pants word in honors English, only to casually drop it into conversation among my peers. "Mr. F— sure can be a sequacious asshole." I got straight As despite barely knowing what I was saying. But the Marine Corps strangled these haphazardly constructed, erudite phrases. Syllables fell away so that fast, technical terms could take their place. Acronyms dominated communication, distilling complex ideas into quick syllable bursts.

Interspersed throughout this alien language is the word fuck; for a civilian, that one word might be the only intelligible thing they could pick out from our conversations on the range. I remember a phone call home during training when I called my parents and got the answering machine. What I thought I said was, "Hey, Mom and

Dad! Doing great here in the Mojave Desert. Training is chugging right along. Miss you guys. I'll call as soon as I can. Love you!" But when my parents played the message back to me it was more like: "Hey, Mom and Dad. It's fucking, um, fucking Tuesday. Hot as fuck out here. Training is going pretty good and shit, fucking hot though. Hopefully we can fucking wrap this shit up soon and get out of here. I'm already sick of this motherfucker. Anyways, fucking love you guys, I guess I'll try and fucking call you guys soon. Take care."

With books, I tried to stave off the slow creep of a complete infantry mind, though the first year in the Marine Corps I only read Corps-related things. I read the Marine Corps handbook, infantry tactics, and the Machine Gun Bible.

Along with the required manuals, I snuck in some military classics, but only because they were on the commandant's reading list. Books on the reading list were sold at the clothing store for overachievers like me. I read *Message to Garcia, Gates of Fire*, and *Guns Up!* I had already read *Guns Up!*, but my machine gun section leader made it required reading. There were practical tips about how to wear ammo belts around your neck: bullets facing outboard, always outboard. The book told us that the only people who die faster in a firefight than machine gunners are second lieutenants. We would die because everyone was shooting at the fire-breathing dragon we were lying behind; lieutenants would die because they were either lost or stupid.

As I started to form friendships in the company, we began to pass these books to one another. A Marine named Russell with chubby cheeks and a muscular body let me borrow a book about a numbered hill in Vietnam that Marines were told to take and hold at all costs. When he handed me the book, Russell said, "Dude, look at the pictures in the middle. There's a dude in there that looks just like you. It's fucking creepy. He's a crazy fuck too, you'll love it." I flipped to the picture and stared at a grainy black-and-white photo of a Marine with a cigarette dangling from his mouth and his blouse unbuttoned. Russell was right; it looked just like me. And I read the book as if it were me. I went on those night missions; I felt the terror as each thumping bootstep might trigger a booby trap that took my legs.

Before I could be counted as a member of the "boots-on-the-ground" club that the news reporters always talked about, I wanted to use reading as a way to live a hundred lives before stepping onto the battlefield. I think the others felt the same way. We read the war books like how-to manuals. Shoot this way. Say this thing. Kill with this or that, but always kill. Never crack, but know that everyone has a fracture point when the pressure becomes too much. We used books to walk in the bloody paper footprints of the Marines and soldiers who came before us.

I had a few close friends in my squad, but none better than Huth. Through the workup to Iraq, and the first few weeks of combat, Huth had become my best friend. I hadn't bestowed that title on a person since I was ten. We shared a filthy sense of humor, a love for old country music, and a desire to prove ourselves on the battlefield. The major difference between us was that Huth had never read a book, ever. He had been an athlete in school and as long as he kept making three pointers, he'd been allowed to abstain from the summer reading list.

Huth possessed a different intelligence. He could train a dog to hunt for him. He could track a buck through the Tennessee mountains. He never missed his target, and his knowledge of his trade as a rifleman was second to none. His mind was full of the tactics espoused in training. Where I pored over the manuals to memorize facts and data, Huth let himself be taught by combat vet instructors, missing nothing. His lack of enthusiasm for reading wasn't an indication of lesser intelligence; it was simply something he had never needed to get ahead. So, when I would lie back with some book that I thought made me look smart, Huth would chide me. One of his favorite expressions was, "Look at dork ass over here, reading another damn book." But as the weeks of our deployment dragged on with nothing to distract us, Huth wanted to know what in the hell was pulling me into those pages while a war carried on around us.

I had brought my high school copy of *The Iliad* with me to Iraq. The burred edges of the book, along with the dog-eared passages I'd marked, made the book look important, something worth poring over and over again. This wasn't lost on Huth. Every time he caught me pulling out the book, it would bring an insult or insinuation of homosexuality. I wouldn't respond with a retaliatory insult about him being tall and gangly, nor would I blow him a kiss. I would simply read aloud: "Closing, Meges gave him some close attention too – the famous spearman struck behind his skull, just at the neck-cord, the razor spear slicing straight up through the jaws, cutting away the tongue – he sank in the dust, teeth clenching the cold bronze."

Huth would smile, and I knew that each quote was pulling him closer and closer into the pages of the Greek epic. "He killed Astynous, then Hypiron, a frontline captain. One he stabbed with a bronze lance above the nipple, the other his heavy sword hacked at the collarbone, right on the shoulder, cleaving the whole shoulder clear of neck and back. And he left them there, dead."

He began to realize that I was immersing myself in war porn. Huth was a war movie junkie like the rest of us. I tried to explain to him the immersion of a book. I told him that the picture is created in your mind with the help of the author, but it is your unique creation. You fill in the untold details with your own perception, images from your subconscious mind rush in to fill the gaps left by the author. I made him understand that books create a symbiotic relationship between author and reader: an alligator letting a bird clean the rotting flesh from between his teeth. I told him that he would be able to decide exactly what it looks like when the bronze sword cleaves off a shoulder – he would control the blood spurt and the expression seen through the war helmet's visor.

Finally, when my quoting no longer sufficed, Huth asked to read it. When I handed it to him, I tried not to act too giddy. The first complete book that Huth would read in his life was one of the greatest works in the entire canon of western literature.

It took him a few weeks to get through it. He would occasionally ask questions, and I pretended I had the answers. We shared some of the same opinions: "That Achilles is kind of a pussy fart, ain't he? It's like, hey asshole, there's a damn war going on, and you're all pouting and shit in your tent. What the hell, man?"

When he finished and handed me back the book, he soberly told me thank you. There were no jokes about it being as gay as he thought it was going to be. He simply asked if I had any more books he could borrow. I never told him that most of the characters in the book were probably bisexual.

Most of the readers I knew carried a small library into Iraq with them. Carefully selected titles, most of them serious books that we wanted to read before we died. Other books came to the Forward Operating Base from moms and grandmas that threw in whatever was collecting dust on their bookshelves. They would send care packages of sweets and wrinkled paperbacks. Most were awful, but occasionally a gem would make its way into circulation. Bret Easton Ellis's *American Psycho* was one. A corpsman had brought the book with him, telling me it was one of his all-time favorites. The corpsman was good looking and unassuming, which may be why I can't remember his name. But I remember the book vividly.

I took *American Psycho* with me everywhere, even to places where reading may have gotten me killed. The story of a psychopath who wore a yuppie costume every day to conceal what was really inside appealed to me, I think, because I was the exact opposite. Since joining the Marines, I adopted the persona of a psychopath to conceal the chubby book lover I really was. If people thought I was a callous man who constantly teetered on the edge of violence, I would be seen as dangerous. I wanted to be viewed as the coral snake, with red touching yellow; a promise of dead fellows to come.

In reality, I was a scarlet kingsnake, hoping to fake it until I made it. Books were a part of this façade. When people looked at me and saw a huge machine gunner, covered in black and gray tattoos of death and strife, I wanted them to think they had me figured out, to know that I was a dumb, dangerous brute. But when I pulled out a copy of Emerson's collected works, I wanted them to know that they had no idea what I was.

The staff non-commissioned officers (NCOs) and officers, in particular, always looked at me quizzically, not quite sure what I was. They would often comment, "Hey, Tellessen. I didn't know you could read." I had a general disdain for officers because they thought their four years of college made them superior, a part of the aristocracy whose positions were attained through the relatively painless trial of lectures. They thought they were smarter than all of us, and they may have been, but I refused to believe it. Books, then, were my small act of rebellion against the aristocracy.

This yearning for a persona started earlier than the Corps for me. In high school, I'd found out what kind of person I wanted others to see. I was a fat kid growing up, fat and horribly ashamed of it. I played sports and would agonize over how tight my uniform fit compared to others. I escaped my blubbery torment by hiding in books and video games. I read Goosebumps and then Stephen King, scaring myself more often than not. All I knew was that I didn't want to be who I was, a fat nerd.

In high school, I dropped the weight but not the books.

I wanted to be athletic and brilliant, but being neither, I forced myself to work harder than those around me. I'm sure it can all be reduced down to evolutionary biology: I was just trying to make myself more attractive to the opposite sex. But most of the girls in my rural eastern Washington high school – a place where kids were bused in from towns with names like Waverly or Mt. Hope, towns so small they couldn't even claim a stoplight – weren't interested in talking books. I was the outsider who was allowed on the inside because I had struggled my way into athleticism. I was the captain of the football team and an honors student. I was a scared fat kid, wearing the mask of a cerebral athlete. Some things change; others never will.

I grew up in one of those lower-class vortexes that never lets people leave. The ones who escape are either exceptional or transient, not content with the alcoholism or drug addiction of rural eastern Washington. I saw my friends around me grooming themselves to become their parents: farmers, laborers, drunks, and drug addicts. I loved my parents, but I didn't want to become them. I wanted to be something different; I wanted to be something I didn't see when I looked around the Friday night football bleachers.

In both high school and the Marines, I carried my prop with me: a book. It was a prop I loved. If I didn't have a book in hand, it was always close by in a bag or vehicle. If I always had a book, I had no excuse not to read every day. I carried a book in my cargo pocket on nearly every patrol in Iraq.

I had a copy of Stephen King's *Gerald's Game* on me when we got the call that some tankers had been hit with a daisy-chained, improvised explosive device along route Boardwalk.

I had started reading *Gerald's Game* on the recommendation of the only Marine in the company who read more than I did. He was from Sweden and joined after watching innocent people leap to their deaths to avoid the flames of September 11th. He felt compelled to make a difference, to fight hate with a righteous hate. He could find no organization more fueled with righteous hate than the United States Marine Corps. As a half-blooded American, it was relatively easy for him to enlist.

He brought with him an accent that was slightly off, a love of milk chocolate, a set of ideals about right and wrong that made him formidable. And books. Others spent hundreds of dollars on video games and DVDs, but the Swede's shelves were lined with books. He introduced me to Cormac McCarthy, offering me a copy of *Blood Meridian,* which we both read as cowboy horror, not yet having the tools to dissect the craft of such a well-wrought novel. All we knew was that it was important, and the violence of the book somehow connected to our lives. We talked about the Judge being the devil, or the evil of mankind, and wondered if there was a difference.

Like many of the other readers in the company, the Swede loved fantasy novels. He gave me his copies of The Dark Tower series by Stephen King, and it reignited my affinity for the horror author. I became obsessed with the series and the author, which allowed me to ignore his disparaging view of grunts as simple fools too stupid for college. King was a hell of a writer, but he didn't know shit about grunts.

On the day we got the call to rescue those tankers, a bruised and tattered copy of King's sometimes overdone prose was stuffed into my left cargo pocket.

I had been sitting in my rack, reading King. Every time I shifted my weight, the fragile red metal bunk bed would creak and moan. I could hear the metallic groans from the beds of the other Marines in my squad, a symphony of discomfort. I twisted onto my side and stuck my book over the edge of my bed to catch the fluorescent light that hummed above. A nameless Marine from the Combat Operations Center pushed through the door, hard. I jumped and sat up, thinking the worst.

"Get your shit on and get to the COC," he said as the door swung shut behind him.

I stuffed the book into my pants that were on the ground next to my rack. The room erupted in wordless motion as we all dressed and donned our gear. As I pulled on my pants, I felt the rectangular shape of the Stephen King book ride up my leg and come to a rest at my left knee.

Some might call a book unnecessary weight when determining a combat load, but those critics are the ones who don't know the power and protection that prose can offer a grunt. My flak jacket and Kevlar came on next, then my gloves and ballistic glasses. Just outside our door, we kept an ammo can full of fragmentation grenades and other pyro: smoke grenades and pop-up flares. Frags weren't allowed in the hooch with us, but I always had the sneaking suspicion that if a frag cooked off outside our door, the thin, particle-board shield would do little to protect us. I grabbed two M67 fragmentation grenades, both adorned with Sharpie art. The first was marked up to look like a testicle, with black ink hairs jutting out in different directions; it contained the tag, "The left nut of the Green Weenie." The other grenade had a rudimentarily drawn smiley face and said, "EAT SHIT AND DIE TERRORIST SCUM." I shoved the left nut and smiley face into their respective pouches and ran across the courtyard in the FOB to the briefing room.

The makeshift base was once a school, located on the northwest tip of Haqlaniyah. It faced a bridge leading to another small city that we called Bonnie-D. It was a central location, a great place for a school and a terrible spot for a Forward Operating Base (FOB). Most of the city had views that looked down into the FOB; it felt like we were in a fishbowl or maybe a colosseum. The FOB consisted of a series of courtyards, presumably once playgrounds, and a series of classrooms turned grunt barracks. They never told us what age group the school used to serve, but I always pictured elementary students. Small boys and girls in uniforms ready to learn about the world.

The run was short, less than fifty yards of flat old playground, before our path dipped down some stairs into the old principal's quarters turned Combat Operations Center (COC). The run was just long enough for us to consider what we were getting into before we reached the briefing room. In that fifty-yard dash, you could create an elaborate plot in your head as to what was waiting outside the wire. Each thumping bootstep jarred loose an image of the possible war. In the beginning of the deployment, my possible war was always filled with glorious combat, fierce gunfights, and near misses. In the end, I imagined only screams and blood.

The CO waited in the briefing room. I don't think any of us particularly liked him, at least I never talked to anyone who had kind words to offer, but we respected the rank, just as we were taught. The CO began to speak as soon as he got the signal from my squad leader, Corporal Gardner, that all Marines were present and accounted for.

"Alright gents, we had some tankers coming up Boardwalk that got hit with an IED. Not sure how bad it is. Expect the worst. We need you to double-time over there and secure the site. We've got mounted patrols headed there now. Get there, secure the area, set up an overwatch. Get it done."

We scrambled out of our seats, our gear and weapons banging off the newly constructed benches, and ran outside. Our patrols were normally slow and methodical once we made it past the bridge just outside the FOB. We would run across the bridge, hoping to zig and zag away from the gunfire that erupted whenever we crossed it. Then we would slow down, try and use misdirection and caution to avoid predictability.

Not this day. This day, we ran across the bridge and just kept running. We bounded from alleyway to street corner, scaled walls, and ran through people's backyards. I was worried we were going to lose someone along the way. I thought of one of us turning left instead of right and running to the edge of the street corner, getting separated and becoming the first Marine captured in Iraq. The first Marine to get his head sawed off on LiveLeak.

The gory fantasy dissolved, replaced with pain, as the air in my lungs ignited and turned to fire. Sweat soaked through my cammies, legs, and back, leaving amorphous silhouettes of moisture anytime I leaned up against a wall or car to cover another's movement. The sweat seeped into the corners of my squinted eyes. I could feel the book resting against my thigh, its rectangular mass bouncing off walls and cars, but I wasn't thinking about whether the heroine would be eaten by the stray dog chewing on her husband's face. I was thinking about the fire in my chest and the tankers bleeding out on the street.

When we made it to the blast site, the Humvee was upside down, wheels still slowly spinning. The explosion had picked up the 6,400-pound, tan, tactical turtle and placed it on its back. From inside the Humvee, I heard a screaming Marine: "Get me the fuck out. GET ME THE FUCK OUT. PLEASE. PLEASE. PLEASE."

Marines stood next to the door. My eyes shifted again to the slowly spinning tire, a small rock wedged into the rubber making its lethargic revolution.

"FUCKING PLEASE."

The rock disappeared, making its way around the dark side of its orbit.

"Okay. Okay. OKAY. CAN YOU PLEASE GET ME THE FUCK OUT?"

A pry bar slid against the metal of the Humvee, its teeth biting underneath the door. A Marine grunted and pried, grunted and pried.

"FUCK FUCK FUCK."

More grunting and prying. I watched for the small rock on the tire to come back around. But the Marine with the pry bar rested his hand on the tire, stopping the slow revolution with the weight of exhaustion. I wondered if that was how all revolutions ended.

We bent the door open, and the first Marine clawed his way out. "Thank you. Thank you. Thank you. Get them out, get them out. Get the others out."

The Marine who crawled from the Humvee had eyes that opened too far. The black disk of his pupils nearly eclipsed his irises, and the wild eyes and blank stare made him look more animal than man. We pulled him the rest of the way out and rolled him onto a litter. Two Marines grabbed the long handles that ran through the green canvas and picked him up. Now that he'd been freed, he pleaded for his friends: "Please get them out, get them out. Just pull them out."

I kneeled at the corner of the Humvee. Another patrol had moved into overwatch, so we were now just aiding with the medevac. I had a strong back and stomach, so Corporal Gardner asked me to help move the other tankers who had been trapped inside.

The next Marine pulled out was a huge man who wasn't speaking anything intelligible. I thought I heard him moan, "Fuck," but it was hard to tell.

Once he was clear of the Humvee, his gear was stripped and a corpsman cut away his cammies with a pair of trauma shears. Blood, mixed with dirt and gravel from the street, was smeared across his face in a textured testament to the blast.

He moaned and looked up, as if searching for relief in the cloudless desert sky. The corpsman had cut off all his clothes, so he lay naked on the litter. He seemed unaware of his nakedness and put forth no effort to cover himself. The violence of the explosion had returned him to a state of infancy, naked and unable to communicate. Blood oozed out of the white bandages spotting his body. It all looked too bright to be real, as if the special effects guy had gone colorblind.

I found myself at the head of the litter, my hands on the poles. The corpsman counted to three, and we lifted. I mentally prepared myself for the strain, expecting him to feel like a ton of rocks. But when I lifted, he almost seemed weightless, like the blast had not only taken his mental faculties, but his physical weight too. When I picked up my end, I accidentally jolted the man. He winced and moaned, then pinched his eyes shut.

I wanted to say something meaningful, something that would make him feel better, but the vision of his body returned me to a simpler time as well. Instead, I just repeated over and over that it was going to be okay, it was going to be okay. Of course, I had no idea how things were going to turn out for the Marine. I think I was talking more to myself than to him. I wanted to believe everything was going to be okay. I wanted to hear what my mother would have told me when I skinned my knee in the driveway. The man shook his head, and I wondered if he knew something I didn't. I suspected he did.

We loaded him in the rear of a high-back Humvee and watched as it took off toward a landing zone somewhere in the open desert. The three wounded Marines would be flown to Al Asad Air Base, where they would be stabilized. Those deemed severe enough would then be taken to Landstuhl, Germany. Then they would fly back to the States where their war would never end.

I moved my machine gun, slung around my back, into my hands and took my place around the cordon protecting the blast site. Marines rifled through the rubbish, eager to find anything they could "acquire." Everything in the Humvee, including weapons and optics, would be written off by the military as a total loss. I saw a

Marine stuff a pistol into his waistband, another nonchalantly put a pair of night vision goggles into a drop pouch. I looked at potential plunder for a while, enticed by what macabre trophy I might bring back home.

I saw a small pocket-sized book leaning against the curb, its plastic cover patterned with desert camouflage. It was a King James Bible, the kind handed out to us on our way to the new holy war, which was how some saw this fight. Not a war on terror, but a war on beliefs. The classic Us versus Other. That's not what I believed. I didn't think I even believed in a god. I surprised myself by picking up the book and sniffing it. It smelled of sweat and sulfur. I had tried reading Dante's *Inferno* multiple times, but I lacked the grit to get past the first few levels of hell. I thought this might be the smell that Dante and Virgil smelled when they abandoned all hope. As the Bible rested against my nose, I wondered if it was what saved the man in the Humvee. Maybe his version of an omnipotent, finger-snapping creator was right, and I was wrong to trust my ever-evolving transcendent ape version of the story. Right or wrong, I stuffed the Bible into my pocket next to Stephen King. I wasn't religious, but I did have a hypocritical belief in good luck.

I dwelled on good and bad luck as we waited for the wreckers to come and pick up the Humvee's metal remains. I couldn't decide whether the Marines who hit the IED were lucky or not. They had the bad luck of picking the wrong street, but the good fortune of not being totally eviscerated. The crew that came to pick up the Humvee walked with a mechanical drowsiness. Whatever pep or vigor had animated their bodies when they first rolled from their racks this morning had vanished, replaced with the autopilot of muscle memory. I could see that they had done this many times. I assumed they would do it many more before our time was through.

The convoy carrying the wreckage left with its metallic casualty headed for the vehicle graveyard outside of the Haditha Dam. That place stood as a testament to the effectiveness and sophistication of an enemy that many of us considered simple "goat fuckers." Much easier to kill a "goat fucker" than to kill an intelligent human being capable of cunning, slyness, and bravery.

Our patrol back to the FOB was slow and painful. The sweat of the day had crystalized in the creases around my eyes, which felt like sand each time I squinted to make out a sniper or IED that wasn't really there. We mustered enough strength for another zig-zagging sprint across the bridge. We were slow and easy targets. Thankfully, the snipers of the city had thought they had accomplished enough for one day. We made it back into friendly lines without further incident.

After the debrief, where Corporal Gardner rightfully criticized our sloppy patrol back to the FOB, I sat outside our hooch. A sandbag wall had been erected outside our door, and we could now smoke outside with no gear on. Alcohol and drugs were forbidden, so other vices grew in proportion to fill their absence.

I lit a cigarette and reached into my cargo pocket, nudging aside the Bible and grabbing the familiar red cover of *Gerald's Game*. The first thirty pages were damp with sweat. I noticed a small smear of blood on my wrist, a reminder that the war was real and no amount of reading could save me. In the luxury of this temporary safety, I ignored the blood and stowed myself away safely in the story of someone else's suffering. I leaned forward on an ammo crate, inhaling the smoke, and letting it lazily escape my open mouth, the smoke rolling up my cheeks and past my eyes. I read until I didn't think my eyes could take anymore. I had four hours until the next patrol.

I stuffed the book back into my pocket and looked out across the courtyard. A patrol was getting ready to leave the wire. They were lined up in formation, waiting for the final word. I saw a member of the book club standing in full body armor. He had a strange-sounding German name that we collectively shortened to Fresh. We enjoyed the same books, but mostly we just drank too much together. Our book club relationship was similar, I think, to that shared by unhappy and overworked wives who flock together to escape their families and guzzle Pinot Noir.

Fresh would make margaritas in the barracks that had so much booze in them, they would turn the premade mix's artificial lime green color a muddled sewage brown. He was from Southern California, raised in a good neighborhood, and from a nice family. He could have been or gone anywhere he wanted to. But like the rest of us, he was a serial romanticizer.

I longed for a night of sewageritas and conversation that had nothing to do with Iraq or IEDs — a therapy session where we could pretend that the most important thing to talk about was whether or not Roland Deschain of Gilead would ever make it to the fucking Dark Tower. We didn't need to talk about Boardwalk and bleeding Marines because we had books. I patted the book in my pocket with a nicotine-and-blood-stained hand. I knew Fresh would love this Stephen King book. I would try to get it to him as soon as possible.

We were all posers to a certain degree, boys desperately seeking identity. We shared books, and we shared the romanticism that has been driving young boys to war since the poets of the oral tradition passed down the stories of Beowulf and Achilles. We were from everywhere, from every background, every social class, every race. None of those usual sources of division mattered.

What mattered to us was physical and mental aptitude, love of country, and love of books. I'm from the middle of nowhere in eastern Washington, the son of a heavy equipment operator who grew up shoveling pig shit. Yet I felt like I was somehow related to a Hispanic Marine named Torres. On the surface, we couldn't be more different. Other than the differing shades of skin pigment,

Torres grew up in Pasadena, California, an alien planet to my Spangle, Washington. He took meticulous care of his clothing. I once watched as he ironed his socks and underwear. Yet somehow, we both manifested the same world view. We had the same desire to test ourselves with a Spartan lifestyle when the world around us seemed to be softening. We were both spurred into action by September 11th, feeling that something had to be done. And if not us, then who? So, when we both read Steven Pressfield's *Gates of Fire*, it was no surprise that we both fantasized about standing next to a King Leonidas and becoming legend. We were all different, we were all the same.

Books kept a lot of us together after our enlistment. In phone calls and text messages we would recommend books to each other. We would often call to tear apart the latest bullshit movie or book about Iraq. Conversations would always lead back to our book club days, those days when we thought we were the center of the universe, those days when there was a clear protagonist and antagonist. It was bibliotherapy in every sense of the word, and books kept us together despite the miles and years that separated us from both the war and each other.

The Marine Corps was the lighthouse that we all saw from our respective high schools and colleges. We were idealists and romantics, nerdy degenerates who grew up with Big Bird and Conan the Barbarian. We believed in good stories, thinking we could live one if only we dared. We were tied together by a unique moment in history, by our voluntary service during a time of war. But what really stitched us together were the stories.

The Marine Corps is built on stories. Recruiters and drill instructors act as bards of an epic poem. They spin yarns of rough and drunken revolutionaries in Tun Tavern that swaggered into a bar and volunteered to create the republic. They elevate The Battle of Iwo Jima to the same status as The Battle of Thermopylae.

We already wanted to serve, but when we heard or read the stories of America's Spartans, we felt we had no choice. It's hard, though not impossible, to make a hero's journey in a backyard, and whether we want to admit it or not, that's what we were all after: a good story. A life worthy of being read.

2. The Making

I joined the Marines because I read *The Iliad*. It was assigned summer reading going into my sophomore year of high school. The book's cover had a stone statue of a Bronze Age warrior with a plumed helmet and a spear held high over his shoulder. The black background to the Penguin Classic Edition exposed a few small fissures in the stone statue. The book sat on my faux oak dresser for most of the summer, staring at me as I walked past it each day. Beneath the book was a white rabbit fur, which I personally selected for a bedding because I thought the book looked more impressive on a dead animal skin, but if the rabbit skin was turned over, it would reveal a novelty roadkill menu that I had bought as a child from the world famous 10,000 Silver Dollar Bar in Haugen, Montana. Once I reached a certain age, I turned the fur over from its satirical dinner choices and pretended that it was a serious piece of room décor. I liked the book being out for display, its black corners starkly contrasting the snow-colored fur. I thought just having a book like that made a person smarter. I would even go so far as to set it out on the kitchen table when company was expected as a conversation starter. "Oh, that old thing? Just a book I'm reading for my honors English class." But still, I didn't read it.

I procrastinated for most of the summer, being sucked in by video games or movies that I had already ingested a couple hundred times. But as the last violent August heat wave arrived, I opened the book. Two-a-day football practices were about to begin, which meant that I had two weeks to read the book before school started back. I read the introduction and can remember being horrified that the book was going to be as dry and boring as the scholarly writing that introduced the material. I chipped away at the introduction like a laborer with a claw hammer, not enjoying the work but knowing that it had to be done. Finally, I turned the page to the first lines of the epic:

> Rage – Sing, Goddess, Achilles' rage,
> Black and murderous, that cost the Greeks
> Incalculable pain, pitched countless souls
> Of heroes into Hades' dark,
> And left their bodies to rot as feasts
> For dogs and birds, as Zeus' will was done.

I was enthralled. Every challenge from champion to champion made me fidget on my navy blue futon. I would shift on my transforming couch-bed and smile, sometimes letting out an audible "Holy shit," before going on. It only took me a few days to finish the book. I read until my eyes burned: the fighting, the bravery, the hubris. Hubris was a word that I wouldn't learn until I finally stepped into class a few weeks later. My English teacher, Mr. Carty Strait, had written it on the board with no definition. He asked, "Does anyone know what this word means?" I wanted desperately to know; I was embarrassed that I didn't know, so I just looked down at my notepad and pretended to scribble notes:

I don't fucking know, please God don't call on me. When no one answered, he carefully placed the two puncturing marks of a colon on the board, then wrote in blue dry erase: an overweening pride. The definition stuck, and the word became one of my favorites. It was a word that I would try and drop into casual conversation when I wanted to sound impressive, not realizing that using words you barely understood made you sound more like an asshole than an intellectual. But I really did love the word. I loved the notion of a pride so powerful that it had the capacity to destroy.

I had always been taught to take pride in my work, that anything worth doing was worth doing right, whether that be building a house or cleaning a toilet, but I never thought of pride as a force that had the power to destroy worlds. But that's what I found in *The Iliad*. It seemed to me, and still does, that pride is a precursor to greatness. Maybe that was one of the messages that Homer was trying to convey, that to be truly great is to know pain and suffering at the hands of the things you hold most dear. But the first time I read the text, I wasn't trying to read between the lines; I was simply reading a war story, and as such, I loved it.

The Iliad jarred something loose in my brain, some unknown mason jar of perspective that fell off the shelf of my consciousness, shattering the old way I had of looking at the world. When I walked onto the football field, I no longer saw plastic pads and forehead acne. I saw unarmed conflict on a hash-marked battlefield, where bronze armor was exchanged for the hard plastic kind, and the warring generals wore baseball caps and taught history during the daytime. I saw simulated battle, and it made me love the sport more than ever. I was never a talented athlete, but I worked harder than most, so it gave me an edge as the game wore on. They could be bigger and stronger than me, and most of the time they were, but they couldn't outwork me. In the third and fourth quarter, I would always start to overtake whoever I was lined up against. They would take plays off, and I wouldn't. I used to pretend that each play was life or death. I pretended that the simulated combat was for real. *The Iliad* was changing my life.

The text had everything a kid could want: huge battles, superhuman heroes, and gods with unimaginable powers. But for me, the allure was beyond that. These characters existed in a world where their lives were dedicated to the art of war. Achilles was supposedly the baddest man of the Bronze Age, but he wasn't my favorite – an irony because Achilles shared the most in common with the ideal United States Marine. He was lethal, prideful to a level of insanity, and he led an amphibious assault on a defended beachhead. But when I read about his deeds and actions, I thought he was kind of an ass. I hated how he turned from the fighting because his feelings were hurt. I thought that if he were truly the greatest warrior to ever live, he would have been able to compartmentalize his wounded pride in order to stay in the fight. I admired Odysseus in all his wisdom and Diomedes in his fearless berserker's rage – a rage so fierce it threatened even the gods. I loved the way Homer depicted combat, the spear thrusts and the sword slashes. The contrast between the orderly ranks of Greek and Trojan lines and the chaos of the actual battle. The book was a gateway story for me. It led me to novels and memoirs that allowed me to charge the beaches of Normandy and patrol through the humid death of Vietnam.

It was in the books on the Vietnam War that I found the Marines. As an American, I always had the Marine Corps in my periphery, but it was an abstract concept to me when I was younger. The Marines were a group invoked in conversation when the speaker needed an example of extreme discipline that bordered the limits of sanity. Any Marine I ever met was treated with a particular reverence – most of the time after he or she left the room. "Hey, did you know Jim was in the Marines? I guess he was in the shit back in Nam."

John Wayne was practically the patron saint of my home, and I can remember watching him play Sergeant Stryker, charging headlong onto the black-death beaches of Iwo Jima. I watched with my father in silence, not knowing that I was weaving the accumulated mythos of John Wayne movies into my moral fabric. It was only when I picked up books about the Marines in Vietnam that I came to realize they were just people, exceptional people, but flesh and blood people just like me. Or, at least people like who I wanted to become.

The first book about the Vietnam Marines that I read was one I pulled off my grandfather's bookshelf. He had been dead for years, but his home in the hills of Springdale, Washington was left nearly untouched. The cabin in the woods had become a shrine to my grandpa, a place where the family could go and remember the man and the world he used to live in. The house and the property served as a kind of Parthenon for my family's mythology. Despite our reverence for his place, we simply called it the ranch.

The ranch always seemed primordial to me in my youth. Maybe it was because the earliest memories of the place involved an old man, bent and gray, working with seemingly ancient equipment and implements. Maybe it was because the woods seemed like they had existed forever and would continue to exist long after any of us were around to see them remain unchanged. A creek ran through the property, and the woods seemed to crawl out of that slim ribbon of water; first on its belly, in the bushes that lined the creek; then on its hands and knees in the broad-leafed, deciduous trees that hung close to the water; and finally, on its feet, in the towering pines and tamaracks that always made me feel so small. The deeper I walked into the woods, as the sun was reduced to sharp shafts of light crisscrossing the path, the more upright and ancient it seemed.

The cabin sits on a hill overlooking a meadow where my

grandpa's cows used to graze. I could always hear the creek before my eyes could locate the liquid fracture that ran through the center of the property. It was in that cabin that I found the book buried in between some classic Louis L'Amour westerns. In bold black print on the white spine of a thin paperback stood the words MARINE SNIPER. I gently pulled the book from the shelf, careful not to let the other dust-covered paperbacks fall to the ground. My grandpa must have been a voracious reader – the bookshelf reached nearly to the ceiling, and there were boxes of books in the backroom. I pulled the book out and turned the cover toward me. A Marine in a ghillie suit stared back, his face painted different shades of black and green, a white feather sticking out of his boonie cover at a dangerous angle. I sat down next to the cast-iron Fisher wood stove and didn't get back up until I finished the book.

The book detailed the life and times of Gunnery Sergeant Carlos Hathcock, a legend of the Marine Corps. There was a picture of him on the back page, sitting in his den, looking unsuspecting and ordinary. He looked a little like my grandpa, a WWII veteran who had come back from the war but kept his story to himself. A glance at Hathcock walking down the street wouldn't betray his skills as one of the deadliest humans to ever pick up a rifle. His eyes told a different story though, even in the black-and-white photo. There was an intensity to them, a vigor that transcended print. He was known for his ability to shoot straight and endure unimaginable pain, all in the name of a single well-placed bullet. He wore a white feather in his cap, a gesture of bravado, a taunt to anyone foolish enough to come after him. Prior to reading *Marine Sniper*, my heroes had been athletes and action movie stars. I forgot about all the muscle-bound actors and leading passers as soon as I read about that sharpshooter from Arkansas who learned to shoot as a small boy, hunting food for his family's dinner table. There were real-life heroes walking past me in the grocery store, and I didn't even realize they were out there. I had a new obsession: the American fighting man.

I read any book about Marines or Vietnam that I could get my hands on. In my search for the next war story, I found a book called *Guns Up!* The book is a firsthand account from the Marine machine gunner Johnnie M. Clark who served in Vietnam. He survived in a world where a machine gunner's life expectancy during a firefight was measured in seconds. The machine gunner was the antithesis of the sniper. Where the sniper remained hidden, firing only that single well-aimed shot, the machine gunner sat behind a roaring mechanical dragon, spewing hellfire and hate, drawing nearly all the enemy fire to himself. The sulfur tips of the machine gunner's tracers glowed like a stream of red hateful consciousness, telling all the grunts in the area where they should be shooting. The consequence of such bravery, though, was that the tracers could be followed to the machine gunner's own position. It was a job that demanded not only the physical and mental toughness needed to carry the weight, but the grit to stay behind the gun when it seemed like you were the only man on the battlefield. The book followed the growth of a Marine from being a boot (barely out of training) to a hardened veteran. It detailed the horror of the Vietnam War and the bravery of the men who waded through brimstone and filth for a cause that seemed apparent only to themselves. Once in Vietnam, they were fighting for each other's survival. Sometimes it's as simple as that. Maybe most times it's as simple as that. The picture of war that Clark painted was bleak and disturbing; it was harrowing and exhilarating; it was beautiful and repulsive; it was both selfless and selfish; it was exactly what I was feeling as a teenager, only distilled to the most potent of spirits. It was everything I wanted.

After *Guns Up!* it was a forgone conclusion: I would become a Marine no matter the cost. But I kept my decision a secret. I wasn't ashamed of service. I was, however, afraid that people would see how I wasn't made of the same stuff they use to make Marines. Like every teenager ever, I was outrageously insecure. If I would have looked in the mirror with any clarity, I would have seen the captain of the football team who was damn-near a straight-A student (fucking math). But all I ever saw were the blemishes, pimples, and pockmarks of failure. The Marine Corps was to be my spiritual Proactiv, my cure-all, my way to kill my weaknesses once and for all.

The only person I consulted about this decision was myself, who was notorious for romanticizing life. I had daily internal conversations that weighed the pros and cons of a decision of this magnitude, but I always rigged the scales, slipping stones on the side of the Corps when my rational brain looked away. Really, I only addressed the negatives so that I could prepare arguments that I might face if people questioned my decision. I expected a few teachers and relatives to tell me I was throwing my life away and turning my back on a promising academic career. But I knew I would have the support of my immediate family. My brothers would be on board, if only because they were too busy to care, and I was certain that my parents would be thrilled that they had raised a young man with such a strong sense of duty. I felt like they had to know I was different, that something like this had always been secretly guiding my azimuth. They had all witnessed my obsession with G.I. Joes and the VHS copies of *Uncommon Valor* and *Aliens* that I used to watch religiously. They had to have seen this coming.

After a secret meeting with a fast-talking recruiter, I felt like I had all the ammunition I would need to tell my parents about my decision to enlist. I had facts, figures, and carefully crafted recruiting slogans that I could regurgitate on command. I had a few rebuttals prepared, should things get out of hand. The first was that I wanted to do something meaningful with my life so that I would have interesting stories to tell my unborn grandchildren. Second, I wasn't sure what I wanted to study in college yet, so why not take a four-year sabbatical to find myself and what interested me. Thirdly, the Marine Corps was literally the finest fighting force the world had ever known, just ask my recruiter. I saw no holes. It seemed airtight. I was excited to see the pride beaming off my parents' faces when I told them the big news.

Like too many families, we usually ate dinner in front of the TV. My mom had brought home Papa Murphy's pizza, and a slice of their supreme pie sat on my lap. The pizza's cheese had begun to ooze off the slice, spreading out in amoeba-shaped blobs over the blue eggshell pattern of the ceramic plate. I stared at the pizza, looking at the bright red pepperonis, the red onions that were more purple than red, and the asteroid-shaped sausages that dotted the slice in a random-impact pattern. I studied the pizza to avoid looking at my parents, who sat in silence, watching the nightly news. I glanced up from my untouched pizza just as a serious-looking news anchor with a crooked nose listed off the current casualty numbers for the wars in Iraq and Afghanistan.

Instead of waiting for the tactically appropriate moment to discuss my enlistment, I quickly blurted out my decision to join. On the TV screen, a Humvee smoldered. My prepared talking points evaporated out my eyeballs. As the awkward silence reached its soul-crushing crescendo, I shoved an inappropriately large chunk of pizza into my mouth and filled the silence with slow bovine smacks and chomps. My futile thought process was that if I was chewing food, I wouldn't have to field any questions.

My dad shifted in his seat, "You're going to do what?" My mom didn't speak. She simply placed both of her hands over her eyes and remained silent as Dad's look continued to bore holes of fatherly disappointment straight through me. "Now why in the hell would you want to go and do something like that?"

I had a contingency plan for this unlikely situation. Although I was expecting a little more enthusiasm, I had gone through this kind of conversation at least a hundred times in my head. I prepared to speak, to bring it all back to my impenetrable talking points, but all I did was shove more pizza into my mouth. I chewed. They stared.

Dad furrowed his brow. "You know there's a war going on, right?"

I took the question as rhetorical and continued to chew. Of course, I knew there was a war going on. The war was the great pull – my chance to prove my worth. If I'd had the wherewithal, I would have told him that I didn't want some other kid standing in my place, simply because I didn't have the spine for it. But still, I only chewed.

Instead of articulating my stance, which was well thought out, I simply told them that I always wanted to be a Marine. Then I got up from the couch, grabbed two more slices of pizza, walked into my room and closed the door. I had a bookshelf in my room teeming with my heroes. I would eat pizza and read about the superhuman feats of the Marine Corps demigods.

***

If I could go back, I would tell them about *The Iliad*. I would tell them that my decision wasn't based on blind patriotism or a desire to escape them. It was something much stronger. There was something that I felt was always pulling me toward war. I would tell them that it wasn't just the fighting that attracted me; it was the discipline, the order of it all. When I looked at my hometown, I didn't see the types that woke up at four thirty in the morning to run five miles and do burpees until they puked. I saw binge drinkers and overweight seasonal workers who were content with the status quo. I wasn't content with my position in life. I wanted the discipline that I saw when I looked at a pair of dress blues. I thought that if I could only taste the legendary discipline of the Marine Corps, I could do anything, anytime, anywhere. My decision wasn't about the next four years; it was about who and what I wanted to be for the rest of my life.

We had watched the towers fall in the same living room where I told them of the path I wanted to walk down. After what we had watched together, on an endless loop for months, how could any able-bodied young man not go off and fight against that evil? That would go against every John Wayne movie I ever watched with my dad. That would go against everything I wanted to be. I believed in the cause. Though experience has an ugly way of showing us the folly of our ways, I never doubted the reasons for invading Iraq. This is a difficult stance to hold today, but all I can say is that I believed what I read. I remember reading Newsweek every Wednesday before my Current World Problems class, entranced by articles detailing Saddam's enormous cache of WMDs. When Colin Powell was on my television pleading the case for war, I believed him. I thought we had no choice; I knew I didn't. Honestly, I think I wanted to be a Marine regardless of the fight. I needed to be a Marine, and what the hell is a Marine without a war to fight?

I don't blame my wonderfully ignorant high school self for not being able to articulate these reasons. As a teenager, talking to your parents about your weekend plans is difficult enough, let alone a decision with the magnitude of military service. Nor do I blame my parents for their reactions. They saw a good student who had a shot at being a college athlete if he worked hard and got lucky. But I was done with the simulated combat that football offered; I wanted the real thing. Mom and Dad eventually came around, even coming with me to the recruiter's office so I could join before I turned eighteen. Dad called the recruiter a lying son of a bitch before signing the papers.

My reasons for joining the fight were largely a byproduct of reading. The romanticized accounts of war that I read created too strong a pull for me to resist. I willingly opened my ears to the siren's song and pointed my ship toward the rocks. I read a history written in blood, horror, and heroism, and wanted desperately for history to repeat itself. Illogically, I never considered that I could be killed; I might have thought I couldn't be killed, that the bathtub in our double-wide trailer was my own River Styx, and my mother the sweet Irish-Native American Thetis. My irrational, youthful optimism selectively omitted the eventual death of Achilles. Didn't I think Achilles was an asshole anyways? But I guess it didn't matter anymore; the papers had been signed, and the date for boot camp loomed on the horizon like a towering cumulonimbus, occasionally scarring the sky with electric bolts of self-doubt and fantasy.

3. Processing

The recruiter's office was in North Spokane, behind the Babies-R-Us that used to be the Toys-R-Us. I don't think anyone visited that street unless they were joining the military or buying meth. I was nervous going in, not sure what I would find behind the glass doors. In my mind I had elevated the recruiter to a level he may or may not have deserved. I was eager to impress, and as a result, was a tangled ball of nerves.

I gave myself too much time to get there, arriving a solid hour before my appointment. I drove past the office, not wanting to seem desperate by showing up too early. I drove past an ice rink and a tax preparation business. I drove past a car wash and then a bar. I turned around and did it again, driving the same stretch of road as the minutes ticked away. I made it back to the parking lot with half an hour to spare, enough time to nervously fidget in my car for ten minutes. I tried to open a book, *American Spartans*, but by the time I made it halfway through the first sentence, I was going through the motions of reading individual words and not comprehending the sentences. I was worried the recruiter would sniff me out immediately. I was worried he would laugh in my face before showing me the door to the Air Force recruiter.

I took a deep breath and stepped out of my car, slamming my door a little too hard. I looked back at the 1980 Cadillac Eldorado and cringed at the sight of the swaying fuzzy tits that hung from the rearview mirror. They were a gift from my older brother, who told me that they tied the whole vehicle together. I thought about going back to the car and throwing them in the back seat, afraid that the recruiter would want some fresh air and see that the potential recruit was some pervert. I would plead to him that I wasn't a pervert. I just had terrible taste and a poor sense of humor. I now worried that a pair of novelty breasts from the local Spencer's would be my downfall, my Achilles' areolas.

I was thinking of plush breasts as a means of destruction when I entered through the front door. The Marine recruiter's office was the first on the right. The building housed a recruiter for every military branch, but I wanted nothing to do with the others. I admired them, but the Marine Corps was at the top of my invented military hierarchy. I opened the front door of the office and immediately regretted not knocking first. The walls of the room were covered in blatant Marine Corps propaganda. I knew it was all designed to entice me to join, but that didn't diffuse any of its effectiveness. The poster that asked if I had what it took stood as an open-ended challenge that I was desperate to answer. Did I? I was both sure of my ability to succeed in the Marines and terrified that I was lying to myself.

Sitting behind a cheaply made laminated wood desk sat my recruiter. He smiled at me when I walked into the room and stood. He was a good-looking Black man clad in dress service charlies, which is the dress uniform of the Marines with the blue pants and short-sleeved tan shirt. Because the man was a sergeant, a thick red line ran down the sides of both his legs. He would later tell me that they were called blood stripes, but I had already looked that up. I read that the stripe was meant to pay homage to the sacrifice of the Marine officers and non-commissioned officers in the 1847 Battle of Chapultepec in Mexico. Years later I would find out that the blood stripe really came to be because it looked good. The Battle of Chapultepec did take place, but it was attached to the red fabric after the uniform changes had been made. It turned out that it was just the drill instructors spinning a yarn, assigning meaning where they thought there should be. But at the time, I looked at the blood stripes with a reverence for the saber-wielding Marines that died a glorious death, building the footing for the legend of the Marine Corps. I was an easy mark.

The creases in his uniform were immaculate, perfectly sectioning off the chest. The ribbons and name tapes were in exact symmetry. I couldn't see a single wrinkle in the uniform. My eyes were drawn to the ribbons, but I had no idea what any of them meant, only that I wanted some of my own. I was impressed with the discipline that it must have taken him just to get dressed in the morning. This wasn't a pair of jeans and a hoodie; this seemed more like a superhero's costume.

The recruiter smiled, but I didn't quite buy it. His smile seemed to be more of a uniform item than the genuine article. "Twenty minutes early, I like it." There was another recruiter in an identical desk to our right. He was talking to a feral-looking teenager who had an unkempt mop of sandy blond hair. The teenager didn't look up at me, but the recruiter nodded in my direction. I followed my recruiter into a back office that was more like a supply closet.

There was another cheap desk and little else. He laid out a series of thick plastic cards with words like "honor," "duty," and "professional" written on them. They looked like his nametag, like he could have plucked one off the table and inserted it perfectly into his nametag holder. I wondered if it was that easy once I left, if all you had to do was pick it up and pretend long enough for the plastic nametag to fit. He asked me to select the words that best described myself. I made sure I selected the words that I thought he wanted me to choose: honor, courage, commitment, steadfastness. The words felt as plastic as they looked as I slid them in front of me. They were words that I wanted to describe myself with, not the words that I thought actually described me. What act of bravery had I ever participated in? I played through broken bones in football, but toughness and bravery are different. Besides, I only kept playing because I didn't want to disappoint my football coach. I had lived too little to describe myself in these terms. And if the recruiter wanted an honest answer, there were words missing from the table: insecure, scared, jealous, petty, lazy.

I tried to anticipate what the recruiter wanted to hear and fed him as much bullshit as he fed me. I told him I had a pretty good ASVAB score. He asked how good, and when I told him, he smiled.

The ASVAB test, or the Armed Services Vocational Aptitude Battery, was administered at my school cafeteria. I filled out the bubble sheet of the standardized test on the same table where hours earlier I had eaten a bowl of chili and a cinnamon roll. I took the menu items – the best cafeteria offerings – as divine providence. It was going to be my day. Some teachers had whispered to us students that if we wanted to avoid a barrage of calls from the various military recruiters, it would be wise to purposefully bomb the test. As I looked around during the testing, I noticed my peers finishing their tests in a fraction of the time needed, their pencils frantically scribbling in bubbles so that they could get on with their high school existence. I finished with scarce seconds to spare. I gave every ounce of intellectual energy I had to that test. Little did I know, I only needed to score a thirty-three out of a hundred to be accepted into the Marine Corps.

The recruiter went over my test scores and told me there wasn't a job in the Corps I couldn't pursue. He told me all my options but tried pushing me toward military intelligence. He told me stories of James Bond-type Marines dealing in top secret information and leaving the wire, as he put it, "Lone Wolf McQuade style." I always wanted the infantry, but the recruiter's fast talking was working. The more he talked about it, the more exclusive he told me it was, the more it appealed to me. We shook hands, and I left the recruiter's office vibrating, an unconscious smile stapled to my face as I walked to my Cadillac. I sat behind the wheel, staring at the fuzzy tits, thinking about how good I was going to look in that uniform.

When I went home, I returned to my books. I read about a Marine grunt turned biology professor. His name was E.B. Sledge, and his book *With the Old Breed* detailed his experience as an infantryman in the Pacific Theater. Sledge's words carried with them a matter-of-factness that presented the horrors of war in a clear and concise manner. His descriptions made me realize that I had experienced almost no adversity in my life, not even a speck of what Sledge had seen. He told of fields of the dead that exploded in clouds of rotting flesh and engorged maggots. His account both chilled and warmed me at the same time. The terror of his existence permeated the pages, but the brotherhood and love that he had for his fellow Marines seemed unbreakable. They walked through hell and made it to the other side by leaning on one another. I wanted what Sledge had; I wanted war, and everything that came with it. I thought an experience like his would fill the cracks and holes that I saw when I looked in the mirror. I hoped conflict could be the mortar that would solidify my soul. I was right. I was wrong. I had no idea what I was asking.

Sledge talked about his disdain for POGs: Persons Other than Grunts. It was apparent that in Sledge's world, there was a clear and distinct in-group and out-group, and in his opinion, if you weren't infantry, you weren't shit. Though my recruiter described the intel community with a particular swagger of their own, a Marine who is not a grunt will only ever be a POG. I wanted to be like Sledge when I grew up. The next time I went into my recruiter's office, I would tell him to tear up the paperwork we had started that had "intel" written on the top. The next batch of papers he would draft up would proudly say 03XX infantry on the top. The irony of tearing up the papers that had intelligence scrawled across the top for a chance at becoming machine gun fodder was not lost on me.

The rest of the process was quick. After you sign the paperwork, they don't have to be nice to you anymore. There is a Faustian quality to the experience. The recruiter waits with bated breath as the potential recruit taps the mass-produced Marine Corps Bic pen on the paper, maybe chewing the tip a little, trying to decide his or her life. Some of the signatures will be neat and elegant, a practiced hand; others will be a scribble, a wavy line that impatiently acquiesces to the sale of four years of life. My signature was careful. I wanted the official documents to denote that this person had thought hard about this decision.

After signing the papers, I was now officially a "poolee," which is the lowest lifeform in the Marine Corps hierarchy. We poolees met every other Saturday for PT. We ran mock PFTs (Physical Fitness Tests) to make sure we were ready for boot camp. The minimum was three pull-ups, forty-four sit-ups, and a twenty-eight-minute three-mile run. But, the recruiter informed us that if any of us scored close to these minimum scores, our lives would become a living hell. The score to shoot for was 300: twenty pull-ups, one hundred sit-ups, and an eighteen-minute three-mile run.

I ran every day, obsessively. My regimen was four miles before school, four miles on my lunch break, and four miles after school. I did sit-ups and pull-ups until my muscles screamed at me. I read whatever I could get my hands on about the Marine Corps. I was trying to act how I thought Marines acted. I always thought that if my life was a movie, this would be my montage scene, my two-minute clip that condensed months of preparation. Maybe I really did think my life was a movie, or some half-cocked adventure novel.

I got a call from my recruiter that I was to report to his office. Apparently, we had a date for me to go to the Military Entrance Processing Station. They call it MEPS because everything in the military has to be accompanied with an acronym, and the actual name itself sounds like a meat-rendering plant.

Spokane's processing station was in the federal building downtown. The building's façade appeared historic and prestigious, but the inside looked like crappy, early-'90s remodeling. The color scheme was light colors of beige and green, with nothing vibrant standing out at all. If beige could also be a personality trait, the building's security screeners possessed it. They took us to a conference room and handed out stacks of questionnaires for us to begin lying through. I answered truthfully where I could, but deceived where I thought the truth would hurt. I finished the stack of questionnaires and consent forms and began reading through them again, reading words but too bored to comprehend any semblance of meaning. I wished I had brought a book, something with enough pizzazz to suck me out of that beige purgatory.

After a time (a long time), a woman came in and read off a single name, not mine. The boy was led away. It went on this way for a generation. Babies were born, couples were divorced, and the world would get serious about leaving Earth for Mars. Finally, my name was called, and I followed the light gray sweater down a series of hallways, twisting and turning until I was certain I'd never escape without a guide. The woman pointed to a small office and told me to go inside. Sitting behind a table was a deranged-looking Marine in dress service charlies. He had a graying crewcut and a blue-purple vein that bulged at his temple. The vein pulsated as the man searched my eyes, trying to glimpse the deepest pit of my soul through my ocular cavities. The vein made me think that the man had to tense his whole body to continue presenting this professional façade. He looked like he wanted to explode, to paint the walls bright red, to start a fire and dance through the orange and blue, but he only sat, asking questions. He held my questionnaire between murderous thumbs as he asked if I was telling the truth. He would re-ask the same question if he sensed I was lying. I believe his job was to sniff out weakness in the earliest stages. I'm sure they wanted to make people confess if they were concealing a felony, but I don't think they really cared about any of the other questions. My recruiter had offered me this advice: "I'm not telling you what to say, because that would be a breach of protocol, but I told the dude I never touched weed. Did I drink? No sir, never. Was it true? That motherfucker wasn't ever gonna find out."

He asked if I had ever smoked weed, which I had multiple times. I said no. He asked if I was an underage drinker, which I transformed into almost every Friday and Saturday night when I could get away with it. I said no. Marines weren't supposed to lie, but I rationalized that they were supposed to accomplish the mission at all costs. I was already learning the mental gymnastics necessary to endure the dichotomy of war.

After the interrogation with Gunnery Sergeant Pulsing Forehead Vein, we were sent to the doctor's examination room. It was a large, sterile-looking room where a coolness seemed to permeate from the floor. I looked for a drain somewhere near the center of the floor where they could wash away the blood after they sent a bolt through our foreheads. Any surface that could potentially be sat upon was covered in disposable paper sheets. They wanted to be able to easily erase all trace evidence that any of our butt cheeks had ever sat upon their uncomfortable medical furniture.

A nurse with a tired, forced smile and baby-blue scrubs told us to "disrobe." A boy asked if that meant get naked, and the nurse offered a genuine smile this time and said yes. The door closed behind her with a metallic thud. We all looked at each other before beginning to "disrobe." The cool silence in the room was briefly interrupted with the clicking of belts being undone and the sound of fabric sliding off flesh. Eight of us stood naked in the center of the examination room. I wasn't quite sure if I should cup my genitalia in a gesture of modesty, or if I should stand shoulder-width apart and try to exude confidence. I awkwardly transitioned between both positions and decided that I was instead going to try and focus on a small piece of real estate on the wall and pretend that I wasn't standing naked with seven other teenage boys in a "processing station."

A geriatric doctor walked into the room holding a clipboard that he looked down at as he talked to us. The doctor made us stand in a line, and we were all forced to partake in the infamous turn-your-head-and-cough exam. Our coughs came out in varying tones that all resembled whimpers. After the hernia exam, he ordered us to do a set of simple exercises. And so, eight naked teenage boys squatted and walked on their tippy toes as the doctor observed joints and muscles to make sure they bent and flexed as naked teenage muscles and joints should. Finally, he told us he had seen enough of our nude duck walks, and he walked into a smaller exam room where he called us in one at a time. We stood waiting, still naked, trying not to stare at each other's privates.

He called my name, and I walked into the claustrophobic exam room. I sat on an exam bed and cringed at how loudly the paper shield crinkled. The noise seemed amplified by the room. The doctor once again looked down at his clipboard. He nodded his head, not saying a word. I wondered if he was going to deliver the news that my embarrassment was terminal, and I'd never recover. He finally told me that everything checked out. I sighed – it was almost over. I began to eye the door, knowing that just beyond the pale door lay freedom, and my underwear. Without pomp and circumstance, the doctor asked me to stand up, turn around, and bend over. It was at this moment that I became concerned. I had endured a sports physical almost every year of my teenage life and had never been asked to do this, but I had also never been asked to duck walk in the nude. I acquiesced, bending over and staring at my toes. I wiggled my toes uncomfortably on the cold concrete floor for what seemed like three hours before the old doctor said that he had seen enough and that I could go get dressed. I did so, avoiding eye contact with the still-naked boys standing in the larger exam room.

The day was filled with blood and urine samples, questionnaires, and waiting rooms. It was an all-day ordeal. I half expected to be treated with a reverence, being a young man willing to volunteer for the Marine Corps infantry during a time of war, but I didn't register on any of their give-a-shit meters. This was the first time I was treated like government property, a number with a pulse, and it wouldn't be the last. I stood at the position of attention in a ceremonial room with red carpet and a dark wooden podium. I swore to defend the constitution against all enemies, foreign and domestic.

I proved that I was healthy enough, and a good enough liar, to join the Marines. My excitement grew. As the date drew near, I felt my confidence begin to grow too. I felt like I was now a part of something bigger, that I was more than just a scared kid from a small school. I was almost a Marine for God's sake, so I decided to start acting accordingly. After years of obsessions and rehearsed soliloquies of love that I never had the balls to deliver, I finally tried to kiss the girl that I had been in love with since freshman year's physical science class.

Her name was Melissa, and I had been madly in love with her for almost four years. I had rehearsed speeches in front of the mirror, professing my love and the multitude of reasons that we should have been together, but when the time came to deliver my love sonnets, I would always find an excuse to keep my mouth shut. I would normally just opt for an attempt at humor. I could always make her laugh, so it became easier just to stick with that, and besides I liked to see her smile. But after I had been approved for boot camp, there was a new swagger in my step, though it was relatively undeserved. I felt like there was more to me now. I had set a goal for enlisting in the Marine Corps and everything had worked out, simply by trying. I knew that I would never be with her if I didn't try.

We were at a party toward the end of high school. The music was too loud, so I used it as an excuse to stand closer to her. She smiled back at me, but then told me she had to go. I was scared to death as I leaned in a little closer, but her smile kept me from running away. I leaned all the way in and gave her a kiss. She kissed me back. I followed her outside and told her goodbye while she stood on her toes to give me another kiss. I watched as she moved to get in her friend's car. She turned and smiled, waving at me before grabbing the door handle. Her foot slipped as she was opening the door, and she pulled the car door directly into her face, shattering her nose. I ran toward her, but she just waved me off and got into the car. I saw her the next night at a basketball game. I like to believe that she was slightly concussed, and medicated, which would explain why she blew me off.

I kept after her, and eventually she succumbed to my dorkish charm. We dated for a few months leading up to boot camp. I was trying to be dramatic when I told her we should break up before I left. I was crushed by how agreeable she was with the breakup that I initiated. I rationalized in my head that I was protecting her, but really, I think I wanted her to worry about me. I wanted to return to her a conquering hero. I was an idiot who had read too many stories and seen too many bad movies.

4. Boot Camp

My mom took me out for one last meal in civilization before leaving for boot camp. It was one of my favorite restaurants. I remember the loaded potato skins, the four-foot-tall wooden troll that stared at me while I ate. We talked about anything other than me going away. My dad called when we were eating. He had taken a construction job in Alaska and called me from the farthest island on the Aleutian chain. He told me to be careful. I could tell that he wanted to tell me he was proud of me and he loved me, but that had never been our way. I heard the tears welling up behind his words, so I immediately looked up at the ceiling to keep myself from crying. I've always wanted to be the "tough guy," but the truth is that I'm a crier, and always have been.

The next morning, I was taken to the Spokane airport and started the journey to San Diego. I told anyone who would listen that I was headed off to become a Marine. This was in 2005, and the country was still clinging to the violent patriotism that arose in the wake of 9/11. Most would nod in approval and thank me for my service. I enjoyed the praise but also felt embarrassed by having solicited it. I hadn't done anything. My only achievement was signing my life away for four years.

The closer the plane got to San Diego, the larger the tangled knot of fear and excitement became in my belly. I had a window seat coming into San Diego and could see the lights from the Marine Corps Recruit Depot. It looked unintimidating from the sky, but I knew that was just a ruse. My tattered copy of *The Iliad* sat in my lap. I brought it for good luck, and to impress strangers. A part of me wanted to read it to find shreds of motivation, but I felt too nervous to focus on the words. As soon as I would begin reading, the sentences would blend into a conglomeration of unconnected words. My mind drifted to the first day of boot camp, or what I envisioned at least: the yelling, the screaming, the barely real threat of physical violence. As the plane was landing, I opened the book to one of the pages I had dog-eared for such a moment of weakness: "Let me not then die ingloriously and without a struggle, but let me first do some great thing that shall be told among men hereafter." It was dramatic and over the top, but so was I.

The Marine Corps had a bus waiting for us at the airport. We all boarded and sat in silence. I didn't look at the young men in the bus with me; I didn't study their faces to see if they were here for the same reason I was. I simply stared at the rough navy blue fabric of the seat in front of me. I tried to find patterns in the closely woven fibers, maybe a face or a hidden message left for just this occasion by the random power of the cosmos. Instead, I found nothing but my own anxiety. The bus stopped, and a brute of a man stepped onto the bus wearing the trademarked Marine Corps drill instructor Smokey Bear hat. He stood in silence, looking at all the new recruits, letting the silence and intensity of his gaze work its way under our skin. His face transformed to a grimace of disgust before he said, "Yes sir, no sir, and aye aye sir. Those are the only words to come out of your mouth. Do you understand?"

The entire bus screamed, "YES SIR."

But it wasn't loud enough; it was never loud enough. The drill instructor yelled, "LOUDER."

We all screamed in unison again, somehow finding a few more decibels in the bottom of our civilian chests: "YES SIR." Our voices bounced and reverberated off the sloped beige walls of the bus, and the interior seemed to vibrate in front of my face. The drill instructor yelled again, and again we yelled back. This was our new form of communication; it seemed simple enough. Just as I was beginning to comprehend the nuances of our new language, we were told to get off the bus. We all scrambled out of our seats to get off the bus as fast as possible, slamming into one another in a bid to be the first to step their feet on the black top, to be the first to place their feet on the path that no longer held any alternative routes.

The night air was hot and sticky as I jumped down from the last step of the bus. A yellow streetlight hung overhead. In stark contrast to the black asphalt were rows of painted yellow footprints. We were being screamed at to step onto them. I took my place in the far right of the front row and stood at what I thought was the position of attention. I watched from the corner of my eye, careful not to turn my head, as teenager after teenager poured from the bus and onto the black top. More drill instructors materialized out of thin air, screaming at those stragglers unfortunate enough to be seated in back of the bus. Once everyone was off the bus and on their own personal set of yellow footprints, we were given the command to file into the building that we stood in front of.

We ran into the building, where the streetlamp's yellow glow was replaced with the harsh glare of white fluorescent light. The mugginess from outside was amplified indoors as we were herded into a large hallway. We were stacked into the hallway like Nabisco cookies in a plastic sleeve, only the aroma was not the indulgent aroma of childhood junk food. Ours was the BO from all corners of the western United States.

The line slowly inched forward. We were being herded into a chute for some reason. As I got closer to the end of the hallway, I could hear the buzz of the hair clippers. I heard a brash, unfriendly voice ask, "Any moles or skin tags? Speak now or they're coming off with your hair." The haircuts lasted less than a minute. It was a picture of efficiency. Average teenagers with long messy hair, the style at the time, walked into the room. What walked out looked much different. It looked like they were prepping us for medical experimentation. My thoughts flashed to the horrors I had read about in Auschwitz and the Japanese Unit 731. It was just hair, but the shaved heads – with chunks of hair clinging to cheeks and foreheads – unsettled me. I waited my turn, listening to the caffeinated buzz of the electric hair clippers.

I stood behind a large towheaded recruit with beautiful blond hair. He shifted restlessly from foot to foot, as if he wasn't expecting to have to shave his head. My hair was already short; I had been shaving my head for years, longing to look the part. The towhead walked through the barbershop's threshold and disappeared. What walked back through the doorway looked damaged, lost, or both. On his shoulder rested a swooping curl of his blond hair, perched like an avian companion, but everyone knows that hair is dead, and the boy with the blond hair was dead, replaced with a scared bald number. The hair drifted off his shoulder, falling to the center of the hallway. The next recruit that walked past him kicked it against the wall.

My turn came. I sat in the barber chair and told the man that I didn't have any growths that were in danger of being sheared off. The barber didn't smile; he roughly pushed my head down and began shaving. He started at the base of my neck and ran the clippers toward my forehead. The industrial-grade clippers didn't get bogged down in my hair but slid over my head, launching a spray of fine brown hair onto my shirt and face. He tilted my head to the side and repeated. I was definitely balder, but not by much. He slapped me on the back of the head and called out, "Next."

My hair meant nothing to me, but I could tell it meant something to others. It meant something to the towhead. It was a part of who he was, a way that people recognized him. I imagined a good-looking girl running her fingers through his hair back in the small town that he probably came from. I wondered if he lied to her like I had to Melissa, or if he was brave enough to be honest. Maybe that's why the hair was so painful for him to lose. The hair they took was a way to strip away whatever identity we brought with us. The goal was to strip away the self, because the old self wasn't good enough. The old self needed to be sacrificed at the altar of the Marine Corps. Every hero worth his salt knew that sacrifices had to be made. Hair would be the first offering. Some would pay with their lives, maybe a limb – others with their sanity. Sacrifices had to be made.

After they took our hair, they took what little belongings we had brought with us. The small trinkets that were brought from home, the good-luck charms that were carried around in denim pockets, were handed over to the United States government for safekeeping. We were told they would give them back, but I didn't fully believe them. The religious could keep their crosses and stars. The room where they led us was filled with rows of glossy, red wooden stalls, each one reflecting the fluorescent lights above them. The stalls were for us to dump our personal effects, so the drill instructors could see if we were trying to smuggle in contraband. We could take nothing from our former lives with us, only what we could hide between our ears. I dumped my small carry-on bag onto the glossy red surface. Drill instructors walked up and down the rows, berating recruits for the things they brought. They would hold up photo albums and love letters, even a pair of pink female underwear, and scream obscenities at the recruit. I tried not to stare.

A drill instructor walked behind me. My back arched a little straighter, and the freshly shaven hair stood up on my neck. He shoved me to the side and rifled through my belongings, briefly picking up my book before throwing it back on the table. It must not have been a big enough infraction to cause an explosion. Maybe he had read the book and approved; maybe he was threatened by it. He moved down the line and began screaming at a recruit for attempting to conceal a Milky Way. I put what was left of my old life into a brown cardboard box, placing *The Iliad* on top of my clothes. I took one last look at the cover, reaching down to touch it, running my fingers over the frayed corners, taking a moment to rest my hand on the cool, smooth surface. I began to wonder if this was how it started for the Greeks and Trojans when they were first tasked with learning the craft of war. But before I could give it much thought, a drill instructor threw a box of personal effects across the room, screaming at the top of his lungs for some perceived slight that I didn't quite catch. I watched as a young man scrambled to put what was left of his life back into a small cardboard box.

The next few days of processing were gear issue, paperwork, and a series of shots. They don't tell you what they are injecting into your arm; you just look straight ahead and walk from station to station. The scent of alcohol swabs filled the hallway, and the pattern repeated itself: swab, stab, wipe, swab, stab, wipe.

It took the better part of a week to completely process us into the system. The drill instructors finally herded us to the squad bay, where we were to meet our actual drill instructors for the first time. The drill instructors that had been shepherding us were nothing but cruel chauffeurs; we hadn't yet met the men charged with our transcendence. It was Friday morning; the recruits had dubbed the day Black Friday.

They led us to the second floor of a concrete building that was erected sometime during the Second World War. We shuffled into a long room filled with two rows of bunk beds and foot lockers. The room looked to be about fifty yards long, with glass windows that ran the lengths of both walls, all of them left open to let in the San Diego air. We sat cross-legged in a cluster at the head of the room, bunched together like scared herd animals, as one of the largest men I had ever seen stepped in front of us. He had mythic proportions, towering over us stinking recruits like a demigod. His black skin shone under the fluorescent tube lights that hummed and flickered overhead. If an artist were to draw this man, it might be commented that he was too muscular, and his features too exaggerated to be believable, but there he stood. His deep voice washed over us as he explained that we were soon to meet our senior drill instructor and begin the path to becoming Marines. He told us that some would not make it out, but if we did, we would find ourselves in the company of the fiercest fighting force the world had ever known. He walked back and forth as he talked, spinning on his heels once he had walked the length of the recruits, his muscles flexing under the sharp lines of his pressed shirt.

Our senior drill instructor walked forward and took command from the juggernaut. By comparison, the senior drill instructor was a less impressive specimen, but there was something arresting about his gaze. The eyes drooped at the corners, but their pale blue irises looked cold enough to burn flesh. He gave another speech about his expectations and the gravity of our situation. I stared at the ribbons on his chest, a neat uniform stack of bright colors and lines. I thought of Tetris, the shapes falling into place but never vanishing, clinging instead to the chest like an exclamation of the miles endured. In my limited understanding, I could make out a couple of Iraq Campaign Medals, a Purple Heart, and a Combat Action Ribbon. This man was the genuine article, not a paper pusher that had decided to play a real Marine for the raw recruits at boot camp. This was a combat veteran. He was who I wanted to be.

I was still staring at the yellow, blue, and red of the ribbons on his chest when he introduced the other two drill instructors who we would be working with. The drill hat, who was to be in charge of teaching us close-order drill, was a tall skinny Black man. He wasn't physically impressive, but like all drill instructors his uniform was immaculate, and he moved precisely, as if his body were propelled by gears and cogs instead of muscle and sinew. The kill hat, who was responsible for daily movement and brutalization, was a short Hispanic Marine covered in tattoos. His hands were dotted with burned scar tissue. We had thought that the burns came from some fiery combat scene in Iraq, some smoldering heroics from the other side of the world. But slowly, the kill hat told us his story, and the rest was filled in by other drill instructors who knew the man.

Our kill hat had run with a gang in his delinquency. He had gotten caught up in the momentum of his shitty neighborhood and was nearly swept away by it. He did what he had to in order to survive. The gang inscribed his skin with their mark. His skin told a story, but it wasn't the story that he wanted his life to follow. He saw a recruiting station that looked more like an escape hatch. The recruiter he spoke with was amiable enough, but told him that he had to get the tattoos removed before they could seriously consider enlisting him. Tattoo removal wasn't cheap, and it would take months to do properly. He did own a car though, and it was old enough to still have a cigarette lighter. He sat in his car on the street, pushed in the cigarette lighter, and waited for the audible click. He pressed the glowing red circles against his tattooed flesh, burning off his history so that he could write a new one. Once the burns healed enough, he went back into the recruiter's office and they accepted him, no questions asked. This was the kind of man the Marine Corps attracted.

The senior drill instructor turned us over to the other hats, and as soon as the door closed behind him, chaos erupted. They screamed commands, some intelligible, others sounding like blind rage. They ordered our every movement. We were to do nothing without being told. They sought to instill in us a knee-jerk obedience to orders, and they got it. I quickly found that if you moved fast and yelled loud enough, you were largely left alone. There were others who had trouble with this concept. They couldn't quite understand that they didn't matter anymore, that they were no longer the center of the universe, that in fact they were the lowest lifeform in the strange and alien planet that they were marooned on.

The punishment for most infractions, whether imagined or actual, was pain through callisthenic or isometric exercises. They would make you do burpees, push-ups, leg raises, eight-count bodybuilders, and monkey fuckers until you were certain your heart would explode. When you knew you couldn't go on, they made you keep going. They were cultivating mental toughness through the rigors of exercise, as militaries have always done. Physical violence was kept to a minimum. Drill instructors were barred from striking recruits, at least openly. It happened in back rooms and hallways where the truth had no chance of escaping the depot.

They broke us down, stripping away everything that we were until we were reduced to our desire for survival. The first couple weeks of boot camp made many of us turn on each other. A mindset of every man for himself began to prevail. People stole from each other when they lost important uniform items. They watched as others were punished for their own carelessness. There is a saying in the Marine Corps: there is only one thief; everyone else is just trying to get their shit back. I was no different. I turned into a thief when it would save me from the wrath of the drill instructors. I stole a uniform measuring stick and a pair of shower shoes from one of my unsuspecting bald brethren. I watched as he dry-heaved from exercise at the front of the squad bay when the drill instructors discovered the absence of his gear during evening inspection. I watched the agony in his face with a mixture of guilt and relief. The atmosphere of self-preservation increased tension, which I'm sure was a carefully crafted construct that the drill instructors employed. It pulled us further away from our civilian selves who never thought they would resort to stealing.

Slowly, we were shown that we couldn't survive on our own. Self-preservation could only carry us so far. We began accomplishing tasks in small teams and squads that could only be achieved through unity. Some tasks were as simple as carrying a heavy log from point A to point B. Though there would always be those who sought to put their weight onto the shoulders of others, in large part we all came to realize that this thing was only possible if we carried our own weight, plus a little more, always a little more.

Everything we did was a competition. Winning was rewarded with brief breaks while the losers had to continue enduring whatever punishment the drill instructors could think of next. We were told that it pays to be a winner as we stood watching the other recruits being thrashed. They referred everything back to combat and killing the enemy. An improperly shined faucet was the lack of attention to detail that led to not seeing a command wire for an IED that killed your whole squad. Learning how to conduct close order drill, which seemed a little too similar to marching band, was somehow going to teach us how to better kill the enemy as a unit. I didn't understand it, but I didn't resist it either. I shined faucets like everyone's lives depended on it. I marched and pivoted like I was pulling the trigger or thrusting a bayonet on some distant battlefield. They made us scream "KILL" before conducting many tasks, and when I screamed it, I meant it. Whatever voodoo they were doing to us was working. I not only wanted to fight, I wanted to kill.

A couple of weeks into training, I developed a rattle in my chest. They called it the recruit crud. All those bodies coming from across the country brought with them their own homegrown germs and bacteria. A teenager's body from Spokane might be well armed with the antibodies necessary to survive in eastern Washington, but it wasn't prepared for what was brought from the inner cities of Los Angeles or the high deserts of Texas. Almost everyone was sick those first weeks. Most got better within a few days. We were given hand sanitizer, and I used it religiously, but the stinging gel that boasted a kill rate of 99.9% was no match for the crud that crawled into my lungs. I told myself it would pass. I wasn't about to raise my hand and tell them that I needed to see a corpsman. I was afraid to show weakness, which in retrospect was its own form of weakness.

The days dragged on, and the faint rattle in my chest turned into something darker. I lost all my strength simply walking across the squad bay. My only plan to defeat the sickness was to drink as much water as I could and try to eat as many calories that I could force down my gullet. The next problem came in the form of dysentery. I quit eating because I was tired of shitting my brains out. I was the sickest I had ever been in my life.

To go from the first phase of boot camp to the second, you must successfully complete a physical fitness test. This was a test that I easily passed when I first showed up in San Diego. But after that first test, the crud had reduced me to a weakling. I was horrified that I wouldn't pass the test, that they would send me to the PCP: the Physical Conditioning Platoon. PCP was a sad place that was unaffectionately called the Pork Chop Platoon because most of the recruits sent there were overweight. They were forced to exercise all day and given reduced rations, all the while stuck in limbo until they had lost the weight and could complete the test. Others in the platoon were just weak. PCP turned some recruits' three-month boot camp experience into a six-month or year-long purgatory. I told myself I would pass the PFT or die trying.

They led us all to a sand pit where there were pull-up bars.

Pull-ups were by far the biggest score-killer on the PFT. Most of the people that failed the PFT failed because they couldn't do three pull-ups. I waited for my turn on the bar. The drill instructor counting pull-ups was being as strict as possible. Any kipping, or not fully extending the arms on the descent, and the reps were not counted. It was difficult for me to make the short jog from the squad bay to the pull-up bars. Self-doubt began to spread from my belly to my brain; I began to think I couldn't do a single pull-up.

I jumped on the bar and immediately pulled myself up for one rep. Lightheaded and nauseous, I lowered myself back down until the drill instructor counted off, "One." I pulled myself over the bar again and lowered. "One." He didn't count the rep, nor did he tell me why he didn't count it. I pulled again. "One." I pulled again. "One." My vision started to blur at the edges. I thought I might pass out at any moment. I needed at least three. I pulled as hard as I could. "Two." I pulled again, knowing that this might be all I had left in my arms. "Two." I was almost in tears. I pulled again, gritting my teeth until I thought my molars would explode. "Three." I fell off the bar, and my vision went black as I stumbled away. I heard the drill instructor calling me a "weak-ass bitch" as I half-jogged over to the sit-up station. I had barely passed.

Crunches are the relatively easy part. A partnering recruit is required to hold your feet and count your reps. If you don't get the max score, your partner is henceforth known as a buddy fucker for not slipping you the extra reps. The minimum score is forty-four, and the maximum is one hundred (most easily hit one hundred). I barely got to fifty, terrified that I was going to shit all over the poor recruit tasked with holding my legs.

The last event was a three-mile run. The minimum time is twenty-eight minutes to pass. Prior to boot camp, I was coming in right around the twenty- to twenty-one-minute mark. I had run miles and miles to get ready for boot camp, and now I wasn't certain

I could make it to the halfway mark. We lined up, and I tried to weasel my way as close to the front as possible. The time didn't officially start until the last recruit passed the starting line. I was hoping to buy five seconds. A whistle blew; I began to run. I focused on the recruits in front of me. I tried to keep my eyes fixed on their bouncing bald heads as I desperately tried to keep putting one foot in front of the other. Less than a quarter mile into the run, I vomited out the little water I had been able to keep down. The vomit was clear; I don't think I had really eaten anything for a couple of days. Left foot. Right foot. That's all I focused on now. There were no more recruit heads to fixate on as almost all of them had passed me. I instead focused on each new turn in the course which ran along the edge of the recruit depot. A twelve-foot cyclone fence topped with barbwire bordered the run. I tried to focus on my feet and the next curve instead of the oppressive chain-link fence that taunted me each time I looked over at it. I wheezed and stumbled but I never stopped moving forward. Left foot. Right foot.

At the halfway marker, a drill instructor stood with a stopwatch and berated my slow time, telling me I would need to eat out the Virgin Mary's asshole for a Christmas morning miracle if I was going to pass this run. I tried to scream out "aye aye, sir," but I vomited in my mouth again. I settled for nodding my head and swallowing back the vomit. Left foot. Right foot. It seemed like I was running in place until I rounded a corner and could see the finish line. Another drill instructor stood there screaming. I focused my vision on him, and everything else blurred at the edges. Left foot. Right foot. As I got closer and closer, my vison kept getting narrower until all I could see was the bright red sweatshirt of the drill instructor – even his face was beginning to blur. He counted down from ten seconds to the twenty-eight-minute mark. Ten. I was going to make it. Nine. Left foot. Right foot. Eight. I stumbled past him. Left foot. Right foot. Darkness.

The next memories come in flashes. Nothing concrete, always a blur. I remember the drill instructor yelling for a corpsman. I remember them pulling down my shorts and ramming a metal thermometer up my asshole. I remember the look on the corpsman's face when he read that my temperature was over a hundred and five. Then the memory washes out for a while, until they start pouring ice over me.

I came to in the hospital with an IV stuck in my arm and an oxygen tube in my nostrils. I had a heat stroke, brought on by overexertion and a horrible case of pneumonia. When I woke in the hospital bed, I was scared that I had been kicked out of boot camp; that this is where they sent the cowards who weren't strong enough to finish. The nurses were all pleasant, but I still sensed a trap. I was uneasy every time they brought me anything.

The next morning, the senior drill instructor came in. I tried standing up, but he put his hand up to stop me, so I just stared at him, waiting for his disappointment. He had taken off his hat and held it at his waist, spinning it between his two hands. I could hear the rim of the hat scraping against his rough hands. I focused on that sound and not the steady beep of the EKG.

"You look pissed off," he said. "That's good. Don't quit."

With that, he left. Not a lot of information to go on, but he didn't make it sound like they were kicking me out. I ate all the food they put in front of me and drank whatever liquids I could get my hands on. I was starting to feel like a human again.

I spent close to a week in the hospital – a few days in an actual hospital bed and another couple in a strange holding area where broken recruits waited in a storage closet for surgeries or separation. They led me to a large room that held old office chairs and desks. Apparently, it was where they stored all the furniture that wasn't in use. Toward the back of the room there were bunk beds set up. This was where the injured recruits spent their days, in the back of a furniture closet, discarded like the purple ceramic lamps that held vigil for them.

I sat down next to a depressed-looking recruit and began to put what little gear I had away, stacking it as neatly and uniformly as I could underneath the rack. The recruit didn't say anything to me; he just threw me a collection of nude pictures cut from a magazine, held together by a reddish-pink rubber band. I didn't really want to touch the paper. I could imagine the things it had seen. But wanting to be polite, and not hating the idea of seeing a nude woman again, I leafed through the pages. Instead of anything that bordered on sexual excitement, I just felt sad for these poor souls who'd been reduced to used furniture.

Seeing that they hadn't wheeled me into the room, and that I didn't have any casts surrounding my limbs, the others must have sensed I was a short timer. They mainly talked about their injuries and if they were going to get medically retired or not. I wasn't thinking about anything but getting back. These guys already seemed defeated. I spent my days doing push-ups and sit-ups while the broken G.I. Joes talked about x-rays and herniated disks. I left virtually unnoticed. The recruits that remained didn't acknowledge my going; they just continued their depressing chatter about the silver lining of a medical retirement. I saw the porno scrapbook peeking out from behind a hospital pillow and was happy to be leaving.

When I got back to the recruit depot, I knew I wasn't headed back to my old company. They had continued training, and I still wasn't deemed medically fit for service. I was under observation for at least two weeks. I was headed for the medical rehabilitation platoon. A sad place, but nothing like what I saw at the hospital. These recruits were broken, but it was deemed a temporary break by the medical staff.

The medical rehabilitation platoon, or the MRP, was located

right next to the depot's medical building, and directly across from the Pork Chop Platoon. I had the brief opportunity to talk to one of their members, who had told me he had lost seventy-five pounds since coming to boot camp. His oversized cammies corroborated his story.

I felt terrible for these recruits that came to boot camp in such horrible shape. They should have been warned, and their recruiters should have faced public lashings. But I only had so much give-a-shit to go around. I needed to get the hell out of this purgatory and back to training. Instead of being excited about progressing from T-29 (Training day twenty-nine) to T-30, I was perpetually stuck at T-24. I began to plan my escape.

The quickest way out was a clean bill of health and a first-class PFT. I had fallen far but I was expecting my body to bounce back. I ate well and exercised every chance I got.

I forced myself to eat and drink as many calories as I could. I thought it would help my strength come back. I turned everything they served into a giant peanut butter sandwich and washed it all down with milk – think a turkey, mashed potato, and gravy peanut butter sandwich. After lunch, I did pull-ups until my arms gave out.

When I first got out of the hospital, my numbers were around four. But after a week of recovery, I was back up to twelve. The poor unfortunate souls of the Pork Chop Platoon that got zero pull-ups had large zeros written on their hands. A common drill instructor joke was to draw the zero into a giant doughnut, sprinkles included.

Though I felt bad for the PCP recruits, it didn't stop me from making them a part of a personal game during the PFT runs. I would hold back toward the rear of the pack, giving them all as much of a head start as I could, and then I would see how many of them I could pass before the halfway marker. My first few runs back were awful, coming in at around twenty-four minutes. But I was getting better. Each run was faster, until I was right back to where

I was before I got sick. I kept my head down and did everything I could to get out.

When they released me, they sent me to a company that was on the exact training day I was on when I went down: T-24. All the new recruits eyed me with suspicion when I showed up, thinking I was some kind of weakling because I was sent back in training.

The day I showed up was in the middle of field day, which is Marine Corps slang for cleaning day. I think field day sounds more masculine; that's why they use it. I showed up, and everyone was in their PT gear and combat boots. It seemed every training company had their own quirks when it came to cleaning attire. The MRP cleaning uniform was a pair of whitey-tighty underwear, a skivvy shirt tucked into the underwear, and a pair of shower shoes. This cleaning outfit was a much-welcomed change.

The drill instructor showed me to my rack and then began inspecting the cleaning process. I could hear him bemoaning recruits' lack of attention to detail as I filled my foot locker with belongings. I immediately stripped down to the uniform of the day and began cleaning. I grabbed a can of Brasso, which is a polishing agent, and began to shine faucets.

We cleaned for hours. Any surface that could possibly be inspected was scrubbed and polished. Beds were retightened, surfaces cleaned for the umpteenth time. All the while we inspected each other's work, always eager to find an infraction that needed immediate attention. Everything was supposed to be covered and aligned at exactly the same length and exactly the same distance. We ran a string line across the bunks to make sure that all the blankets were aligned. Tailor's tape measurers were used to check the distance between racks.

Of course, the cleanliness was never good enough, nor was anything ever properly organized if the drill instructors' moods swayed them. Many times during these field days, a drill instructor would erupt from his office and tear the squad bay apart, tipping over mattresses and throwing foot lockers across the room. Only later could I see these field days for what they were: just slow training days, invented by drill instructors to occupy us. At the time though, I took it deadly serious and watched with bated breath as the drill instructor moved across the squad bay, inspecting our work. I was always devastated if something that I had cleaned or aligned didn't pass.

It didn't take long for the new recruits to warm up to me. I made friends with most of the squad leaders and the other high performers in the platoon. I wanted to be a high performer, so I figured the best way to get there was by hanging out with the guys that acted how I wanted to act. The day after I arrived, we took the PFT that had to be passed in order to go to the second phase of boot camp. I passed all the events easily and managed to avoid getting a thermometer shoved up my ass. It was a good day.

***

The second phase of boot camp is conducted at Camp Pendleton. This is where they teach recruits how to shoot a rifle and exist out in the wild. Marksmanship is one of the cornerstones of the Marine Corps, so they seem to really emphasize this portion of training. The stress levels are dialed back during marksmanship training, and the previous drill instructors turn recruits over to instructors who are foils of themselves.

Most of the marksmanship instructors I encountered were laid back and eager to teach us. One of the most noticeable differences between these marksmanship instructors and the drill instructors was their headwear. Instead of the Smokey Bear hats of the drill instructors, the marksmanship instructors wore safari pith helmets. From the neck up, they looked like they belonged alongside Teddy Roosevelt.

Almost all the marksmanship instructors were infantry combat veterans. The ones that weren't kept their mouths shut around the combat vets. I noticed a hierarchy among them. The combat grunt was alpha. I began to realize that this was probably the case throughout the entire Marine Corps, even among the drill instructors. This made me happy about my decision. I was going to become an alpha chimp and looked forward to flinging poo at the lesser primates.

General John "Blackjack" Pershing of the United States Army famously said, "The deadliest weapon in the world is a Marine and his rifle." I saw this quote inscribed on walls and echoed by both our drill instructors and marksmanship instructors. I began to believe it. By the end of the training and qualification, every recruit could kill a man at five hundred yards with iron sights. An impressive feat by any stretch of the imagination.

The shooting filled us with a sense of self-confidence, and that's what this second phase of boot camp was all about. The first phase stripped us of our identity and broke us down to nothing. The second rebuilt us – rebuilt me – as something nearly unrelated to the high school kid I'd shown up as.

The time spent out in the field finally started to make me feel like a Marine. I had wondered when we would get into the bayonet charges and the muddy obstacle courses, and this was it. During the first phase, I felt like I'd signed up to be an incredibly fit janitor. It's a trend that would continue in my early years of service. When I first arrived at the actual Fleet Marine Force, I was asked if I knew what PFC stood for. I promptly responded that it stood for Private First Class. I was handed a cheap white toilet brush by a senior lance corporal who shook his head and said, "Wrong. It stands for Professional Fucking Cleaner."

All the obstacle and assault courses we trained on were named after Marine Corps Medal of Honor Recipients. That was part of the brilliance of the Marine Corps: its history was integral to our training. Our manuals were filled with the deeds of Marines that came before us, and we were required to memorize the dates and people who built the Corps as it now stood. A drill instructor could give a history quiz at any moment, and the punishment for failure was always severe. There was a saying that "pain retains," and I can honestly say I never missed the same question twice.

Before we tackled each obstacle course, the drill instructor would gather us in a circle and read us the Medal of Honor citation. There were stories of heroes stretching all the way back to WWI. The Marine Corps had created its own pagan warrior cult and elevated its past members to the statuses of heroes and demigods. After listening to a citation of untold bravery, it was impossible not to imagine myself in their position later as I scaled the wooden obstacles in the relative safety of Camp Pendleton. I pictured myself storming the beaches of Iwo Jima as I crawled under the barbwire and the drill instructors threw smoke grenades and artillery simulators. The history and Medal of Honor citations made me feel indebted to the legacy of the Marine Corps, as if I was being entrusted to carry this reputation into the twenty-first century. The responsibility felt real. It made you feel like you really were part of something bigger, something almost eternal. I had given myself completely over to the Corps and longed for the chance to charge across a smoke-filled battlefield, bayonet attached. I was desperate for the opportunity to prove that I was worthy. Of course, this is exactly what the training was meant to do. I didn't resist; I simply surrendered, happy to be a small cog in the people-eating Rube Goldberg war machine. My disillusion would be delayed until I could peek behind the curtain and see that a citation never tells the whole truth. Yes, bravery exists, and the simple act of putting on your combat boots in a warzone takes a certain measure of it, but bravery is a moment in time, chopped up and frozen in the stale words of an officer's imagining of the events. The citation never told me about what comes after the moment in time, when the combat operations have to continue, when the hero of the story has to walk back to friendly lines, past the ghosts of his friends. When the hero must keep trying to live up to his own bullshit day after day, and the looks he gets when people realize that he is not special, he is just a memory of a moment in time.

The second phase ends with what is called the Crucible. It's a field training exercise that is supposed to test the mental resolve of the recruits and see if they can endure sleep deprivation and limited food. The event is three days, and you are given approximately a thousand calories a day. Each day is filled with obstacle courses that are meant to build teamwork. This is where the notion that you are only as strong as the weakest person really comes into focus. All obstacles are designed so that they can only be completed through collaboration. During the training, we were read historical accounts of Marines who endured hell on earth. I think this was meant to show us that what we were going through was nothing compared with what we might be asked to endure in the name of the Marine Corps. They read us stories of the Chosin Reservoir in the Korean War, stories of frozen limbs and wave after wave of Chinese soldiers outnumbering the Marines ten to one.

I wanted my own Korea. They were inducing a strange kind of psychosis that made us yearn for war and the chance to get an obstacle course named after us. It was a strange power they held over us, and they wielded it masterfully.

The Crucible culminates in a forced march, ten or so miles. This comes at the end of the exhausting three days, once sleep has evaporated. As we hiked through the night and into the early morning, I couldn't stop smiling. This was the event that supposedly made us Marines. We would no longer be considered recruits after the Crucible, and I knew every step took me closer to what I had been fantasizing about for years. The last hill of the hike was known as the reaper, and on top of that hill rested our Eagle, Globe, and Anchor pins that would signify us becoming Marines. The hill was nearly vertical, with deep trenches cut by rainwater. The fine powder of the beige dirt kicked up around the marching boots and caked to whatever exposed skin it could find. It stuck to our teeth and gums and filled our mouths with grit. I smiled a muddy smile as the lactic acid filled my muscles and tried to make me succumb to gravity. But as with my bout of heat stroke during phase one, I focused on my feet. Left foot. Right foot. All the way to the top. The sun was rising over the California hills as we made it to the top, which I'm sure was precisely calculated by the drill instructors. They were trying to create a religious experience, and it worked.

At the top of the hill, they ordered us into platoon formations. I looked at the dirty, exhausted faces and thought that I could see a difference; somehow, we had all changed going up that hill. I'm sure it was all in my head, but what difference does that make if you are a true believer? The company commander and chief drill instructor gave speeches about our responsibility to uphold the Marine Corps' highest traditions. They told us that the weight of the tradition of excellence and tenacity had just been placed on our shoulders. They handed us a black Eagle, Globe, and Anchor. The Eagle was a representation of the United States. The Globe represented the Corps' readiness to fight on any clime or place in the world. The fouled Anchor represented the naval genesis of the Marine Corps. The three parts taken together were a talisman that America's warrior cult fought under. I clenched the sigil in a closed fist, relishing the pain the sharp edges inflicted on my palm. I had drunk the Kool-Aid. I was a full-fledged cult member.

***

The third phase of boot camp was all spit and polish. We took our final tests and conducted close-order drill until we were as near to perfection as humanly possible. We marched around the depot in perfect synchronicity, our boots pounding the asphalt at the exact same moment, creating an ominous smack and thud as we marched from place to place. We all stood a little taller and puffed our chests out a little more. We were more than we were.

Most nights after I had devoted a certain amount of time to studying the handbooks they gave us, committing as much Marine Corps lore as possible to memory, I would read letters from home. My mother wrote every week, and she would always close her letters with a famous quote. My favorite was the quote often misattributed to George Orwell: "People sleep peaceably in their beds at night because rough men stand ready to do violence on their behalf." I had read *Animal Farm* in high school, but I had never read any of his essays. I read the quote over and over again, and now looking back I wonder what Orwell would have thought of boot camp. I wonder if he would have admired how the Marine Corps used language as a mind-control device, or if he would have been horrified at the power that the tradition and pageantry held over such young and impressionable men. Orwell commented on the power of history in *1984*, writing: "Who controls the past controls the future. Who controls the present controls the past." I think Orwell's opinion on the matter can be found in those lines, and his words a warning label that should accompany the weaponization of history. But at the time, none of that mattered. I was trying to become one of the rough men who was ready to do violence on behalf of a nation that really didn't care what we did as long as they didn't have to see it.

I wrote to Melissa, and she wrote me back. I agonized over every word, horrified that I might sound like an idiot. I often wrote three drafts of the same letter. The first draft would include everything that I wanted to say: that I loved her and made a horrible mistake breaking up with her. The subsequent drafts would become more detached, trying to play the part of a confident man who had the world figured out at eighteen years of age. I should have been honest, but I had an image to uphold and I was bound and determined to keep up with appearances.

Graduation day came, and it was the spectacle that I had come to expect from the Marine Corps. When the families of the soon-to-be-Marines showed up, we were conducting our last run. We dressed in silkies and tight skivvy shirts to show off our new, hardened bodies. We thought the outfits made us look like Marines, but they also could have easily been costumes in a 1970s porno. The shorts were incredibly short and made from a 100% lightweight nylon tricot that felt and looked like silk. We ran in formation, singing cadences that the Marine Corps was famous for. "Mama, Mama, can't you see, what the Marine Corps done to me." "Don't let the green grass fool you." "If I die in a combat zone." And all manner of left, right, left, right cadences. We yelled at the top of our lungs. We wanted to impress the visitors. We wanted to show them that the recruiting slogans weren't just gimmicks. This was real, and we were a part of it.

My family had come from Spangle to watch the graduation. I knew they were there, but I didn't spot them until after the ceremony. My brother told me that when we went marching by in our cammies, and my mom saw me for the first time, she lost her breath, grabbing his arm. When he first told me this, I was proud of the transformation. But looking back now, I try to put myself in her shoes and wonder what was mixed into those emotions. I'm sure there was pride, but I also imagine a deep sorrow underpinning everything she felt that day. Her little boy had died, and something else was walking around in his skin. I was all self-centered pride that day, not stopping to think how horrifying this must have been for a parent. Their little boy or girl changed fundamentally, in a place that represents war, on a path that leads straight to the gnashing teeth of combat. It's almost impossible for teenagers to truly empathize with their parents, and I was no different.

After graduation, I gave everyone in my family a big hug. I tried to act different, more serious, so they would know that things were different now. Waiting in the car to drive me to the hotel was Dwight Yoakam on the stereo and an ice-cold Miller High Life, my favorites at the time. Sure, they were giving an underage kid alcohol, but I think my dad agreed with the adage that if you're old enough to die for your country, you're old enough to have a beer. That night we went to dinner and a movie. *Jarhead* was playing in the theater, and they thought I would like to see it. I had read the book and acted like I was thrilled at the notion. But anyone who has read the book or seen the movie knows that it isn't exactly a positive portrayal of active duty. I tried to act indifferent, but the themes of death, a willingness to kill, and insecurity made me uncomfortable.

We stopped at an arcade on the way back to the hotel. After all, I was still just a kid.

5. The School of Infantry

I went home after boot camp. Not much had changed. Everyone I left behind was still drinking their lives away. No one had any real plans other than saving enough money to buy that new car or truck they always wanted. I felt like I was better than them, but when I got home, my own wheels started spinning in the alcohol-soaked landscape. During the month I was home, I put my young liver to the test. I didn't exercise once. There would be consequences when I checked into the School of Infantry.

The School of Infantry, or SOI, is where young Marines go to learn the basics of being infantrymen. POGs go to Marine Combat Training. It is here where the vast chasm between infantrymen and POGs widens.

SOI is where grunts are separated and selected for their respective MOS (Military Occupational Specialty) in the infantry. There are the 0311s, which are basic riflemen and the backbone of the Corps; 0331s, which are machine gunners and often considered the balls of the infantry; 0341s, which are mortarmen or the indirect fire specialists; 0351s, which are assaultmen, our demolition and missile-launcher experts; and 0352s, which are TOW missile gunners or anti-armor gunners. We were told to make a wish list of the jobs we would like.

The combat instructors gave us all a brief description of the jobs available. A combat instructor representing each profession would take center stage and describe the merits and challenges of their respective jobs. These presentations were mostly a demonstration of shit talking, where each MOS expounded on their trade's superiority over the others. Being a rifleman – the actual tip of the spear, the true purpose of the Marine Corps – was alluring. Everything in the Corps was designed to support the riflemen, and I liked the idea of being the center of the combat universe. In his spiel, a TOW gunner told us that it was the most intellectually challenging profession in the infantry, and that they didn't have to hump everywhere, as TOW missile systems were vehicle mounted. For a moment, I felt myself wavering, falling for his sales pitch. But then I remembered *Guns Up!* I remembered that to be a machine gunner was to be the hardest man in the patrol. I remembered that all my favorite Medal of Honor citations involved machine gunners mowing down hordes of enemy combatants. It involved white-hot barrels and fighting to the last man, running out of ammo and having to pull out a pistol and a KA-BAR. The decision was easy. I would become a machine gunner, following in the mythical footsteps of Gunnery Sergeant "Manila John" Basilone.

They used our ASVAB scores to dictate who got what job. The higher the ASVAB score, the more likely you'd get your choice. For machine gunners, they also considered your size. If you were big, and it looked like you could carry the weight, you got the job. If you were a small man and still wanted the job, you would have to prove that you truly wanted it. Luckily, I was an ogre with a high ASVAB score. They gave me what I wanted.

The first month of infantry training is all basic infantry skills:

shooting and surviving out in the wild. They taught us how to make it from point A to point B using a map and compass. We were taught how to dig fighting holes. We were taught to dig holes that we were supposed to shit and piss in. They taught us how to stab someone in the neck so that the sentry's screams didn't alert the other bad guys. It was everything I had wanted the Boy Scouts to be when I was a kid.

The first day of basic infantry training would be spent on the grenade range, something I had fantasized about since forever. As a kid, I would always pretend that the black and gray chunks of basalt lying around my yard were grenades. I'd pretend to pull the pin with my teeth before hurling the mafic grenades at imaginary enemy pillboxes and then watching them erupt in the flames of my childhood fantasy. Throwing a grenade during training was literally going to be a dream come true. I had been watching grenades explode ever since my older brothers let me watch too-violent-'80s-action-movies when I was four. I couldn't wait to throw the death orb with all my might and feel the radiation from the fireball that erupted on the range. I would still have to imagine a fictional enemy, but I had a more concrete image in my mind now. It wasn't the Cobra Commander anymore; it was a military-aged Middle Eastern man with a suicide vest and an AK-47.

We first practiced with dummy grenades, inert chunks of metal that thudded heavily into the ground but only kicked up a small plume of dirt. I was surprised at the weight of the dummies. They were heavier than I thought they were going to be, but still I thought them stupid – they were dummies after all. I had been practicing my whole life for this moment; I didn't need to log any more hours throwing fake grenades. But the wait wouldn't last forever, and eventually we all lined up in our respective order. We would each be given one live grenade to throw, which we had to sign for. They took one Marine at a time. It took all day.

We all waited behind a hill, listening to long silences, briefly and violently interrupted by explosions. The explosions shook the earth. While we sat waiting our turns, I began to fidget in the dirt as the day dragged on. I drew pictures in the dirt with my finger. I told jokes, attempting to make anyone who would listen laugh at my inappropriate and ill-timed bits. Then I settled into spinning yarns. Everyone's life story carried tiny inflations here and there, and we let each other get away with it as long as the lie was small enough. It seemed that I was surrounded by almost-college-football stars and near CEOs. But talking was better than silently considering one's life, seated in the powdery dirt of Camp Pendleton, even if every conversation carried with it an aroma of bullshit.

They called my name, and I followed the combat instructor over the hill to a concrete bunker. He asked me if I remembered the procedure. Of course, I remembered. I had been throwing grenades in my head for a lifetime: pull the thumb clip, pull the pin, prepare to throw, throw. The Marine Corps version of grenade throwing was broken into these four parts, unlike the teeth-pull method of my youth. As with most things in the military, the official procedure was mechanical and slightly awkward. They expected you to take a Johnny Unitas stance, with one arm pointed at your target and the arm with the grenade cocked back behind your head. Then you were to throw the grenade in more of a pushing movement than a traditional baseball movement. I was impressed by how the Marine Corps could take something as simple as throwing and make it feel foreign. I just wanted to chuck the damn thing like I had been throwing baseballs and rocks all my life. But if this was the price I had to pay to be the star of my own action movie, I would gladly pay it.

We walked up to a chest-high wooden table where a few combat instructors stood. On the table were wooden boxes that looked like they belonged in a WWII drama. My instructor reached into the box and pulled out an olive drab cardboard cylinder. I followed the instructions on the tube, pulling a wire along the outside to open the cylinder like a can of Pillsbury crescent rolls, sliding the heavy piece out of the cardboard sleeve and into my hand. I carried the grenade to the four-foot-tall concrete bunker that was going to protect us from the explosion's shockwave that would surely blow us back twenty feet. I walked reverently, as if I was carrying a religious artifact. Once inside the bunker, I was given the command to throw the grenade.

I swept the thumb clip, pulled the pin (not with my teeth as I would have liked but with my middle finger), and prepared to throw. "THROW." I threw the grenade as far as my muscles would allow and quickly ducked behind the concrete, waiting for the explosion that would send fire and debris over our heads. There was an explosion, and the ground did shake a bit, but the blast was a disappointment. There was no giant fireball, no car that exploded with a gymnastic flip. There was only a large bang and – when I popped my head up to look at the carnage – a small dust cloud wisping away in the California air. It was a bust, my first official disappointment in the Marine Corps.

Afterward, we marched back to the barracks, none of us really wishing to tell the others what a colossal letdown the M67 fragmentation grenade was. Training continued, and after some time on the rifle range and a few forced hikes, we were turned over to our MOS-specific instructors. Most of the friends I had made in boot camp were going to be machine gunners like me; freaks of a feather flock together. The structure of this training was no different than any of the other training so far. We were taught practical information which included both classroom and field training, alongside historical accounts that demonstrated grit and proved the legend of the Marine Corps machine gunner. All the instructors were combat veterans, and each morning before class they would show us a moto video.

A moto video is a montage that military members put together after a deployment. The music is always heavy and dark, and the footage always shows Marines kicking ass. All the clips of us getting our asses kicked are cut out for motivation's sake. The videos showed the streets of Iraq filled with smoke, dead bodies strewn about the streets, machine gun tracers making insurgents dance, Marines cheering and yelling in primal triumph. The videos worked; I was motivated to practice my new trade. We all were.

We spent time familiarizing ourselves with the weapon systems. There was the M-2 50-caliber machine gun which was designed at the close of WWI and has remained in service from 1933 to the present, its design largely untouched. Gripping the wooden spade grips of the M-2 is like holding onto a time machine. They are the same grips that were squeezed as Americans fought German and Japanese soldiers, and the same grips that held back enemy waves in Korea. Those grips represented the machine-gunner lineage. Whenever I thought of the connection they represented, the grips inspired awe in me. It was horror, heroism, and history sitting peacefully on a tripod.

We were also responsible for the Mk-19 fully automatic grenade launcher. It fired a modified 40-mm grenade and had a maximum effective range of nearly 2000 meters. Our instructor described the machine as if it were the vengeful hand of the Old Testament God, a belt-fed Yahweh.

The last weapon system that we were responsible for was the M240 Golf, a medium machine gun, and the true backbone of the infantry. The 240 was what the ground-pounders walked around with. It was the machine gun you saw hefted over the shoulder of Marines and soldiers as they marched toward the sound of war. The 240 represented the true essence of machine guns and machine-gun gunnery.

In between fondling machine guns, we were taught the rules of machine gunnery and told they would serve us for the rest of our lives. Since the Marine Corps seems held together by lore and acronyms, it was fitting that the tenets of machine gunnery could be condensed to this: PICMDEEP G, which we pronounced "pick 'em deep g." It stood for Pairs, Interlocking sectors of fire, Coordination of fire, Mutual support, Defilade fire, Enfilade fire, Economy of rounds, Protection, and Geometry of fire.

I took this information as my new gospel. These tenets of machine gunnery were learned in the jungles of the Pacific and the frozen wastelands of Korea. They worked and had years of proven efficacy. Rewriting them over ten years later after learning them makes me realize how they've infiltrated my personal philosophy beyond machine gun employment. If I were to distill the acronym down, I would say: you can't do it alone; find good people and watch each other's backs; make sure your effort is aimed at the right goal; you only have so much time and resources, so plan accordingly; think through your circumstances and always have an exit strategy for when the shit hits the fan.

It seems like you could do much worse than machine gunnery as a personal ethos.

The training days kept ticking away, and along the way we had developed an inter-MOS rivalry. Everyone thought that their selected MOS was superior. It was like having a favorite baseball team; supporting numbers and statistics were thrown at each other, along with famous banner carriers of the given occupational specialty. Marines invoked names like John Basilone and E.B. Sledge as if they were arguing over Babe Ruth or Hank Aaron. Everything we did became a competition. It wasn't enough that we thought we were the most elite branch of the military; we had to continue breaking ourselves down into sub-groups until we were certain of our status over other Marines. We were all so similar – the only thing separating us was a few weeks of training – and yet we clung to our new sub-groups for the sheer exclusivity of it.

The last training event of SOI is a twenty-kilometer hike. For weapons-platoon Marines, it would mean we had to carry the standard grunt load out as well as our weapon systems. This was a rite of passage for all the Marines going through SOI, but particularly so for the weapons-platoon grunts. We would carry the most weight and make sure that the regular grunts never forgot it.

In passing, while discussing the hike, our machine gun section leader said that he had never seen anyone hump the 50-cal receiver the whole twenty-kilometer hike. To hump is gruntspeak for hiking. Tim O'Brien described it best in *The Things They Carried*: "In its intransitive form, to hump meant to walk, or to march, but it implied burdens far beyond the intransitive." Though we had yet to experience combat, we humped the weight of knowing real violence was just beyond the horizon. We humped the weight of knowing that we hadn't proven ourselves. We humped the weight of knowing we wouldn't truly know our worth until the first bullet flew past our heads. I took these thoughts with me on the hump. I also took the section leader's observation as a personal challenge. When the hike began, I took the sixty-five-pound rectangular chunk of hardened steel and threw it over my shoulders. I had something to prove, and this was the only way I could think to do it. We stepped off, and I began my left-foot, right-foot mantra, not focusing on the miles to come, but only on the next ten feet. I kept my head down and focused on my steps and the steady rhythm my boots made on the trail.

Marines began to fall out all around me, succumbing to the accumulation of pain that grew with each step. I watched as mortarmen struggled to hand off base plates and mortar tubes, hoping for a brief reprieve from the weight. Each Marine that fell out motivated me, each person who fell back meant that I was doing something they couldn't, and I used it as fuel. Left foot. Right foot.

We humped into the high hills of Camp Pendleton. It seemed like the combat instructors had found a physics-defying incline that had no crest. We kept climbing, and as soon as we were certain that we had reached the peak, we would realize it was an illusion. There was always one more hill. We climbed all morning through the early dark of the day. I imagined that when the sun broke, as in boot camp, we would reach the summit. I was wrong. When the sun came up, it only illuminated the fact that we still had miles to go. I continued to watch the ground in front of me, careful not to twist an ankle in the deep trenches carved out by rainwater.

The machine gunners hiked valiantly. Just like the Marine Corps attracts a certain kind of person, so does the machine gun occupation. We all thought we were John Wayne, and the Duke would never show weakness. But even these sadomasochists were faltering, handing off the guns regularly. I kept my head down and kept marching, the 50-cal receiver balanced on my shoulders. Left foot. Right foot.

When we finally crested the mountain, most of us assumed it would get easier, but going downhill had perils of its own. Marines fell often, all of us stopping to pick each other up. I got a thrill from watching people succumb to the pain; their faltering rarified my ability to keep pushing. Still, I knew we were in this together, and we had to lean on each other when the time came because in the end, we would only have each other. So, we picked each other up, we took gear that the other Marine couldn't carry any longer and carried it ourselves. There was always a look of relief mixed with shame in the eyes of the Marines that handed their gear off. It was apparent that they had a healthy level of self-loathing for not being able to carry their own weight. Marines strapped extra packs to their bodies and extra rifles to their packs.

We followed the trail as it slithered down the mountainside, snake-like in both its shape and treachery. Marines were beginning to trip and fall from exhaustion and the increased pace of going downhill. The weight seemed to get easier as the miles ticked away. The gear dug into the fleshy tissue of my shoulders, but the sense that I was going to complete the hike with the 50-cal receiver propelled my feet. We stopped twice throughout the hike to change socks and hydrate. We sat our packs down in uniform rows along the edge of the trail and leaned against them, peeling our socks off like the second skins they had become. The more intelligent Marines changed their socks to save their feet; others were too lazy and let the moisture dissolve their skin. As I looked up and down the row, I saw the pink exploded blisters of young feet that had only just begun to develop into the necessary callouses all grunts need. I envisioned my brain blistering too, and the hard shell that would grow over it as time passed. It wasn't just our feet that would need to be calloused.

Stopping almost made it worse. Having to mentally re-engage, stand up, and put the pack back on was its own struggle. But the hike was almost over, and it represented another milestone in our young infantry careers. After this it was to the fleet, and soon after to the mountains of Afghanistan or the cities of Iraq – both for some.

The squad bays rose out of the horizon, its towering gray effigy an instant ocular shot of Novocain. We marched back to the courtyard that sits in front of the squad bays and began to shed our gear. I unloaded the 50-cal receiver, its weight straining and pulling at my shoulders. When its metal body touched the concrete, it made a metallic clink, surprisingly slight for such a large object. Shedding the rest of my gear felt euphoric. I stacked my gear up, with the 50-cal receiver proudly displayed on top of my pack, then eagerly awaited the praise of my combat instructor. Surely, he would spread the word of my achievement throughout the Marine

Corps and my own legend would begin to grow. I was certain that the instructors had been watching my heroic hike with awe as the miles ticked down. I stood ramrod straight, sticking out my chest when the instructor walked by. I knew I didn't have to say anything because he had been following my journey from beginning to thrilling conclusion. My eyes traced him as he walked nearer, his brow furrowed in concentration as he counted the young Marines in his charge. When he got to me, he simply walked by. I thought that this might have been because he wanted to tell the whole machine gun section what had transpired, but he kept walking. As he got farther down the line, one of my buddies, Berg, said, "Sergeant, did you see? Tellessen carried the 50 the whole way. You said no one had ever done that before." I loved Berg for saying exactly what I was thinking.

The instructor looked at me before saying, "Bullshit, I didn't see it," as he kept walking.

6. The Fleet

After the hump, SOI was all but over. There was nothing left to do but find out where we would be spending the next three and a half years of our lives. After a weekend spent drinking with my brother in San Diego, I returned to SOI with a purpled face and eyes turned crimson by popped blood vessels. I had to make up an elaborate story about coming to my brother's rescue after he was accosted by some local hooligans in San Diego. I left out the part about me being the chief instigator: During our night cap, I'd purposely shattered my empty pint glass on the bar's dance floor, then picked a fight with a half-dozen bouncers who rightfully beat the ever-living shit out of us. The tale got a little more extravagant with each telling as I regaled my fellow Marines with details from my heroic struggle. But when I spoke with the sergeants and staff sergeants, my story was an exercise in concision. I said as little as possible, hoping the whole thing would blow over before the fumes ignited into a toxic shitstorm.

To conclude SOI, there was a brief ceremony, and we were given diplomas that said we were officially riflemen, machine gunners, mortarmen, assaultmen, and TOW gunners. After my multi-day hangover subsided and the swelling went down, I was finally starting to feel like a Marine.

They gathered us in the squad bay after graduation to tell us what unit we were headed for. The decisions were made solely by alphabetical arithmetic. My fate was tied to the letter T, as it would be for the rest of my Marine Corps experience. The names toward the beginning of the alphabet were going to stay in Camp Pendleton. I found myself repeating the alphabet in my head to gauge how long I'd have to wait. It became a nervous tick, A-B-C-D-E-F-G-H-I-J-K-L-M-N-O-P-Q-R-S-T – over and over again. The instructor got to the letter H, which heralded a new destination: Twenty-Nine Palms. The name sounds like a pleasant retirement community, but Twenty-Nine Palms is legendary for the never-ending supply of misery it provides its inhabitants. The base was in the middle of the Mojave Desert, a wasteland filled with poisonous spiders, translucent scorpions, pit vipers, and generations of salt from the evaporated tears of young Marines. It was a place so awful I was certain that I was going to be stationed there. But as they reached the letter L, the destination changed again.

The rest of the alphabet was heading for Second Battalion, Third Marines. I had absolutely no idea where that was. The instructor shook his head in disbelief before calling us a bunch of "lucky cocksuckers." Second Battalion, Third Marines was housed at Marine Corps Base Hawaii, decidedly not in the Mojave Desert. We were headed to a tropical paradise. I tried to refrain from too much cheering, out of respect for my friends who had been sentenced to the desert, but the excitement was just too much. I wore a goofy smile on my face for the next few hours. I truly couldn't believe my luck. I was going to Hawaii with almost all my boot-camp buddies.

We went straight from graduation to the airport. A van would be waiting for us in Honolulu. My mom and brother, who had both been in San Diego with me over the weekend, stayed for the graduation. When I told them the good news, they seemed happy for me, but my mom still wore that weekend's terrible events around her eyes, looking tired and concerned for me. I hugged them both but was too entranced with my own upcoming adventure to think about what they were going through. I boarded a plane that morning and would arrive at the Honolulu International Airport late in the night.

When we arrived at the airport, we were greeted by the sticky Hawaiian night air and a pissed-off sergeant. He spoke little to us, communicating only in short, sharp commands, telling us to grab our gear and follow him. We all got on a small bus, and the sergeant drove us to the base. I remember being disoriented, losing my sense of direction, and having anxiety because I didn't know which direction true north was. The excitement evaporated, and I was left with a pang of loneliness as the streetlamps and neon signs blurred beyond my shuttle window. I was truly away from home now. The sergeant didn't speak a word for the rest of the trip.

It was pitch black when the sergeant dropped us off at the barracks. We were checking in first thing in the morning and had to be wearing our service-alpha uniforms when we went through the strange ceremonial process. The service alphas are the iconic, olive drab suits with red chevrons. I spent most of the night making sure my uniform was properly squared away, re-centering my only ribbon, the National Defense Service Ribbon, three times.

A lance corporal, wearing a baggy sweatshirt and carrying a beer, woke us up at four in the morning. He got us on line and made us police call the grass for cigarette butts. To police call is Marinespeak for picking shit up off the ground, and the bulk of a young Marine's career will be spent police calling. Little did I know that this would be my routine for the foreseeable future. It was the first morning, and I already couldn't wait to be one of the assholes flicking cigarette butts.

Our battalion had just gotten back from a deployment to Afghanistan, and the only Marines from the battalion that were on base were the ones that didn't have enough leave days. Their deployment to Afghanistan had been a Spartan existence in the mountains, hiking for days and fighting the Taliban on their own turf. Though many of the Marines responsible for us were only a year or two older than us, they seemed a generation older, like they had lived a lifetime during their seven months in Afghanistan. I looked up to them with admiration, which made how poorly they treated us sting worse.

After the police call, we were told to get in our service alphas and stand by for an inspection. I went over my uniform once more, ensuring that no stray fibers, or Irish pennants, would detract from the impressive green uniform. First, I put on a white undershirt and the long-sleeve khaki shirt. One of the uniform secrets that makes Marines look so sharp is the black elastic shirt stays that run from shirt to socks. They looked ridiculous and were somehow even more uncomfortable than they were unsightly, but they gave the appearance of an immaculately tucked-in shirt that would never come untucked unless the dreaded happened and a shirt stay popped off, threatening the genitalia with the slap of black elastic. I got my shirt stays in place and looked at myself in the mirror. If garter hoses were worn by women to attract men, then surely men's shirt stays were meant to repel women. I quickly put on my jacket, adjusted my tie, and placed my gold tie clasp between my second and third buttons. I put my cap on and ensured that it tilted down on my forehead just as the drill instructors had shown us. I stared again at the mirror, this time not at the male garter-hosen, but at the black-and-purple hematoma that still clung to my face. I knew that I was going to have to tell the story of the black eye at least a hundred times before the day ended.

We walked out of our rooms and into the common area, which was a sort of living room in the barracks with a few couches and a foosball table. We stood and waited to be inspected. A man walked in wearing woodland cammies. He was a tall, light-skinned Black man with gray eyes and carried the rank of sergeant.

The sergeant was belligerently checking our uniforms, critiquing the smallest infraction, and screaming over the more glaring ones. A Marine hadn't worn his tie clasp, and the sergeant informed him that there would be consequences. After the inspection, we followed the sergeant to the company office where we were to meet the company commander. Marines were beginning to trickle back into the barracks from leave as we walked to the company office. Many of them yelled obscenities at us as we walked past: "Eat shit and die, boot scum," was a popular insult. I looked straight ahead, not giving them the satisfaction of seeing my emotions.

Once in the office we stood at parade rest, our hands behind our backs in a faux-relaxed posture. Each Marine would check in individually. The procedure was simple. Knock on the door and ask permission to enter. Once granted, the Marine was to walk into the office, centering himself on the desk, and snap a salute, stating his respective name and rank, closing with, "Reporting for duty." One by one, the Marines in front of me walked into the office and reported for duty. I simulated the proper procedure over and over again in my head before it was my turn, going through each motion and word spoken.

The Marine directly ahead of me walked out of the office, and I stepped toward the door. I had to come to a lurching stop because I almost barged straight into the office, forgetting to ask for permission. My entire rehearsed procedure was thrown off. I slammed three times on the door and asked permission to enter. I stepped in and went through the motions, trying to act like I knew what I was doing. I stuttered out my name, then looked forward until the captain told me to stand at ease. My arms slid behind my back, and I finally looked down at the man. He was tall and fair-skinned, with a narrow face and a long nose. His small eyes stared back at me. There was a silence before he said, "Jesus Christ, Marine. What the hell happened to your face?"

"Got into a fight in San Diego, sir."

"So, you like to go out in town and raise hell?"

"No, sir."

"That's good, because we don't tolerate any liberty incidents in this company. Dismissed."

That was my big introduction to the company commander. I remember reading accounts written about and by company commanders from WWII to Vietnam, men who inspired by sheer proximity. Maybe he was holding back, but I didn't feel the slightest spark. We changed back into our cammies and waited for a Marine to walk us around and finish the check-in procedure.

Checking into a Marine Corps base is like a two-day excursion to the DMV. It's a series of waiting rooms with high-traffic carpet and wooden chairs, waiting for a small signature to confirm that you survived a specific waiting room. We walked everywhere. There were no more shuttles from place to place. After a couple days of checking in, we received our gear and were ready to begin training.

The company I was assigned to was Golf Company. They were a former amphibious assault company, but for Iraq and Afghanistan they had traded in their zodiac boats for desert-appropriate gear. The Afghanistan deployment was the first combat deployment for Second Battalion, Third Marines (2/3) since Vietnam. During the Afghan deployment, 2/3 were a part of the infamous Operations Red Wings and Whalers that involved the doomed Navy Seals of *Lone Survivor* fame. The operations were successful in recovering the bodies and rescuing the lone survivor, Marcus Luttrell, while largely destroying the enemy responsible for the attack. The Marines of 2/3 walked straight into mountainous enemy territory, fighting both the enemy and the crushing Afghanistan ecosystem that seemed designed to punish foreigners for thinking they could fight in it. The Afghans and their mountains had been kicking western asses since the fair-haired Alexander the Great led his armies through the same valleys and mountains that the Marines would patrol thousands of years later. It was a land of perpetual warfare, and the Marines that came back from it seemed tempered by the place.

The Marine taking us around the area was incredibly tall. The arms that hung from his rolled sleeves were long and roped with muscles. A skull tattoo on his forearm signified some form of allegiance with death. But when he spoke, he never used a curse word, which was a rarity in my limited experience in the Marine Corps.

His name was Lance Corporal Hall, and he eventually became my squad leader for the workup. It was slowly revealed to me that he was a hardline, born-again Christian who had found Jesus somewhere in the desert and was doing his best to atone for his prior life of sin. I was never outwardly religious and always loved to start arguments. Later, when I got to know him a little better and wasn't such a terrified boot, I would ask him questions of dinosaurs and the fossil record, about whether he believed in evolution. Most of these things he attributed to Satan. I would laugh and keep trying to poke holes in his beliefs, but the certainty in his eyes startled me. When he looked at me like that, it felt as if he knew something I didn't. I was jealous of the comfort he must have felt in believing he knew what came after death. I didn't know, and still don't, but always leaned toward nothingness, which isn't without its own grace. We both believed that what we did mattered – he because it was an all-seasons pass to paradise, and me because I knew this life was the only chance I had.

Our seniors' treatment of us made this time in the Corps difficult. We came to the fleet expecting the respect we thought we had earned through completing boot camp and SOI. We soon realized that respect was only earned after a deployment. And since we were at war, respect was only truly earned after combat. I could understand this sentiment, though it was still hard to swallow. They shaved our heads again, just as they had at boot camp. Seniors wanted to be able to easily identify the boots in the crowd, as if it wasn't apparent enough.

Once we were secured for the day, the boot's main objective was remaining out of sight. The barracks was a rough place, akin to a beer-soaked roadhouse. The only difference was that after a night of chaos, the barracks magically returned to its immaculate condition, mostly through the servitude of us indentured boots. Cleaning the barracks in the early morning hours could be a dangerous task. I tried to avoid the watchful, sometimes nefarious eyes of drunken combat veterans full of whiskey and hate. Hazing abounded in those days. Some of it helped cultivate the combat effectiveness of a new Marine, but much of it was short-sighted and only designed to humiliate. I had told myself that I would only do the things that made sense from a training standpoint. Anything that I could justify as training I would endure; anything that crossed the line I'd fight. I think the senior Marines sensed this attitude and largely left me alone, though others were not as fortunate. One night, I remember seeing two mattresses that were duct-taped together come flying off the third story of the barracks. When two boots reached the mattresses, they cut the duct tape and found a third boot inside. He stumbled out from between the mattresses and gave two thumbs up. Cheers roared from the third deck and empty beer cans rained down on the discombobulated boot.

After finishing check-in, we were assigned to our specific gun teams and squads. Our new section leader was a tiny man with glasses named Sergeant Tardiff. Built like a toy breed, Tardiff was the antithesis of your typical machine gunner. He was a nerd and had the glasses and video games to prove it. But when he stood before us and called our names with a deep commanding voice, we all fell in line as if the voice belonged to a man that was a foot taller and a hundred pounds heavier. Looking down at a clipboard, he called names and organized his new machine gun section. He called my name and told me that my team leader would be Lance Corporal Skalitzky, or Ski, and my gunner was going to be Lance Corporal Plutchak.

Ski was short but stout, with curly red hair and a joker's face. His arms were covered with traditional Sailor Jerry-style tattoos, and he was constantly smoking cigarettes. Plutchak, who had a Nordic face, was tall and hunched. Neither of them took anything seriously unless it came to machine gunnery.

The next day at formation, I was introduced to the concept of "bull in the ring." Senior Marines often treat their new boots like fighting dogs, mainly for their amusement, but the aggression and competition was also good training. They would pit boot against boot and form a crowded circle around them. The boots would sit back-to-back on the ground. The rules were simple but allowed for small variations depending on who was the commissioning senior lance corporal at the time: no standing up, whoever taps the other Marine out and makes him submit wins. Sometimes small five-inch punches were allowed, but it was mostly a grappling affair. Once the boots were back-to-back, the commissioner would say fight, and it was a fight until either the left or right boot cried uncle. I was bigger than the average boot, so my team leader had high expectations for me.

Though I had wrestled in high school and shown up in Hawaii with barfight injuries, I still was far from an accomplished fighter. The only thing I had going for me was that I told myself I would die before I tapped out. As I looked at my first bald-headed opponent, I didn't think he was ready to die for this silly game like I was.

We sat back-to-back, our shaved heads touching. I looked over and watched as my team leader and gunner smoked cigarettes. I was a ball of nervous energy. My stomach pulsed with electricity. I imagined an insurgent's back pressed up against mine, not a fellow Marine.

"FIGHT."

I spun around as fast as possible and was on the Marine's back, an assaultman whom I barely knew. I had him flattened out on his stomach in seconds, but in high school wrestling there aren't any submission moves. About all I knew was the sleeper hold that I learned watching the Undertaker wrestle Yokozuna as a kid. Not knowing what else to do, I grabbed the Marine's head, each hand finding an ear, and squeezed as hard as I could. I was simply trying to inflict as much pain as possible. The Marine beneath me began to scream in agony before tapping out. I was thrilled, but I didn't celebrate; I just stood up and shook the Marine's hand. But it wasn't over. One of the rewards for success in the Marine Corps is that you will be called on again and again to repeat your success. I fought again and again. Most of my rudimentary submission skills involved being meaner than the other guy. I would twist and pull at limbs and necks until people quit. As the days and fights went on, I developed techniques and moves specific to this bull-in-the-ring system. I beat everyone they put in front of me.

My grappling success only added to my hubris. I was wildly overconfident in my fighting ability. Months later, I would meet the champion boot of Fox Company. It never occurred to me that I could lose. My opponent was built like a red-haired refrigerator. He had run through his own company just as I had run through mine, but surely I would be able to beat him. After all, I wanted it more than he did.

The stars were out when we finally decided to get down to it. It was after hours, so we both wore our civilian clothes. We walked behind the barracks and at this point there were no senior Marines around. Us boots had become obsessed with the contests and had whispered, from company to company, about who was the meanest boot in the battalion. I knew if I could beat the red-haired giant, I would hold the title. We sat back-to-back on the cool, damp grass as a crowd of boots began to circle around us. Each of us had a promoter of sorts, a guy who was talking us up. There may have been betting involved, but I was too singularly focused to notice. The giant was a machine gunner as well, so I knew he was mentally tough, but I told myself I was mentally tougher. He was bigger and probably stronger, but I told myself that I was meaner. Then, out of the night air, came the word "FIGHT," and it began.

I spun around and put an arm around his neck, catching him in an awkward choke hold. But the red-haired giant easily swept my arm off his neck and dragged me in front of him, then slammed me onto the ground. All my air escaped out my mouth as I struggled to get back up. Each time I tried to stand, he grabbed my back leg and drove me back into the dirt. I was a half-hearted high school wrestler who had done the sport merely to stay in shape. By the way this Marine was throwing me around, his first love must have been wrestling. It had been my standard operating procedure that if I couldn't beat a Marine fairly, I would cheat and fight dirty. We were always taught that you should never enter a fair fight, but instead create an unfair advantage. I couldn't use a club to bludgeon the Marine, so I did the first thing that came to mind. I reached through my own legs and grabbed ahold of his testicles, squeezing as hard as I could. I wasn't proud of the move, but I had used it with success in the past. Normally, when I implemented the ball crusher, the Marine would howl and let go, giving me the chance to get some separation before gaining the upper hand. But this boot grunted a "What the fuck," before repeatedly slamming me on the ground like a giant toddler with a stuffed animal.

As the match continued past the five-minute mark, both of us entered a state of sheer exhaustion. Once again, he flattened me out on my stomach, but this time when I got back to my knees, he slipped a giant red-haired arm around my neck. I had fallen for his trap. He put the squeeze on, and I watched as his muscles tensed around my windpipe. I knew that if I just held on, I could break his arm loose and finally gain the upper hand. What I didn't realize is that your brain shuts off when there is no blood flowing to it. I reached up and grabbed his arm as things faded to black.

When I came to, I saw the grave faces of Marines kneeling next to me. Apparently, I'd passed out, then started convulsing on the ground like I was having a seizure. The big red-haired man now looked worried sick. It turned out he was really a gentle giant. I apologized for grabbing his balls, and he apologized for kicking my ass. We both had cuts and scrapes, but I was in much worse shape – a grass burn stood out on my forehead like a smear of red paint, and my lip was swollen from an accidental elbow. I chalked it up to accidently running into a force of nature and vowed that I would get better. There weren't too many fights after that, and I was thankful.

The fights were largely a byproduct of boredom. Most of military enlistment is spent waiting around, which is where the term "hurry up and wait" comes from. You are always running to get from place to place, only to sit on your ass for hours after you arrive. This was particularly true for Marines in Hawaii.

While Hawaii is an island paradise, it is severely lacking in quality training facilities. We were on a base where we couldn't shoot machine guns, which made it difficult to train machine gunnery – difficult but not impossible.

Since we didn't have access to the big ranges like the mainlanders did, we had to get creative with our training. We would check the machine guns out from the armory and do gun drills until our senior Marines got tired of watching us. A gun drill harkens back to WWII, where the machine gun is set up on a tripod, and the team works as intended with the team leader, gunner, and ammo man all contributing to the machine gun's setup. The squad leader stands in an open field and calls off the direction and distance of the enemy, and the machine gunners scream back the commands at the top of their lungs. Once the command is given, the machine gunners rush the field and set up their guns. Because everything in the Marine Corps is a competition, if your team isn't first in setting up the gun there is pain to pay. Burpees and all manner of calisthenics are the consequences for losing. The senior Marines were trying to drill into us the idea that in combat the consequence of losing is death. Maybe not your own death, which is at least palatable for most Marines, but the death of the Marines that you are covering. Machine guns are the great force multiplier on the battlefield, accounting for seventy percent of a line company's fire power. So, when the riflemen scream "GUNS UP," the whole company is depending on the machine gun team to get set and start turning the tide through an overwhelming wave of sulfur and lead.

We would also conduct mock patrols through the base. I'm sure they were odd exercises to see for the rare civilians who found themselves strolling through Marine Corps Base Hawaii. During mock patrols, we stayed out of base housing, though everywhere else was fair game. Sometimes we would work with the riflemen so we could experience the actual structure of a patrol, but other times we just patrolled with our machine gun section. I'll always remember the juxtaposition of a Marine in full body armor, carrying a machine gun, standing in front of a McDonald's golden arches. I hoped it wasn't an image of things to come.

When all else failed and they let us take the guns out of the armory, we would practice disassembly and reassembly. We normally checked out at least two guns, so we could compete against one another. We ribbed each other while we worked, speaking of one another's mothers and girlfriends in all manner of sexual situations. We went after each other's origins too. There were racist remarks on all sides, and there was an elegance that made me believe we had finally found the cure to racism. We reduced it to a joke, a meme. We used humor to diffuse racial tension, so much so that it almost disappeared entirely. When nothing was off limits, and the limits of our humor pushed all social boundaries, it opened a world to us where race really was an afterthought. Perhaps much of this came from making competition our singular focus. It didn't matter what color you were; it only mattered if you won. A good Marine was a good Marine.

When the senior Marines got tired of watching us do regular dis and ass (disassembly and reassembly), they would bring out blindfolds and make us work the machine gun by feel. Slowly, the machine gun became an extension of ourselves. Just as you could run your left hand up your right arm and feel the bumps, moles, and scars you have accumulated since birth, so too could we find familiarity along the charging handle of a machine gun in the dark.

We cross-trained as much as possible. Marines from other disciplines taught us classes about their own crafts, and we taught the rest of our company about the violent art of machine gunnery. There was a dry-erase board in the common area of the barracks where most of our classes were conducted. Most lessons began with erasing a phallic mural from the board. After that, we'd sit cross-legged on cheap carpet and learn how to breach doors and call for fire support. All the while, we frantically took notes in case there was going to be a test.

The only real, live-fire training that can be conducted on Hawaii involves a plane ride to the Big Island. The Big Island, as the name implies, is huge. It is the only island to have four of the five climate zones and is home to arguably the most beautiful beach in the world: the Punalu'u Black Sand Beach. But the Marine Corps, being the entity that it is, bought the center of the island – a post-apocalyptic wasteland where no vegetation grows, and the ground is paved with razor-sharp lava rock. It looks like the end of the world, so it is the logical place for the Marine Corps to conduct training.

It is called the Pohakuloa Training Area, or PTA, and is a rite of passage for Hawaii Marines. It was in those obsidian-filled fields that we finally got to shoot our machine guns and conduct company operations, with the entire company working like the war machine that it really was. All our gear was shipped to the big island on boats while we followed on commercial flights. Once on the island, we were bused past the beautiful beaches toward PTA. The road climbed higher and higher in elevation, the snowcapped Mauna Kea mountain looming in the distance.

After the gear had been unloaded and all Marines and equipment were present and accounted for, we took military trucks into the center of the training area where we set up a bivouac site. A bivouac site is just a much cooler way of saying campground, because essentially that's what we were doing: camping in two-man tents, or just under the stars, and playing war. Despite the lack of amenities and the constant barrage of cold wind, I thoroughly enjoyed myself.

We qualified with machine guns at the School of Infantry range, but this was the first time we would be firing the guns since we got to the fleet. The qualification shoot for machine guns is a huge paper target with rows of tombstone-like targets. The objective of the qualification is to put a three- to five-round burst on each one of the tombstones. The machine gun is mounted on a tripod and manipulated with a metal crank that moves the gun in small clicking increments. If used properly, the gun is incredibly accurate when mounted. All of us boots were set to qualify, and as usual, it was a competition.

We lined up at the range, lying on our bellies in the prone position behind the guns. The team leader lay next to the gunner, ready to feed ammo into the gun and direct fire. I lay behind the gun, nervous but confident. I fired in short, controlled bursts, just as I had imagined back on MCBH when I was only firing rounds of imagination. I slowly squeezed the trigger and then twisted the dial that was below the gun, moving it to the next target. When the last bullet was fired, I looked down range at the target, smoke rising from my barrel in a slender white wisp, contrasting starkly against the black and red rock that the range was built on. We cleared the weapons and waited for the squad and team leaders to tally up the scores.

The boots gathered in a small circle, huddling together against the wind. We talked about how we did; some of the Marines boasted that they wouldn't be surprised if they had shot a perfect score. My own confidence slowly eroded with the wind, until I was positive that I had not qualified at all, that I had actually missed all my targets. Soon Sergeant Tardiff, the section leader, called us all over to a tall wooden table, which looked cartoonishly large in comparison to the tiny Marine.

Sergeant Tardiff looked furious; all the squad and team leaders looked down at the ground. He launched into a tirade, decrying us as worthless pieces of shit. There had only been one Marine who had qualified today; the rest had failed. I thought Torres had probably qualified – he was the squared-away Mexican Marine who always seemed to have his shit together. After what seemed like a twenty-minute speech, Sergeant Tardiff finally said, "One goddamn Marine qualified. One. Fucking Tellessen is the only one of you assholes that qualified. That is unacceptable. Go get the guns off the line. We're done shooting for the day, but we're going to do gun drills until I get tired of watching." I kept my eyes fixed on the ground, trying not to smile. The hubris I had been cultivating since boot camp grew a little larger. I was starting to believe my own bullshit.

We weren't a terrible machine gun section, but we were out of practice. We could be experts in handling our weapons and setting them up, but you only get better at shooting by shooting. Unfortunately, more trigger time was in short supply for Hawaii Marines.

After the crushing pressure of qualification, all our performances improved. The PTA training curriculum culminates in a company-level assault on a target. During a company-level assault, all the company's assets work together as a single creature. Mortarmen launch indirect fire on the target so that the riflemen can get closer to the target. Meanwhile, machine gunners get into an elevated position so they can cover the riflemen's movements while the assaultmen breach obstacles and soften the target with missile launchers. This is how a Marine rifle company is designed to operate.

After extensive hours of preparation and briefings, we were in the staging area. We had run through the operation countless times at the sand table, where we had recreated the range using rocks and MRE boxes. We had a plan – all we had to do was execute. As we stood around the staging area, we began to hear the mortars exploding on the target. This was our signal to start moving. We would patrol to the bottom of a large hill, aptly named machine gun hill, and wait for the command to take the hill. We slithered through the range, staying close to the mountain where vegetation still grew. We moved from tree to tree, trying to use the flora and natural depressions in the ground as cover. It was training, but the lump in my throat made it feel real. We made it to the base of the hill and waited for the command to take it. I felt like I was in WWII, getting ready to fire belt-fed hate down on the Imperial Japanese military. And who knows, I could have been training on the same hill John Basilone trained on, as the PTA training facility was used for the WWII Marines who fought so valiantly in the Pacific theater. As I held the gun in my hand, I felt connected to history. I felt like I was finally living my dream.

"GUNS UP."

I ran up the hill like the entire company operation depended on me. In my mind, the stakes had never felt more real. This wasn't training; this was life or death, victory or defeat. My legs fired like pistons, and I left my team leader behind as I charged up the hill. I dove onto my belly at the hill's crest and sighted in on Green Ivan targets. The Green Ivans were a carryover from the Cold War. They were Russian-faced plastic targets that carried rifles and never seemed to stay dead. They were designed to fall after being impacted by a specific number of bullets. After they were shot down, they would pop back up, ready once again to spread a plastic communism across the free world. My team leader reached me, and we set up the gun. The plan was to open with a fifty-round burst once all the guns were in position. This huge initial burst was meant to shock the enemy. I never took my eyes off the army of Ivans, but waited until my team leader slapped me on the back and screamed, "Fire!" I squeezed the trigger and shifted my hips to the right, spraying the Ivan targets from left to right. The ratcheting targeting system we had used to qualify was now unlocked – I could move the gun freely on the tripod. That first fifty-round burst ripped through the row of green plastic targets, and I watched as they fell backward in their temporary graves. I can't be certain, but while I awaited their mechanical resurrection, I think I was smiling.

The range was a success. We performed much more admirably on this range than we had during qualification. We did well enough for our section leader to gain some recognition from the battalion commander. Plus, we weren't met with the same speeches of unworthiness when we made it back to the debriefing area, so I knew we had done alright. It was an experience to see the cogs of the war machine working exactly as they were designed.

The last training event was a twelve-mile hike back to the Quonset huts we had driven past when we first showed up. Clean beds and hot showers awaited us. I was still on a high from the range when we left for the hike. We hiked in silence, a giant green centipede armed to the teeth, a hundred individual bootsteps crushing the black rock in near unison. It was a forced march, but it felt to me like a parade of conquering heroes.

After we made it back to the Quonset huts and dropped our packs, we got together for a picture, all us machine gun boots, and had a mortarman take the picture. Our faces were covered with dirt, making our baby faces look a little older than they were. We clung to each other in the joy of accomplishment and the euphoria of exhaustion. It was just a training exercise, but we were all one step closer to not being boots. We were one step closer to Iraq. And the completion of PTA meant the senior Marines would let us grow our hair again. It was a good day.

When we got back to Marine Corps Base Hawaii, we immediately began preparing for our final training operation before stepping off for Iraq. In preparation for a fight in a Middle Eastern desert, the Marines train in the American Mojave Desert. Twenty-Nine Palms housed a fake Iraqi city, erected out of shipping containers and inhabited with role players who acted as Iraqi civilians and insurgents. Essentially, it was high-level LARPing.

When we got to Twenty-Nine Palms, we were set up in metal Quonset huts with sand floors. The camp was meant to inoculate us to the austere living conditions of Iraq, though I had a sneaking suspicion that there wouldn't be a chow hall, Post Exchange, or hot showers where we were going. The toilets flushed and didn't require a burning detail, so I knew we were living like kings at Camp Wilson compared to what awaited us in the Middle East. It was a rush to get to the camp and get set up, but once there we waited in limbo for days. The temperatures soared, so we mainly drank water and slept like dogs in whatever shade we could find.

We shot a few ranges, but it was almost a week before they took us out to the shipping-container city. There was a small camp next to the city that we were going to treat like a Forward Operating Base. By this point, I had fallen into the peer pressure of smoking cigarettes, so the days revolved around chugging water and smoking cigarettes. Our first mission into the city was going to be with Simunition. Simunition rounds are 9mm chalk bullets that are fired out of rifles like civilian paintballing. Only, in this case, chalk hurts a lot more and the concussion of the 9mm projectile sounds like a rifle going off. It's as real as you can get to a firefight without shooting live rounds at each other.

We patrolled into the city like we knew what we were doing. But the other Marines lying in wait chewed through us like we were amateurs. The confidence we had built in PTA was quickly destroyed, and we were made to realize that we had a tremendous amount to learn before our deployment. We got better with each patrol, but the entire battalion had to go through this training and there was only so much time.

The Explosive Ordinance Disposal Marines had set up a course to illustrate the IED threat we would face in Iraq. It was horrifying. They informed us that in most cases, by the time you see the IED it's too late. Insurgents commonly hide IEDs and their wires beneath trash and debris, so it seemed like all we had to do was keep our eyes trained on any trash in the street. The catch was that the simulated training streets – and ostensibly all the ones we'd encounter in Iraq – were covered in trash and debris. They told us if we were lucky, the insurgent would be careless, and we could catch sight of a wire or a strange collection of trash that looked too well put-together to be random. But they also said many of these IEDs couldn't be spotted with the naked eye.

By the end of our training, the biggest takeaway was that the battalion wasn't ready. We scored poorly on the urban assault ranges, showing that the mountainous combat experience my seniors had learned in Afghanistan was not directly translatable to city settings. In an urban environment, our threat could come from three hundred and sixty degrees. We needed more training, desperately, but there was no time; we would have to learn through experience, the cruelest of instructors.

The training also let us weapons-platoon Marines know that when we got into country, everything would be different. We would no longer be a machine gun section. We would be separated and spread out among the regular platoons. There was a chance that we could remain in our small teams when we were tasked out, but there were no guarantees. During the training in our fake city, I had been attached to a squad of riflemen and had begun to make friends with some of them. I immediately struck up a bromance with a tall Marine from the hills of Tennessee named Huth. He told me he was from a town called Dunlap, and I asked if that was kind of like what you saw at Walmart. He asked me what the hell I was talking about and I replied, "You know, those people you see at Walmart, when their bellies Dunlapped their peckers." It took him a moment, but he laughed, and that was all it took.

He came from a place that time had forgotten. In this southern hometown, the Ku Klux Klan still held annual rallies. He talked about it in a matter-of-fact tone, but I think the disbelief in my eyes made him uncomfortable. He told me that he never went, and none of his family was involved, but it was a fact of his life in Tennessee. Huth wasn't outwardly racist – you really couldn't exist in the Marine Corps if you were. Our fates were intertwined with the races and creeds of the Marines that made up the company, which was far from a picture of whiteness. We had to lock arms and wade into the uncertain future together; any gaps of racism or ignorance and we would simply be washed away. The Marine line company acted as the ultimate social experiment in racial equality.

Huth had brought with him a small MP3 player filled with old country music and Tom Petty songs. During the lulls in training, we would sit next to each other and listen to Tom Petty and the Heartbreakers. We would nod our heads to the slow, steady rhythm of Hank Williams III and close our eyes to the pain we heard in the gravelly voice of Johnny Cash. All this we did through the haze of cigarette smoke. I had been repulsed by smoking when I was younger, thinking it a disgusting and idiotic vice, but there I sat in the desert sand, a constantly lit cigarette held between my fingers. I smoked Marlboro Reds because I thought that's what John Wayne would have smoked. Little did I know that Marlboros were originally designed as a woman's cigarette, its red filter meant to conceal lipstick smudges. I thought these were the cigarettes of the wild men who tamed the west, and that's how I wanted to see myself. Maybe I really smoked to ease the tension of being unprepared for combat, hoping that the cigarettes concealed how green I felt.

We were given a thirty-day block of leave before the deployment. The week prior to leaving for home, we were told it was a good idea to write a will in the event that we didn't make it back. I sat in a large room, staring at the form that would direct all my earthly possessions to my family. I didn't have much to give away, just some books and childhood artifacts that I had carried from home. There was a small worry stone my father had given me, pictures from a not-too-distant childhood, and a wallet my mother had bought for me after boot camp. The wallet was a light tan, with the words "Bad

Motherfucker" stitched onto the front in bold black letters. They were my most prized possessions at the time. I left everything to my parents, to include the $400,000 life insurance policy that the military takes out on all its members.

The will triggered something in me, and I started obsessing over my own death. I became certain that I would die in Iraq, and strangely, I didn't mind so much. I wrote a death letter to my parents, telling them I loved them and that they gave me the priceless gift of a happy childhood. I wrote another letter to my brothers, telling them to take care of Mom and Dad, and I even told them I loved them. My family was never big on the "L" word, and it was something we had all come to avoid. But I told them I loved them in my scrawling chicken scratch. It was much easier to write my feelings than it was to speak them, a fact that has always been the case for me.

The certainty of my death was affirmed by my namesake, Great Uncle Olaf, who had died serving in the United States Army during the invasion of Normandy in WWII. His black-and-white picture hung in my grandmother's home, and the resemblance was there for the world to see. I have never been a religious person; maybe I've always feared the implications if the texts were true, but I've never been able to escape my ancestral superstition. I had a strange feeling that kept forcing its way into my mind; I thought that my family had sacrificed a son to the nation in WWII so that they could have a chance to chase the American dream. I thought that there was another debt owed, and the poetic symbolism of two Olafs sacrificed on the bloody altar of American freedom was just too much for me to ignore. Still, I wasn't afraid. I think the same strain of romanticism that led me to the Marines twisted my thoughts into thinking that my terminal fate in the desert streets of Iraq would be a beautiful death, something worthy of remembrance.

I prepared for home, ready to say my goodbyes like they were the real thing. The flight from Hawaii to Seattle was about four-and-a-half hours. I read a Stephen King book and tried not to think about what my parents would look like at my funeral. The flight attendants gave me all the free booze I could handle. I think they felt like they were doing their patriotic duty, one airplane bottle at a time. I was happy for the gesture.

When I arrived in Seattle, I tried to sober up a bit, stopping at Ivar's for a bowl of clam chowder. It's a short flight to Spokane from Seattle, but when the flight attendants offered me a dark beer, it was too good to resist. After all, this was to be my final vacation. I landed in Spokane, and my parents were there waiting for me. My mother looked at my arms, which were now covered in tattoos, and I could see her trying not to appear disappointed. I gave them all big hugs, but once again avoided the "L" word. My middle brother, Dusty, was there as well. He threw me a set of keys, and I watched as the sun caught the metal, making them sparkle. I watched them all the way until they hit me in the upper sternum. I was still slightly drunk, and my reflexes were soggy. I bent down to pick them up and realized they were the battered keys of my old Pontiac Firebird that I had bought my senior year of high school. It was a real fixer-upper. Since I had little to no mechanical skills, I was certain that it would remain a shit box forever. I asked how she was running, and he told me better than ever. We walked the rest of the way to the parking lot, and I saw my old car. The car was transformed entirely; instead of a calico pattern of brown, gray, and black primer, the car was now a glossy midnight black. I stared at my own reflection on the driver's side door. My parents and brother stood beside me, their bodies bent and stretched in the glossy black paint. I looked at the distorted image and knew that everything was going to be different, that nothing would ever go back to the way it was. When I got in the car with my brother, he turned on the radio and Motörhead exploded from the new speakers. As we flew down the highway, the chaos of "Ace of Spades" added an extra fifty horsepower to the motor. I looked over at my brother – a huge smile spread across his face. It would be the image I'd conjure every time I thought about him in Iraq.

My mom went out of the way to make my leave experience everything it could be. She stocked her pantry and refrigerator with my favorites and planned an enormous going-away party. I wondered if she sensed an end coming as well.

I drank too much and made an ass of myself more than once. I desperately wanted to see Melissa, but she always seemed out of reach. It wasn't until two days before leave was over that I finally got to see her. She was attending Eastern Washington University and pursuing a degree in speech pathology. She rented a house in the small college town of Cheney and invited me to come over. She was more beautiful than I remembered. I could still make her laugh, and that smile of hers threatened to stop my heart from beating. I brought booze, but we didn't drink any. We stayed up talking all night until we fell asleep, tangled in each other's arms. I kissed her in the morning, certain it was the last time I would ever see her.

My parents drove me to the airport, and I tried not to cry as I gave them a quick hug at security. I told them I would see them soon, then turned around before the full effect of my mother's tears made me sob like the child I really was. I savored the view of Washington's expansive skies as I flew back to the island and closer to the desert.

7. Going

The City of Haqlaniyah in the Al Anbar Province of Iraq sits beside the fabled and ancient Euphrates River. Since the inception of civilization, humans have been living and fighting next to these waters. Upriver from the city sits Iraq's largest hydroelectric dam. Built in collaboration with the Soviets in the early '80s, the dam is vital to Iraq's overtaxed infrastructure. The Soviet-inspired gray concrete heights of the Haditha Dam created the artificial Lake Qadisiyah. Seen from the International Space Station, Lake Qadisiyah looks like an ancient serpent in the middle of digesting some fierce barbed prey, as the inlets from the artificially swollen water shoot out in every imaginable direction. It is a fitting analogy, as the artificial lake swallowed one of the oldest archeological sites in Iraq: a forty-three-century-old village named after the ancient virgin war goddess Anat. It would seem in 2006 the war goddess was alive and well, spewing forth her poison from the Red-Army-built concrete structure.

The Haditha Dam makes the northernmost point of the Haditha Triad, or the Triangle of Death to the more dramatic. It consists of the three municipalities of Haditha, Barwanah, and Haqlaniyah. All three of the cities were built off the bank of the Euphrates, giving their streets a steep incline as they rise from those ancient waters. Haqlaniyah herself rests on the west side of the river, rising all the way to the top of the desert plateau. On one block there are towering three-story stucco structures with marble floors and guest houses, and on the next block are half-built stucco structures where families squat in absolute filth. Open sewer trenches flow down the steep city streets, carrying the population's refuse towards the gentle current of the Euphrates. Garbage litters the streets, the inhabitants employ an out-of-site-out-of-mind policy with their garbage, dumping their refuse over the high stucco walls that surround the courtyards of their homes.

The houses themselves seem built for war. Almost all the houses are at least two stories, and all have roof access with adequate cover and concealment for rooftop snipers. Each house is surrounded by a high stucco fence, some upwards of seven feet tall. An illogical pattern of alleyways and small side streets twists through the city, making navigation almost impossible for the uninitiated.

After the invasion in 2003, the roads lost their Iraqi names. The American forces renamed the streets after Major League Baseball teams and American landmarks. Like the formerly cursed Boston Red Sox, route Red Sox was constantly plagued with misfortunes. Most of these misfortunes came in the way of Improvised Explosive Devices. The IED was Iraq's biggest and most ominous killer. The insurgent fighters had become experts in cobbling together old munitions and household goods, turning them into powerful bombs with biblical implications. Explosives scraped out of old Russian artillery shells were the explosive of choice. They created IEDs that were meant to maim, only taking off a heel or a toe, maybe a whole leg, in order to cause chaos on the battlefield. These were often mixed with well-coordinated ambushes. Other IEDs were built with the destructive capacity to liquefy humans and twist metal like demonic origami.

The main drag that runs all the way from Haditha to Haqlaniyah was named after the game-ending piece of blue real-estate from the Monopoly game: Boardwalk. Boardwalk ran alongside the lush palm groves that bordered the river, offering the area's farmers an oasis to grow dates and graze their goats. The farming culture of the area has endured centuries of war with scattered generations of peace. Stone structures built off the water tell of the Roman occupation of antiquity. The farmers survived the invading Mongols who rode like death on a sea of horses. They survived British rule. They survived the brutality of Saddam. They would survive the Americans as well.

It's 8,388 miles as the crow flies from Marine Corps Base Hawaii to Haqlaniyah, Iraq. But the giant metal birds of today rarely fly like their crow forefathers. Our plane had to fly to Alaska, 2,777 miles, and then across the white and icy expanse of northern Canada where almost nothing can survive, to Germany, another 4,048 miles. While on board we were given prepackaged meals of chicken or beef by good-looking blonde flight attendants. They looked like clones in their matching blue skirts as they went up and down the aisle, making sure rifles and machine guns were in their upright and locked positions. The airplane stopped in Germany for the amount of time it takes a Marine to smoke six cigarettes. With more smiles and performances on what to do if the plane crashes, our metal bird ascended into the air again. It flew over southern Europe and into the Middle East, another 2,439 miles. The bird landed its big wings in Kuwait, and we boarded tour buses headed for a city made of plastic tents in the Kuwaiti desert.

The city itself is a strange growth in the desert landscape. It looks like it has been there for years, but it also looks like it could vanish if a strong-enough sandstorm came along. A walk through the white sand streets reveals strange facsimiles of American Burger

Kings and coffee shops. Small shacks selling new cars and travel packages crowd the fast food restaurants and trinket shops. Though it's an American military base, most employees of the fast food joints and barbershops are Indian men, not the Kuwaiti people who own the desert.

Our stay would be brief. Dressed in tan uniforms, we attended classes and briefs about cultural sensitivity and life on the Kuwaiti base. In less than a week, we would be loaded onto a military C-130 and strapped in for a flight into a combat zone. The flight would be less than an hour, to another city made of plastic tents, this one reinforced with concrete barriers. People were a little more serious on this base than the last, but not much. There were the plastic façades of American businesses here as well. A poorly constructed Subway sold sandwiches that in no way lived up to the land of milk and honey's moniker. More briefs, more cultural sensitivity classes. They threw in some IED-preparedness training as well, the main sentiment of the PowerPoint presentation being that every piece of trash in the city could explode, and of course the streets would be covered in trash. As I sat in the plastic tent, it became apparent that our soon-to-be area of operations was currently the deadliest in Iraq. The takeaway from this particular PowerPoint on enemy activity was that it would get worse before it got better.

We prowled the base in unsullied tan uniforms. I alternated between feeling like an excited child on vacation and like a man on death row, punished for a crime I hadn't yet committed. I watched with fascination as the other men in tan uniforms spent their final moments in quasi-civilization. Some tried having a bowl of ice cream before they ventured out into the wilderness. Others frantically wrote home, already telling war stories to the pretty girls who waited for them. Some watched war movies, hoping that they could learn something from Colonel Kurtz before they traveled into their own Heart of Darkness. A few read. There were copies of *On Killing* by Lieutenant Colonel Dave Grossman making their rounds. There were even a few of the classics floating around. *The Sun Also Rises* hovered above a Marine on a green cot. The novel seemed like it belonged. There were many who could be found at the gym – one last chance to get a proper pump in. More than a few of the men in tan uniforms stared off at nothing, worrying about what was at the other end of the impending helicopter ride.

The helicopter came in the all-consuming darkness of the desert night. I shielded my eyes from the sand and pebbles that were kicked up from the CH-53's massive propellers. War was no longer an impending fate; it was now a current reality. All of us raced with our gear to the lowered rear door of the helicopter. The grit of desert sand coated my teeth as I shuffled up the rear hatch, carrying hundreds of pounds of gear. I found my seat and collapsed into it. All our collective gear sat in the middle of the helicopter, all our lives packed into two sea bags and an ILBE pack. The stack of gear was just low enough so that I could see the faces of the Marines seated on the other side of the helicopter. I stared at their faces as the crew chief inspected the loaded gear and secured the rear hatch.

There was a red glow from the cargo lights inside the helicopter. When I had imagined going to war, I imagined hard men with grim faces, staring through space and time, anticipating and making calculations for the fighting to come. I imagined the weathered jaw lines of Tom Berenger, or the stoic face of R. Lee Ermey. I don't know why I didn't imagine this: the red light reflecting off the smooth faces of teenage boys, most of us barely nineteen, some younger. We were kids, barely old enough to vote. Only a handful of us had any war experience, but that was in Afghanistan, which may well have been Mars for all the good it would do us here. I hoped I didn't look that young, sitting there in full body armor. I wanted to look menacing, but I suspected that my baby face glistened just like the rest.

The helicopter rose into the pitch black. Once we left the view of Al Asad Air Base, the landscape was shrouded in total darkness. We could have been flying over the ocean, and I wouldn't have known the difference. The stinging scent of fuel filled my nostrils. I looked to my left to see an older staff sergeant sleeping, his head hanging forward, swinging to the rhythm of the helicopter's movement. Maybe he already knew what was waiting for us and decided to try and dream of home. I couldn't stop myself from picturing what was waiting below.

The CH-53 banked hard and swung over a few flashing red lights in the darkness. Every time the helicopter banked, I could see the four small red lights blinking. The helicopter's circles got smaller and smaller until it leveled out and came to rest on top of the Haditha Dam. As soon as the rear hatch was dropped, the non-commissioned officers screamed at us to unload the helicopter. They weren't screaming at us in anger; screaming is just the way Marines communicate.

We formed a human chain and began unloading the packs and gear. In silence we toiled, as NCOs walked up and down the human chain, hurrying our actions along with verbal commands interspersed with profanity. Finally, the helicopter was unloaded.

I knelt next to a uniform stack of green sea bags, resting a hand on the bottom row. I let out a sharp breath as I felt a knee dig deep into my side just below my tan flak jacket, which scared me more than it hurt me. I stood and spun in anger, ready to fight. Immediately, my eyes were drawn to the collage of chevrons and rockers that hung heavily from the bald man's collar. He outranked me by about a thousand years of hard service. He struck the center of my flak jacket with an open palm and knocked me backward.

"How about standing at the position of attention, you disrespectful little fuck?"

I thought about tackling him into the concrete, just to see what would happen. Or maybe I could come up with a smart-ass quip to make him feel like an idiot. But then I saw the bags they were loading onto the helicopter we'd just gotten off. The long black bags carrying bodies. Their contents looked small and diminished but still human. I snapped to attention and stood staring at the bags as others carefully hoisted them up the rear ramp. I knew that seven months ago, the Marines in those black bags had walked down the very same ramp I just had. I later learned that they were on their last convoy to the dam when an IED swallowed them whole. As I stood there and gave a salute, cold sweat beaded on my forehead. The fallen Marines, meanwhile, began their journey back to moms and dads who would never smile again without feeling the pain of a phantom's knife digging deep in their bellies.

I had seen a version of this before. It was an echo of the opening scene from *Platoon*. The major difference, though, was that this scene atop the Haditha Dam was actually fucking happening to me. I had to live through all the cut scenes and backstage production. I didn't get to bitch about the catering or renegotiate my contract for a better air conditioner. This was reality. I could no longer hide in stories of human triumph and defeat. I had to step into the unknown and hope that my character came close to matching my heroes of the silver screen and written word. But as I've come to realize, nothing ever turns out quite like the movies.

8. Into the Wild

I stood in the dark, feeling like a child who couldn't find his parents, disoriented, nervous, and scared. I focused on the purring hum of the idling military vehicles that waited to whisk us away, covered wagons that we would ride into the frontier. A voice called for us to transform our weapons from the docile condition three to the deadly condition one. Condition three is a magazine inserted and the bolt closed on an empty chamber; condition one is a magazine inserted and a round in the chamber. The difference between the two is life and death. We lined up in a row behind the red clearing barrels. The barrels were 55-gallon drums cut in half and filled with sand. They were designed to catch bullets that inadvertently fired during the loading process, an accident that wasn't rare enough.

I waited my turn behind Huth. There were few men in the company who I looked up to, but Huth was one of them. My eyes were drawn to the shaved base of his head. I had been put into the newly formed fourth platoon, which was a collection of all the company's bastards who'd been sacrificed to make up this fourth grouping. He and I would not only be in the same platoon, but also the same squad and fire team. I counted myself lucky to be among the bastards. Huth made his way to the clearing barrel and racked a round into the chamber, pulling the charging handle slightly to the rear to see the gold shimmer of the brass, then smacking the forward assist to close the chamber. He closed the small stamped metal ejection port cover with a click and spun to the side, waiting for me. I pulled my Beretta pistol from the drop holster on my thigh and racked a round into the chamber, doing a one-handed brass check by sliding my shooting hand around the top of the pistol and pulling it back, looking for that slight golden glare.

They were supposed to have a machine gun waiting for me, but there was no gun with my name on it, which reduced me to a pistol. Machine gunners are issued pistols as a backup because in close quarters a pistol is a hell of a lot easier to use than a full-sized machine gun. The pistol gave me a realistic range of twenty-five yards; that is, if my nerves held. I slid the pistol back into the drop holster and hoped that a machine gun was waiting for me at the FOB.

Huth must have seen the worry on my face. He turned to me and said, "Hey man, don't stress it. If I die, you can have my rifle. Russian style." He laughed as I punched him in the arm. We loaded into the back of an armadillo, which is not the dinosaur-like mammal, but an armored seven-ton truck, and drove into the wild.

Everything outside the armadillo's headlight beams was black. My imagination created the city that lay beyond the headlights. I saw men with rocket-propelled grenades on rooftops. I conjured the grinning faces of trigger men hiding behind corners, their fingers hovering over the stereotypical bright red button that would ignite a daisy-chained IED and eviscerate the entire patrol. I would be a casualty within my first few hours in a combat zone.

I once again found my sense of direction mangled, feeling a slight panic for not knowing which direction true north was. I thought of the ditty I had learned as a boy scout to remember the cardinal directions: Never Eat Soggy Worms. But the dark and the fear tangled the worms, and all I knew now was that we were driving deeper into the city.

When the armadillo stopped, I was able to peek over the side. A Marine got out and pulled aside a hooping strand of concertina wire. The Marine ran back to the armadillo and hopped onto the sidestep. We drove through the open c-wire and stopped in a large courtyard next to a row of other seven-tons and Humvees.

I stepped down the truck's rear metal stairs, trying my best not to become a casualty of my clumsiness. My dad once told me that he had an old childhood dog like me, Sox. She could walk into a room to lie down and end up knocking over every glass and plate in the room. I tried to be conscious of the old dog as my feet searched for the metal steps that were suspended in mid-air. When my feet found the hard-packed earth, I instantly felt better. The Marines that got off before me were huddled in a group, like a pack of scared herd animals looking for comfort in each other's presence. I shuffled next to the group, hoping for the relief of proximity too. The air was filled with a cacophony of blue-colored scents: exhaust fumes, body odor, diesel fumes, and human shit. Over the heavy drone of the diesel engines, I heard the familiar voice of our company gunny yelling at us: "Grab your shit and follow me."

I didn't particularly like the company gunny, but the familiar voice in the darkness was comforting. I grabbed my shit and followed, happy to be told what to do. A beam of white light danced to the rhythm of the gunny's steps. He stopped to make sure we were all following him, the light from his headlamp blinding me. I tried to blink away the spots as he led us through another courtyard and up some steps. The steps were crooked, and I caught my foot on the second to last step, almost falling on my face. Fucking Sox.

Gunny pushed open the makeshift door to our hooch; it was

made entirely of particle board. As the door slid open, I heard the friction of a rope sliding against wood and the sound of something bouncing off the back of the door. I followed the gunny, and the door slammed shut behind us unaided. I looked back to see two water bottles fashioned into a pulley system that acted as a self-closing door. I smiled at the ingenuity of the Marines who had slept here before. The ability to make something out of nothing has been a hallmark of the Corps since its inception.

The room itself was a twenty-by-twenty walk-in closet. The room was filled with frail red bunk beds, stained mattresses sprawled over top like vagrants on park benches. Small clumps of garbage was gathered on the floor: a discarded water bottle, a Red Vine licorice wrapper, small candy-coated chocolates of some unknown brand, bloody tissues, and a small segment of a magazine cover. The upper portion of a blonde-haired woman stared up at me from the dirty floor, a single green eye observing the newcomers with suspicion: Would they be as careless and dirty as the last group?

After the last Marine had shuffled in, the gunny commanded the attention of the room. He was a small man who didn't have the usual hardness associated with company gunnies. A company gunny was normally the toughest man in the company, a grizzled veteran who had, as Clint Eastwood's Gunny Highway so elegantly said, "Drunk more beer and banged more quiff and pissed more blood and stomped more ass than all of you numbnuts put together." The gunny reminded me more of a wise-cracking barber with his round face and mop of graying hair than he did the senior enlisted hard ass of the company. Nothing screamed Marine when he spoke, but we were trained to listen to the rank and we did.

The gunny cleared his throat before speaking. "All right, Marines. Anytime you leave this hooch, I want you in full PPE (Personal Protective Equipment). I know you can all smell the shitters, so just follow your noses if you have to shit. The piss tubes are directly across the courtyard, which means no pissing in the shitters unless you are in fact taking a shit, then it is fully authorized. If you decide to circumvent procedures and piss in the shitters, I don't really give a damn, because I'm not burning shit. You are."

The gunny bent over slightly and peered underneath the bunk closest to him. He grunted, sliding something out with his boot, before kicking it across the room. A water bottle filled with brownish-yellow liquid skidded across the floor, sliding all the way to the far end of the room before slamming into the back wall. "The last shit bags that lived here left a cache of piss bottles under the racks. I'm here to tell you right now, the first sergeant has made it his personal crusade to eliminate piss bottles from this corner of the Marine Corps. Something about the sight of the piss bottles disturbs him. So, if you use your little brains for a minute, you can figure out that piss bottles are strictly forbidden." He pronounced forbidden as forbaden. "If First Sergeant sniffs out any piss bottles, I can assure you: life as you know it will become a living hell." I stared at a yellow stain on the bunk mattress in front of me. "I would get some sleep if I were you guys. Fourth platoon takes over post at 0530." Gunny grunted at us and then disappeared, the water bottles slamming the door behind him.

I looked at Huth, and we both shook our heads. Marines were killed coming to pick us up from the dam, and it seemed like the singular focus of the command was whether or not Marines pissed in water bottles. It was more of the same: command seemed more focused on trivial matters like grooming standards than they were preparing for war. I had an instructor tell me that it was an illusion, that they weren't concerned with the grooming standards, or whether or not someone walked on the grass, or pissed in a bottle. What the command was really focused on was discipline and the fear that Marines were getting too comfortable. In theory, a comfortable Marine, with all the niceties he could ask for like plumbing and air conditioning, would soften. The best way to house a fighting man was in standards that kept him from getting sick but prevented him from fully relaxing. If it looked like Marines were settling in, a senior enlisted Marine would send out word. Maybe hair had grown out of regulation, maybe moustaches were threatening to extend past the corners of mouths, maybe some Marines didn't think it was necessary to shave at all when dodging bullets. The command would then enforce the grooming standards with harsh punishments for any infractions. They would start by punishing the Marine responsible, then they would start to go up the chain of command, punishing team leaders and squad leaders. Normally, once a team leader or squad leader was punished, he would likely take it out on the Marine responsible. Shit does indeed roll downhill, as physics and the infantry can attest. The process had already begun in Iraq.

There is another reason for the seemingly single-minded focus on insignificant grooming standards, and that is the concept that they are not so insignificant in the first place. There is the notion that discipline is not a finite resource, but a muscle that needs to be exercised. By enforcing the smallest details, the hope is that discipline will permeate all aspects of the Marine's duties. This concept makes perfect sense to me, but when you are an eighteen- or nineteen-year-old kid, it just seems like you are surrounded by assholes who aren't seeing the bigger picture.

We cleaned the room, ensuring that we wouldn't be caught holding another man's piss bottle, and then set to organizing our living space and cleaning our weapons. There would be no sleep for us that night.

I tried to close my eyes before post, but I was too excited, too nervous for what the day would bring. I couldn't shut my brain off. The imagination that had illuminated the city in broad strokes of differing shades of crimson and black was still painting a picture of my potential futures. I created scenarios that I considered likely, or fantasized about what I would like to happen. The base would be assaulted by the largest insurgent force ever assembled, and our untested platoon full of boots would be the only thing standing between the FOB and total annihilation. It was partly fantasy fiction, but much of it was a horror story that involved overrun positions and decapitations. Of course, I imagined myself the last man standing, heroically manning my machine gun until the barrel glowed white-hot and melted, forcing me to draw my KA-BAR and charge the enemy in a last-ditch effort at survival.

I was deep in my fantasy when I heard our squad leader putting on his gear. I looked down at my watch and pressed the little button to make its face glow radioactive green. It read 0330. He was getting ready two hours before the patrol. Our squad leader was an older Marine from Baton Rouge, who called himself Guard Dog.

His real last name was Gardner, but I think he wanted to avoid cultivating the image of a woman in a farm dress bent over radishes. He had been in the Marine Corps in the early-'90s and had been regaling us with stories of his former glory. He went from the Marines to the Navy Special Boat Teams, then spent the late-'90s working as a police officer in the shadier parts of New Orleans. He kept his head razor-bald and had a jawline that could have been taken from a '50s-era combat comic. He constantly frowned and would cry "bullshit" at anything that didn't agree with him. He told us he had been a sniper back in the '90s and had been on a few combat missions in Eastern Europe. It was impossible to verify his stories, but he told them with such passion and detail that I started to believe him. I put my faith in a leader I had known for a month. I hoped he was for real.

The sun was just starting to turn the sky purple when we walked across the FOB to the briefing room. I sat with the rest of the squad, crammed into a small room partitioned off by particle board. The room was silent except for the uncomfortable shifting of the Marines around me. I don't think it was a physical discomfort, just the discomfort of not knowing what to expect. Our collective combat experience came from old books and shitty movies.

I heard another shift, and a rifle smacked into the wooden bench. An aerial map was stretched across the wall in front of us – a black-and-white satellite image of Haqlaniyah. The city sprawled in every direction, roads and alleyways splintering and twisting like cracks in a broken windshield. The map became too nauseating to look at, so I stared up at the stucco ceiling instead.

Overhead, an orange industrial extension cord had been nailed to the center of the ceiling. The cord connected to a hanging construction light that emitted a harsh fluorescent light, a working man's chandelier. I heard a door open and close, and when I looked back down, a Marine stood with his hands on his hips. It took my eyes a moment to adjust; there was a huge white blob on the Marine's shoulder and torso from the overhead light. "Good morning gents," he said. It was the Marine who would be conducting the turnover brief for us. He oversaw the guard for the unit that was still occupying the FOB. There was supposed to be a weeklong change-over, where the Marines who knew better would take us out on patrols and show us the area and our posts. The Marine at the front of the room paced back and forth, the white blob following him across the room as he walked to the aerial map.

"As you would expect, this is a map of Haqlaniyah. Most of us here just call it the Haq. There are a thousand and two ways to die out there on the streets, and your job, while standing post, is to keep them the hell out there. There are twelve manned posts and four supplementary posts that can be manned as quickly as QRF can get their shit together. Each post has all manner of rockets, frag grenades, and pop-up flares."

I blinked my eyes to try and expel the white blob that still clung to the outer circle of my vision. I squinted at the enormous bags that hung from the Marine's eyes. The chevrons on his shoulders told me that he was a corporal, just like my squad leader.

He pointed to a black-and-gray schematic of the FOB. "There are two posts that have Iraqis standing up there with you. So far, we haven't had any issues. But to paraphrase Lord Mattis: 'Wear a smile but have a plan to kill every motherfucker you meet.'" The Marine smiled at his own cleverness, looking across the room to see if his quip had registered. I couldn't stop the slow crawl of a smile across my face. "Now these two posts that have Iraqis are the two with machine guns. I don't know why that is, but that's just the way it's always been. The first is the Entry Control Point, and the second is Post 6. My guys on post will give you all the ins and outs of your sectors of fire. It's my recommendation that you stay on your first post for the whole deployment. With nothing to do but stare at the city, no one is going to know that chunk of city better than you."

He walked to the center of the aerial map and turned his back to us, staring at the black and white. Then he spun around on his heels, looking at each one of us in turn. "Bar none, this is going to be your worst duty here. You might do worse shit, blood and guts shit, but nothing is going to press on your brain like standing post. Hour after hour, locked in a wooden box. That's not normal human behavior, and it starts to wear on a guy. Just know that while this may be the shittiest detail, it's also the most important. We can all close our eyes because Marines are on the wall, keeping the wolves where they belong. You're going to get complacent up there; it's damn near impossible to avoid. Just try and remember that everyone in this FOB is depending on you. Corporal Gardner, do you have anything for them?"

Corporal Gardner was standing against the back wall, his arms crossed. He walked next to his corporal counterpart. I fully expected him to repeat exactly what was just said. A large component of being an effective military leader is being an effective regurgitator. But Gardner simply nodded and clapped his hands. "All right, Marines. You heard the man – this is the real fucking deal. Time to earn your big-girl panties. Head outside to the breezeway for inspection."

The breezeway connected the COC to the chow hall and a few hooches. At one time the FOB was a schoolhouse. Classrooms once filled with young Iraqi children now held sleeping Marines who dreamt of violence. The principal's office, desk included, now belonged to an infantry captain, whose job I imagined was surprisingly similar to that of a grade-school principal: keep the kids on task and make sure everyone follows the rules.

I stood with my back against the wall, looking down over my flak jacket to my leather boots and the concrete floor. Corporal Gardner walked down the breezeway, checking all our gear, making sure the kids hadn't forgotten anything.

The two corporals led us each to the post we would be standing. Corporal Gardner told me that I would be standing the Entry Control Point, or ECP, because it had a machine gun on it, and it was one of the most important posts in the FOB. It was the entry and exit point for all FOB traffic. I stood a little taller when he told me this.

I was the second-to-last Marine taken to his post. When they finally got to me, both corporals walked in front. I was hoping for some last-minute advice, but we walked in silence. Now that the sun was high enough to illuminate the FOB, I finally got my first real look at our new home. It was much smaller than it appeared in the dark. There was the courtyard that separated our hooch from the COC, and in it, a few CONEX boxes that stored water and MREs (Meals [supposedly] Ready to Eat). When I looked above our hooch to the roof, I could see the sandbags of a post that sat directly above our room.

I followed the two corporals through the first courtyard and down a ramp into the motor pool. From here, I could smell the shitters. It was a smell I'd have to get used to. Two large Caterpillar diesel generators droned on as we walked through the Humvees and seven-tons. More than one of the Humvees had a fiery bite taken out of its front end. There were mechanical casualties of IEDs, but these were the Humvees that had been going slow enough that the explosion occurred beneath the front end instead of underneath the crew.

On the farthest wall of the motor pool, a hole had been sledgehammered to create a crude passageway. At the base of the hole stood cruder wooden steps, lopsided and deformed, probably made by a self-styled Marine craftsman who had fibbed about his construction experience to pull FOB duty. The corporals and I climbed the stairs, which creaked and groaned under my considerable weight. The corporal who gave us the brief pointed down a pathway that led to the ECP. "There you go, right down those steps. The Marine standing post will give you a proper turn-over."

I looked to Corporal Gardner for some sage advice, maybe an old story that I could cling to on post, but he simply nodded, his bulldog frown still fixed to his face. He slapped my shoulder and turned to walk away. I took a deep breath before walking down the path.

These wooden steps leading to the ECP were built by somebody who knew what they were doing. I walked up them and looked at the green sandbags that surrounded the post in tightly stacked rows. They looked like they would stop a bullet, but I wasn't so sure about an RPG.

There was a Marine and an Iraqi on the post. The Iraqi was overweight and sweating profusely. He had a thick handlebar mustache and looked like he could have been one of Saddam's famed body doubles. He stared back at me with scared brown eyes.

It looked like this was the last place on earth he wanted to be. The Marine standing with him looked tired but happy; his bloodshot eyes contrasted with pearly white horse teeth.

While we stood together, Horse Teeth spent most of the hour talking about what he was going to do once he got back to the States. He was a surfer and had intentions of blowing most of his survival money on a van and a new surfboard. I could have used some advice on the post, the do's and don'ts, the places to stand so you wouldn't get shot, little things like that, but I liked listening to his plans. They were the happy contemplations of a man who had spent the better part of a year refining them. The sun glinted off those white Chiclets, which made me happy. When he left the post, I missed him instantly.

By early morning, the heat was already staggering. Sweat rolled down my face and back in rivulets. I put a hand on my lower back, underneath my flak jacket. My blouse was already soaked through with sweat. I looked over at the Saddam doppelganger. Sweat poured from his face and dripped onto the table he sat beside. The post had two machine guns, one American and one Iraqi by way of Russia. They pointed in opposite directions. There were two wooden tables, built to hold the machine guns and ammo, and a tall wooden chair next to both. I had been told this was the only post with a chair and I felt lucky for my good fortune. Next to the machine gun sat a yellow bullhorn, some pop-up flares, and an ammo can with a few hundred rounds of 7.62, patiently waiting to be fired. The post had thick bulletproof glass that went around its entire perimeter. The thick glass let the sun's radiation in and kept the air out. The byproduct was our sweaty misery.

I looked around the post at the graffiti, of which there was plenty. Bullet holes in the ceiling rafters and walls had been dated and named by the Marines who had dodged them. A few of them were converted into the eyes of crudely drawn smiley faces. One bullet hole was used as the meatus of an enormous veiny penis, with the words "Green Weenie" written on the shaft. The wiener drawing was the unofficial mascot of the delinquent lance corporal. They belonged to a crude, base sense of humor, and they never failed to make me laugh.

A Chuck Norris joke was written on the rafters: "They once had a showing of Walker Texas Ranger in 3D. There were no survivors." I laughed to myself and felt the Iraqi staring at me out of the corner of his eye. He must have thought I had lost my mind to the heat. I read the joke aloud to him, hoping he had picked up enough English to get the joke, hoping we might actually be able to converse. After the punch line, the Iraqi's eyes widened, as if to tell me he had absolutely no idea what I was talking about. He let out an uncomfortable laugh and exclaimed, "YES" before turning his head back to the city. It seemed like he was just as out of place as I felt.

The city came to life as morning dragged on, and I could look far enough down the road to make out the edge of a marketplace. There, it looked like people were getting on with their daily lives. I'm sure most of them couldn't care less about Saddam or the Americans, as long as they could go to work and pay their bills – just like the rest of us. I watched with fascination. Women walked the market in long black chadors, with only the small slits of their eyes showing. I thought that if I was a bad guy, I would just dress like a woman. The baggy dress would conceal a rifle and grenade belt and get an insurgent through most check points. When I was in the middle of picturing myself dressed in a chador, I noticed a woman walking awkwardly in the market.

She was walking at an angle, in the direction of the FOB, her gait a strange bow-legged waddle. I thought maybe she was pregnant, but it was so exaggerated I second-guessed myself. The longer I watched her, the more I expected her to pull an RPG from between her legs and blow up the ECP. When she made it halfway across the street, she stopped and looked in my direction. I shifted to behind the machine gun, resting my hand on the handle, not pointing the weapon at her, but knowing that in less than two seconds, I could be. Suddenly her dress flew up. A toddler came running out. He had been playing a game with his mother. I swallowed the spit in my mouth and went back to sweating and observing.

The day lurched forward, dragging itself along at a gastropod's pace. Despite the lethargy, I was certain our post would be attacked at any moment. I fought it as hard as I could, but the heat fried my brain into a state of complacency – the c-word our drill instructors took so much effort to warn us about. I looked at the architecture of the buildings and considered the slope the city was built on. I studied the landscape more than I looked out for terrorists. I turned to face north, where the small city of Bahnidahara sat, or what the Marines called Bonnie-D. That was where the bad guys were supposed to live.

I took my oversized military binoculars and scanned Bonnie-D, looking for stereotypically dressed terrorists, black ski masks and AK-47s at the ready. I just saw people living their lives. I scanned to the left of the city, into the open desert, and saw a cloud of dust rising out of the earth. I focused my binoculars and saw two men riding nut to butt on a motorcycle. I thought they were probably just a couple of friends taking a joyride through the desert. I used to do the same thing with a friend back in Spangle. He had two Honda Trail 90s, but one or the other was normally broken down, forcing us to ride doubles on our way to whatever mayhem we planned to cause that day. The memory made me smile as I watched the motorcycle stop in the desert.

One man stayed on the motorcycle as the other fidgeted with something on the ground. They were small colored blobs in the two magnifying tubes of my binoculars. I watched as a cloud of dirt enveloped the red blob standing in the desert, and I heard a barely audible thump. I watched the blob as the dirt began to drift off.

An explosion shattered my complacency in a mixture of sound and fire. The explosion was probably three hundred meters away – harmless despite the loud, echoing boom. With another thump, a second dirt cloud plumed, this time about a hundred and fifty meters away. The bikers were firing mortar rounds. I heard a shuffle to my left and looked over just in time to see fake Saddam running from the post. I stood behind the glass watching the explosions. The window gave me a false sense of security, as if the bulletproof glass was only a television screen broadcasting a combat reality show. The reality, though, was if one of those mortar rounds dropped on the post, it would be completely destroyed. The two men were too far away to shoot at, so I brought the binoculars to my face and watched them drop another mortar round.

This round exploded closer, but it was still about a hundred meters away. They were walking their rounds onto my position, just like our mortarmen would do. I watched as the men dropped another round, and I knew this one would be even closer. I thought I heard a whistle, like the cartoon effect of Wile E. Coyote falling from a cliff.

A small stucco shack, about seventy-five meters away, went up in a blossom of orange fire and beige rocks. The explosion shook the post, knocking all the Iraqi's plastic-packaged pastries off his table and rattling the bulletproof glass. I felt the explosion's rumble transfer from the bottom of the post, through my boots, and all the way to my clenched teeth. The motorcyle men floated away in the distance, and the indirect fire ceased. I was lucky they didn't have a couple more rounds to walk onto the post.

While that last round was hanging in the air, and I was focused on the strange whistle, it seemed like time had slowed; the arc of the round through the blue desert sky lasted a lifetime. I had time to think of my own destruction, and there was a calm to it. This was when I realized that I wasn't afraid to die; this was when my belief solidified that whatever happened was destined to happen, and no amount of wishing or worrying could change it. I had started on a path and I intended to keep walking down it. I reached down and grabbed one of the Iraqi's Honey Buns off the floor, then tore the package open with my teeth. The first bite sent small shingles of sugar down the front of my flak jacket. It was the best thing I had ever tasted.

***

Post continued for a few days, each day bonding and morphing into the next. I didn't experience anything near as exciting as the indirect fire we took. We were shot at a few times, but the marksmen were unskilled, or maybe afraid to actually look down their sights, or perhaps some of them didn't actually want to hurt anyone. The most significant thing that happened was my introduction to the soul-crushing experience of the post routine. The post standing itself was awful, as time seemed to stop inside our small wooden boxes, but after post the responsibilities of maintaining the FOB fell on us.

After post, we would collect trash and take it to the burn pit, then clean whatever needed cleaning. The staff non-commissioned officers that roamed the base were always finding new projects for us, and if they couldn't think of anything for us to do, we would fill sandbags. We were normally given a quota: say, two hundred sandbags after post. You could attempt to short the sandbag count, but there were people on the FOB with nothing better to do than count sandbags. Though a small thrill came from cutting corners, the punishments were normally so severe that it was easier to just do as we were told.

The most memorable of the after-post duties was shit burning. Every few days, one of us was tasked with dragging the halved

55-gallon drums from underneath the sandbag-fortified wooden shitters, and then sliding them across the motor pool. Once it was a safe-enough distance from vehicles and non-shit-burning humans, the Marine who drew the short straw would dump diesel onto the shit and ignite it, sending a black smoke offering to the gods of misfortune. As the shit burned down, the short-strawed Marine kept stirring, ensuring the flames burned everything. The process seemed to take hours; I never timed it, but each burn took me closer to middle age. It was commonplace for a Marine to come back into the hooch soot-faced from burnt shit.

Ours was shift work taken to the extreme. Instead of punching out at the end of each shift, we simply moved onto another assignment. Each post rotation was a week long. It was one week of post, two weeks of patrol, and then one week out in a combat outpost.

The post Marines were also responsible for putting up a QRF to supplement the posts, or to conduct quick reactionary patrols around the FOB. A Marine from the COC would come into your room, scream a wake-up call, and inform you that you needed to be in the COC five minutes ago. Most of the QRF calls that first week were drills, but no matter how fast we were, it was never fast enough. But one night, deep into the dark hours, a runner showed up at our door and told us that it was for real. A dark figure had been spotted prowling the blind spots around the FOB.

Our room erupted into chaos as soon as the door slammed behind the winded runner. The light was too bright, and my eyes were still crusted over with sleep, so I didn't recognize the Marine's face or voice, but it sounded real this time. Flak jackets and Kevlars flew across the room as we all went on autopilot, throwing our gear on like an army of newly risen zombies. Huth's flak jacket struck me in the nose as he swung it over his shoulders, but I was in too much of a hurry to call him a clumsy asshole. I had to go one hooch over to borrow a rifle from the 4th platoon squad that was still on rest. The Marine who I took the rifle from grunted in acknowledgment – this wasn't the first time I'd needed to borrow it. I ran out of the dark hooch, jumping down the stairs and running across the courtyard in the dark.

By the time I made it into the COC, whoever had briefed Corporal Gardner was gone. All he said to us was that we were leaving the ECP and patrolling around the perimeter of the FOB. We filed out of the tiny briefing rooms and lined up in patrol formation in the courtyard. We should have been conducting our pre-patrol inspections, but it was deemed that there was no time. This was going to be my first time outside the wire on foot. As we stepped off, a butterfly orgy commenced in my stomach.

When we left the circular strand of c-wire, there was a palpable difference in the atmosphere. I'm sure it was entirely psychosomatic, but what difference does it make if the feelings are real? It seemed like there was electricity in the air as we turned corners in the dark. My night vision wasn't working, so I followed close behind Huth, who acted like he knew where we were going. Huth was the point man, and I was right behind him. He twisted around back alleys and side streets like he had lived in the city his whole life.

Huth had once confided in me that he had never read a book and that his ASVAB score was barely good enough to get him into the Marines. But watching him move through the city, it became apparent that intelligence isn't confined to standardized testing. Huth had something different, call it a natural predatory instinct or street smarts. When we smoked cigarettes outside our hooch, Huth would bring out a map and study terrain. It seemed to me like he already had all the street names and corners memorized. I stayed close behind, knowing that without him I could easily be lost in the dark, trying to wander my way back to the FOB in a city that would be indifferent to my internet-published decapitation.

We patrolled around the FOB and found nothing but the thrill of being outside friendly lines for the first time as a squad. I felt exhilarated, even though it was more or less a casual stroll around several city blocks. We made it back to the FOB for a debrief, but there wasn't much of anything to report. The dark, shadowy figure could very well have been a figment of the post-standers' imaginations, a collective hysteria that produced man-made shadows, plotting to slit all their throats. Or, it could have been a man or woman made of flesh and blood, probing the FOB for weaknesses and blind spots. Maybe it was both.

***

With our first week of post completed, we were set to begin our first week of patrols. Everyone seemed excited. Marines were already returning to the FOB with stories of bullets, bombs, and bravery. I became jealous when I heard other boot Marines in the chow hall share their first experiences under fire. I desperately wanted my first time to be over. I was already mortared, but what else was there to do but stand and watch? There was no real action I could have taken. I still had no idea how I would respond when the bullets started flying.

Our first week of patrols came and went without incident. There were firefights all around us, but we never walked into one. We could hear gunfire coming from across the city, and no matter how fast we moved toward the sound, we were never fast enough. Week two came and went with the same results. We were learning the city, finding the occasional IED, but we weren't finding the shit, even though it flowed in open trenches down city streets.

By this time I had finally received a weapon of my own. It was an M249 Squad Automatic Weapon, which we called a SAW. It was a baby version of the machine gun I was used to, but at least it was mine, and at least it was belt-fed. No longer would I have to play hot rifle with Marines that were returning from patrol. I spent the workup training with a different machine gun; all my fantasies had involved a 240. Now, I would have to adjust my dreams accordingly. But as the armorer handed me my inferior machine gun, I thought that I could learn to love her, like a mother loves an ugly child. I took her into the hooch and broke her down, learning her internal organs, seeing if there were any burs or bits that would get in the way of our new relationship. I named her Lucrezia, after the poisonous fifteenth-century predator of Roman Catholic fame. I remember reading in seventh grade that Buffalo Bill Cody had named his 1866 Springfield rifle the same name, and it always stuck with me.

We had survived another week of post. It was miserable but uneventful. Back on patrols, we all felt like our chances for grunt work improved exponentially. But our first patrol of the new cycle was ending, and we were still combat virgins.

The patrol seemed to have covered the entire city. We patrolled through all the hot spots looking for a fight, but so far nothing had happened. On this day, we had set out in the early morning hours, but the late-afternoon sun now beat down on us. The depression and sweat rolled down my back in equal measure. Corporal Gardner passed the word through the squad: RTB. Return to base.

We were patrolling back down the slope of the city and toward the FOB when a halt was called. Each of us took a position that offered some sort of cover. I looked down the street and saw kneeling Marines hiding behind corners, like toddlers who hadn't quite figured out the rules of hide and go seek. Gun barrels pointed at empty windows and down avenues of approach. We tried to cover every possible angle, but deep down we all knew that was impossible in an urban environment. We could have been kneeling on buried IEDs for all we knew. I watched as Gardner kneeled next to the radio operator. They exchanged words, but I've always been a terrible lip reader. Eventually, we received word that we were to cover an integrated squad of Iraqis and Marines as they crossed the bridge into Bonnie-D.

The Marines with the Iraqis were part of the MiTT Team, or Military Transition Team. These Marines were plucked from various positions throughout the company, all of them squad or team leaders, and told to lead Iraqis on combat missions. The idea was to shape the Iraqis into disciplined warfighters. The now-Corporal Hall, a machine gunner who showed me around when I first showed up to the fleet, was one of these Marines. When he told me the news, I felt uneasy for him. The thought of trusting the Iraqis out on patrol, with loaded AK-47s and belts full of grenades, sounded like a white-knuckle existence to me. There was no way of determining where these men's loyalties truly lay.

The point man diverted the patrol and took us toward the edge of the city to overlook the bridge. We patrolled up to a steep hill that led down to a clearing. We would have to traverse about a hundred yards of no man's land to get to the other side. Our fire team prepared to cover the rest of the squad as they made it across.

One by one, they slid down the hill and ran across the clearing, some of them resorting to sledding down the hill on their butts. The terrain was made entirely of loose gravel and dirt banks. It would be an easy place to bury an IED. But they all made it across, scurrying up the far side of the clearing to an abandoned building. When they gave us the signal to cross, our corpsman Zeb and I brought up the rear.

A corpsman is a Navy medical technician, much like an EMT. Because all Marines are considered combatants, our medical personnel come from the Navy, and as per the Geneva Convention, all medical personnel are considered noncombatants. But the insurgents' guerilla warfare ignored all laws of war, with a particular disregard for the Geneva Convention. The insurgents would go so far as to target medical personnel, the large medical bags of the corpsmen becoming a target for enemy snipers. Losing a corpsman was guaranteed to both simultaneously take away the lifesaving capability of a squad and erode their morale. Zeb knew this and often talked about it over shaky cigarettes. Zeb was different than we were; really, all corpsmen are different than Marines. Generally, I find corpsmen to be better humans, more compassionate, more caring. That's probably why corpsmen enjoy an elevated position among Marines, because they tend to be everything we are not. Most of them join the military because they want to support the cause, but don't want to do it with the business end of an M16. They want to save lives, not take them.

Zeb ran in front of me, holding down the top of his helmet like it was going to blow away in the wind. A rifle shot cracked through the silence and a round impacted the hillside directly above Zeb. I couldn't help but smile. This was everything I had been working toward. But as we ran through the naked ground of the wadi, I realized something was wrong. Zeb wasn't moving.

I watched as bullets inched closer to Zeb. They created plumes of dirt that danced around him. It looked like the invisible hand of a giant, drumming on the ground with impatient fingers. Each machine gun burst – a pinky, ring, middle, index, and thumb – flicked dirt into the sky. I ran as fast as I could to Zeb's side, grabbed him by the back of the flak jacket, and pushed him toward cover. Zeb stumbled like a drunk. I strained and pushed to get him up the other side of the hill while his legs simply refused to work. I focused on the abandoned building's open door, not the bullets that impacted all around us. I pushed Zeb into the building's first floor, then bolted upstairs, taking them two at a time. Rifle shots from Corporal Gardner and Lance Corporal Alonzo echoed in the stairwell. By the time I made it to the roof, the shooting had stopped. Silence and the smell of sulfur hung in the air. The enemy had fled. We called in the incident to the COC and informed them that we were in position.

The FOB was barely out of view, but I could see the bridge directly in front of the FOB. A large Marine with a radio on his back began sprinting across the bridge in a serpentine pattern. We were told in a brief that the only way to go across the bridge was in an armored vehicle or a dead sprint. This first Marine had taken the advice to heart. Another Marine charged across the bridge before a clumped mass of Iraqis began to cross. While the Iraqis crossed, all hell broke loose.

Fire erupted from across the bridge. An abandoned industrial park to our north flashed with the orange explosions of enemy barrels. Everyone on the roof picked a muzzle flash and began firing. When my SAW jammed, my hands worked without thought, muscle memory clearing the blockage. I fired more, jammed again, cleared it. I heard Marines screaming in pure elation, like we were having a snowball fight instead of trying to kill humans. Time seemed to slow as the bullets impacted the wall in front of me. The SAW in my hand bucked from the controlled explosions that exited the barrel.

The Iraqis on the bridge were integrating themselves nicely into the chaos, shooting in all directions with no care for where their bullets landed. I had heard of the tactic, but this was the first time I had ever seen it live. It was called the Iraqi death blossom, and it truly was a sight to behold. Once the first shot was fired, the Iraqis picked a direction and held down the triggers of their Russian- and Chinese-built assault rifles. They waved the rifles back and forth as the 7.62 by 39 mm projectiles spewed out of the barrels. The Iraqis didn't care where their bullets went as long as they were putting rounds downrange. There was a common sense to it – sometimes the sound of fire being returned is enough to make the enemy flee. But the consequence of the deadly desert flower was that the bullets didn't care if you were supposed to be on the same team. There had been American casualties of the Iraqi death blossom. I was first told about the death blossom in the Mojave Desert, by a grunt turned desert instructor. He said you better make sure your ass is behind cover from all the Iraqis with AKs – enemy and not. As the misguided friendly bullets slapped into the wall in front of me, I felt like I finally understood the lesson.

Then, as quickly as it began, the riflefire ceased. Silence pervaded. We prepared for a counterattack. I checked my ammo and told the squad leader that I had plenty left for another fight. The rest of the Iraqis and Marines made it across, disappearing into a building right on the other side of the bridge. I looked out over the wadi that separated the two cities and caught movement. The first signal that ignited in my brain came from somewhere deep in the storage shelves of familiar images. It said *rabbits*: the same kind of rabbits that had gotten out of their pens at my childhood house and multiplied like some furry science-fiction epidemic. As a kid, I was constantly catching rabbits' movements out of the corner of my eye. Another of the never-ending progeny of Rocky and Snowball, I'd think. But standing on this Iraqi rooftop, another thought clicked into place. These weren't rabbits, but two grown men running up the hill to the decrepit industrial park. I sighted in on the man in a white track shirt, leading him slightly.

Calmly, probably too calmly, I told Corporal Gardner what I saw. He put his rifle to his eye, using the scope to try and see any weapons. He couldn't see any at first. I asked him if I could fire. I had no idea what I was asking for, only that this was what I had trained to do, the chance to see the enemy in an open field. My finger moved from its straightened position, where it had rested on the trigger guard, and slowly shifted to the crescent-moon-shaped trigger. My finger caressed the trigger, slightly rubbing it on the back side where the metal turns from smooth to rough. I waited for the one-word death sentence for the two men. Corporal Gardner wanted to be sure.

Despite the depiction of Marines as bloodthirsty killers, we are primarily creatures of discipline. Justifiably, any shots fired, or people killed, are subject to heavy scrutiny. Our deployment came in the wake of the Haditha Massacre, where Marines led a bloody, revenge-fueled assault on a house that resulted in the death of a family of innocents. The world was watching the Marines. The chain of command had told us that no quarter would be given to those who violated the rules of engagement or decided to take justice into their own hands; they would be punished to the fullest extent of the Uniform Code of Military Justice. I like to think that those words were echoing in Corporal Gardner's head, informing his mental calculus. By the time he opened his mouth, the men were at the top of the hill, where a white car waited for them.

"Fuck it, FIRE."

An amateur machine gunner will squeeze the trigger and try to ride the bucking dragon in his hands. The professional, the true machine gunner, will squeeze the trigger in tight, controlled bursts. Tiny burps of fire will leave the barrel in five- to seven-round increments. I aimed at the bottom center of the car's rear door, where I saw a man hop into the car. I squeezed the trigger. Holes manifested themselves in the back of the car, large gray holes pocking the metal. I squeezed again. And again. And again. The car's tires lurched forward, and the vehicle vanished behind the buildings, where I would never see it again.

I looked around the rooftop at the other Marines. They all stared at me, most of them smiling. I think some were jealous, others proud. This was our mission, our purpose in life ever since stepping on the yellow footprints at the Marine Corps Recruit Depot. My finger extended from the trigger guard as smoke rose from my SAW's barrel. The smell of gunfire filled my nostrils, a stinging but welcoming scent. It reminded me of a childhood of shooting soda cans. Now that scent memory coalesced with this moment: my first time in combat, and the first time I ever shot at another human being.

I never saw a body or any blood. I never saw a skinny man in a white track suit staring up at the sky with dead eyes. My squad leader told me that a car matching our white car's description was found with a dead body inside, just to the north of our AO. The car was riddled with bullet holes, the trunk filled with munitions: a medium machine gun, grenades, and cases of ammunition. I felt nothing when he told me the news.

I worried that my non-reaction made me a sociopath. All I'd felt was recoil, and satisfaction, knowing that I hadn't frozen when the bullets began to fly. As the news of the firefight spread around the company, Marines began slapping me on the back as I walked past. Others looked at me with contempt because I was in the right place at the right time. I think war was still a game to us then. It wouldn't last. Stray bullets can only remain stray for so long. Fictional IEDs would become oh-dear-god IEDs. Death as an abstraction would dissolve and show us its true rotting face. But in that moment, we were still unscathed kids.

As if to underscore our naivete, we had taken a picture together on the roof after the firefight. It was something a bunch of high schoolers would have done after winning a tough football game. I don't know what the hell we were thinking, but I still have the picture. I'm standing on the far left, my SAW resting on my hip, barrel pointed at the sky. Corporal Gardner is in the center back row without his helmet on, staring into the camera with squinted eyes. The other face I always focus on is LCpl Alonzo, who stands on the other side of the back row, opposite me. Along with Corporal Gardner, Alonzo was the only other Marine in the squad with combat experience. He was one of the Afghanistan vets. There is a subtle smile on his face, like he was pleased with how his boots reacted under fire. The only man not in the picture is Zeb. He was the one taking the picture.

When it was over, we patrolled back to the base, like conquering heroes. We had survived our first firefight; we finally had a story of our own. When we entered the FOB, we were met with a hero's welcome: twin fecal pyres. The dueling flames licked the air as they spewed black diesel smoke into the sky. I watched as the squad walked past the burning shit like dead ancient warriors entering the great hall of the afterlife. The flames coming off the burning excrement exuded heat waves, the blurred lines of a dream. It sure felt like a dream; the only thing that anchored me to reality was the visceral and primordial smell of shit and fire.

We smoked cigarettes for hours after the debrief, everyone telling of the near-miss bullets that smacked the stucco just to the left of their faces. We were high on adrenaline and nicotine, but both would wear off; exhaustion would come like a great flood and wash both away. Zeb was one of the last ones to go back into the hooch. He sat quietly as we all talked, staring at the ground and trying to laugh at the crude jokes and gallows humor that we used as shields, a fragile barrier that we tried to wear against the creeping horror, as thin as cellophane and only slightly stronger. One by one we went into the hooch, knowing that if we didn't take advantage of the sleep, the moment would pass, and we would be forced to walk the streets in more of a haze than we already operated under.

I walked past Zeb, lightly squeezing his shoulder. Once, later on, Zeb thanked me for saving his life, but I don't know if I did or not. That day, we didn't talk about it at all. Instead, I lay in my rack, trying to keep my eyes open, the red glow of laptop batteries blinking throughout the dark room. I listened as Zeb undressed and slid into his bunk, the metal squeaking as he tried to find some level of comfort. It started as a whimper, like he was trying to cover his mouth and hold it in. Then it became more pronounced. I'm sure he hoped that the dark and exhaustion of the men around him was enough to act as a veil for his tears. He must have felt like he let us all down; he had stared death in the face and frozen when his moment came. I felt terrible for him and knew that I needed to get up, try and talk to him, offer a hug at least. But I gave in to the comfort of the darkness and closed my eyes as a friend suffered. Zeb may have frozen that day, but so did I. It wasn't the bullets I was afraid of; it was the fear that Zeb's tears would wash away my veneer of courage. I was the coward after the bullets stopped.

A dreamless sleep came. We would have another patrol in a couple hours.

9. Death Comes

We had all been dodging bullets and shrapnel like young matadors, twisting and gyrating our hips, whipping our flak jackets to the side like capes as the superheated shards of metal charged at us. Most rounds fired at the Forward Operating Base were so poorly placed that they had to have a dash of luck to even hit a guard post. They were the untrained shots of amateurs, taken by fathers and brothers who were thrust into war by either circumstance or their ideas about the sacred duty of jihad, neither of which involved professional combat training. It was our brief age of innocence. We had been largely unscathed by the true essence of war. Roadside bombs had left marks on a few of us. Concussions caused by grenades were joked about. Shrapnel left in the fleshy tissue of camouflaged buttocks was a source of hilarity. A Marine named Gabriel Odum had been shot on his first patrol, the bullet passing through his right hand and one lung, but a few lucky centimeters away from fatality. We believed we were invincible. The casualties were serious, but everyone would walk away, bearing the kinds of scars that would make them celebrities at their respective V.F.W. cantinas.

A couple of weeks into our deployment, everything changed. A deadly sniper was on the loose in the Haditha Triad in Anbar Province. Marines were no longer being wounded; they were dying, to the echo of expertly executed rifle shots. Whispers trickled into the unit that the marksman was European, a mercenary paid by the enemy for each American killed. The rumor mill churned out stories of a German man operating in the area. It's possible that we had seen too many movies, that we sought a story larger than reality, that a Nazi mercenary with cold blue eyes made more sense as an antagonist than a frail teenage Iraqi with a brown, bony trigger finger that never trembled. Whoever was firing, he didn't miss as our friendly neighborhood terrorists did. His hands knew what they were doing when they adjusted for windage and elevation, plugging data into the black circular knobs on top of the rifle. Marines of Fox and Echo Company soon fell. But my Golf company was the first to lose a man.

Pfc. Christopher Riviere had just started his shift on Post 2, beginning his four-to-six-hour sentence of solitary confinement in a wooden box no bigger than a closet. A radio check went around, starting at Post 1. Marines chimed in, one by one, letting the sergeant of the guard know that they were still awake, still alive. Riviere checked in from behind the thick glass. The sound of a rifle shot bounced off the beige buildings that made up the city, but most of us didn't think much of it. The city was a constant echo chamber of M16 and Kalashnikov percussion, a violent symphony of rage.

The posts around the forward operating base were constructed out of two-by-fours and plywood. Rows of green plastic sandbags lined the outside of the post and were laid on the roof. The bulletproof glass let us watch our sectors of fire; small openings in the glass were left so a rifle barrel could fit through and fire. But there were also a few unintentional gaps in the layered, laminated glass; maybe a post was built a little too wide, and the glass was just a little too short. Riviere's post had a two-inch gap, small enough to seem insignificant and irrelevant, but wide enough to allow a slight breeze of fresh air to slip in.

One shot from the marksman came from a window or rooftop that we would never find. It traveled through the city, over the heads of butchers and mechanics, mothers and their children, maybe even over the heads of Marines on patrol, looking for exactly that kind of window or rooftop. The bullet flew closer to our base, closer to the post with our Marine on it. The bullet found the small two-inch gap that normally let in only fresh air. Riviere was standing behind it. He was wearing all his proper personal protective equipment. His helmet was securely fastened, and his ballistic glasses rested on his nose. His hands were sheathed in fire-resistant Nomex flight gloves, safeguarding his hands but thin enough not to impede dexterity. His flak jacket was properly adjusted to fit his small frame. Riviere had the thin body of a teenage boy, but the protective plates were positioned right where they were supposed to be, covering his organs. He was doing everything right, but the bullet didn't care. It found the tiny void in the glass and passed through it. Then it cleared the plate and slid into the flak jacket just above the life-saving armor, easily cutting through the Kevlar, which is only rated to stop pistol rounds. The projectile entered Riviere's chest cavity from the upper right, crossed through a number of his vital organs, and came out his back on the lower left. He fell to the ground where he stood.

Cpl. Chris Mauzy, the sergeant of the guard that shift, heard the shot and ordered a radio check. Post 1 finished the check and listened for Post 2 through the black handheld radio. Marines waited impatiently for the response, their wait answered with a maddening silence. There could be many reasons that a Marine might miss a radio check. One guy had already been busted for masturbation, his pants around his ankles, his eyes closed in deep concentration on a memory instead of looking in the direction of his assigned sectors of fire. There was another who had been found on post sleeping, his boot kicking as he slumbered in the warm embrace of the poncho liner that he had wrapped around his exhausted body. Mauzy might have hoped that Riviere was engaged in any of these acts, but it would only take a few minutes for him to suspect something much worse than a breach of protocol.

Mauzy sprinted up the steps that led to the post, taking them two at a time. He burst onto the rooftop and dashed across the last thirty feet that separated him and Riviere, coming to a rest at the entrance of the post, a hand on the wooden frame of the opening. He saw a young Marine in full body armor lying on the floor, frozen in a moment that had already passed. Mauzy frantically removed Riviere's body armor and began administering whatever lifesaving skills could be shaken from his already-shook mind. Battle dressings were slapped on, chest compressions were administered; the sergeant of the guard even went so far as to try to breathe life back into Riviere, to inflate his chest and reanimate his body with the very essence of his own being, but the Marine's life had already leaked onto the stucco floor of the guard post. The medical corpsman who rushed up to the post also tried, in vain.

A Marine had walked up to Post 2 in full battle armor, weapon at his side, but what was carried back down the stairs seemed so much smaller, like the fragile bird bones of adolescence. Riviere's face was untouched, unbroken, unmarred. If not for the gray-purple color, I might have been tempted to shake him awake. Get up, you're on duty, Marines can't sleep on duty. Didn't you read the rule book? Death had come to Golf Company. Reality would no longer be ignored.

Pfc. Christopher T. Riviere was 21, and he loved the Miami Dolphins.

I watched with the other Marines, the other kids, as his body was taken away. I wasn't standing post. I wasn't there in any of the moments that mattered. I smoked cigarettes outside my hooch while he died. My knowledge would be formed in the collective scuttlebutt heard over cups of instant coffee and MREs. A chunk of flesh had been gouged out of the collective, something stolen, though I'm not sure any of us could have said what. We still had six more months of deployment to think of what was lost, what would be lost, and the pieces of us that we could never take back home.

10. The Palm Grove

Combat never stops for death. If there's time, there are memorials, words spoken, tears shed, before the survivors grab their rifle again and climb the wall. Our story was the same. Death, and the disfigurement of friends, became new topics to ponder when there was nothing to do but hide inside my own mind. I could try and push the thoughts away with sports statistics, or the intricate plot of an Agatha Christie novel, but the corpses and gore were always hiding behind leading passer ratings or Detective Poirot's words. We all just kept moving forward because behind us were moments too terrible to reexamine. I knew it would catch up to all of us eventually, maybe right when we touched down in the States, maybe a decade later. It catches up with everyone eventually.

My squad was tasked with clearing palm groves that clung to the edges of the Euphrates River. They extended about a hundred and fifty meters from the water's edge, before the desert and the city strangled the vegetation.

Word from the intel shop was that the palm groves harbored the largest weapons cache in the AO. Each time we were briefed on the subject, the weapons cache grew and grew. It was like the bass your uncle caught in the '80s; it got bigger the longer the story fermented. The mythical cache was said to be guarded by all manner of trip wires and booby traps. If there truly was an enormous cache that sustained the insurgents' daily operations, it would be well-guarded, not just by booby traps and victim-initiated IEDs, but with sniper fire and machine gun positions. At least that's the way we would do it.

We prepared our gear, packing extra ammunition and frag grenades for the fight we expected. Huth whistled cheerfully as he reassembled his rifle, sliding the bolt carrier group together and slamming the rifle back into one piece, doing a function check and setting it to the left of his sweat-stained flak jacket. I asked him why he was in such a jolly mood.

"Fucking Nam, man. I always wanted to be in the war in Viet-Fucking-Nam and I figure the palm groves is the closest I'll ever get. It's gonna be a good day."

I shook my head and called him an idiot, but I was having the exact same thought. I grew up on sentences and paragraphs that ran straight through the humid hell of the Vietnam jungles. This probably was the closest we would ever get, and if nothing else, it was going to be a brief vacation from the barren desert and urban decay of the city.

This was a fairly big operation for the company. A mounted patrol would follow us down the palm grove and offer heavy machine gun support if shit decided to hit the fan. Another foot-mounted patrol would snake through the city, hoping to sneak up on snipers and trigger men. The plan was to patrol down to the palm groves and then get on line, more or less police calling the palm groves. It sounded both stupid and exciting; a perfect Marine Corps mission.

We began the patrol by sprinting across the bridge, zigging and zagging in drunk-driving patterns. The patrol down to the palm groves went smoothly. We scaled fences and took back alleys until we popped out into the greenery of the palm groves. There were times when we first started patrolling that I would question Huth's routes, thinking we were headed in the wrong direction, but he always got us there. Today was no different.

Once down in the palm groves, we spread out on line, the seven-tons and Humvees rumbling on the road closest to the palm groves, their heavy and medium machine guns protruding from their turrets. The sight of gun trucks, with their long 50-caliber machine gun shafts, was enough to stop some fights from ever starting.

When we began our sweep, it felt dangerous. Maybe that's just because it felt so different from the streets and rooftops we had been prowling. There were reports of insurgents hiding artillery shells in the green mopheads of the palm trees so that the explosions rained down on Marines and soldiers from above. My eyes swept the treetops, certain that they'd come to rest on a cluster of pointed cylindrical artillery shells. There were always buried IEDs to worry about too, which was much more likely. It's hard to say how many IEDs I walked over that day, and the days that followed – how many times I walked over a small satchel that had the power to vaporize my story in a flash of light and a spray of crimson.

The palm groves were used for agriculture, for growing golden dates and vegetables that graced the city's markets. Water pumped from the Euphrates sustained the resilient life that sprouted in the desert. Farmers' water pumps and generators lined the river. Corporal Gardner was convinced they were part of a terrorist plot. He wouldn't listen to the line about peaceful farmers trying to make it in a world made hostile by desert and warfare. Corporal Gardner fragged all the generators, asking each of us to give up our hand grenades so that he could. We took turns handing them over, thankful that we brought extra in case an actual threat presented itself. He would set a grenade, and we would watch as he sprinted from the position, trying to hide the glee in his face as he ran away from the explosion.

Any boat we came across received the same treatment. Any people seen floating the river were deemed insurgents and were dealt a swift death. The insurgents were known to ferry munitions and men from one side of the river to the other in small boats, but I imagine there were a thousand other reasons to captain a boat on the Euphrates. I didn't question the Rules of Engagement when they told me I could kill someone; I only questioned them when they told me I could not.

We swept all day, finding only what was supposed to be in the palm groves: crops and palm trees. The mounted patrol that followed us upriver picked us up and gave us a ride back to the FOB.

There is a general rule in combat operations that you are supposed to mix up your patrol times and never take the same route twice; constantly changing your movement and behavior is a way of making yourself a hard target. If you decided to stick to a routine, the enemy could set their watches to your movements and plan accordingly. The commanding officer wanted us to sweep the palm groves again, at the same time, in the exact same area, the very next day.

The next morning, we found ourselves patrolling the palm groves again. The commanding officer wanted to find this cache. If there's one thing a company commander loves racking up, its battalion-level brownie points. So, he made the calculated risk with our lives and sent us out again.

It was late morning when I made it to a small clearing next to the water. A low-hanging, broad-leafed tree provided me shade. I took a knee in the damp and black dirt and thought I could feel the coolness of the earth through my knee pad. The gentle flow of the river offered the soundtrack as I looked beyond the water to Barwanah, another cityscape of beige stucco boxes. Brief dashes of color came in the way of painted metal doors and clothes hanging from drying lines. It was impossible for me not to think of a Roman soldier kneeling in the same patch of mud, heavy kit on his back, blood painting his short sword as the city burned. Were we the new Legions? Was this a war of territorial conquest? Or was it a fight for the collective soul of humanity? Honestly, it didn't matter. Legionnaires and Marines would be out of business if they spent too long questioning intentions. I stood up and stretched my back, then brushed the earth off my knee and turned north. We still had miles to go.

I looked to my left at the rest of the squad as they caught up. They moved like tired but determined men. I was still watching when machine gun fire cracked over our heads. Everyone ducked in unison like a collective hive organism. Red tracers flashed overhead as we each sought small earthly depressions into which we could pour ourselves, hoping the inch of cover would be enough to protect us. I was lucky – there was a small fragment of ancient stone wall within crawling distance. I reached it on my belly, just as I had been taught on the obstacle courses at Camp Pendleton. The earth gave off a sweet smell of decay as I held my face just above the black soil. I flipped onto my back; I could see the rest of the squad looking for something akin to what I had. Some of the Marines just settled on trees that were too skinny to protect them. Large explosions walked toward us, the unstoppable steps of approaching mortar fire.

I peeked over the wall and watched as the explosions inched closer. There was a pause in the buzzsaw machine gun fire, and I could hear the metallic clank of an enormous metal bolt, piston-pumping in and out. It was the familiar sound of an MK-19, one of my beloved machine guns. These were American bullets and bombs, fired by Americans, chewing the dirt around us. I could see the radio operator through the chaos as he screamed into his handset. I thought about shooting back, but two wrongs rarely make a right, so I just kept my back to the wall and waited for one of the 40mm grenades to find me. It would be death by irony in the greenery of the palm groves.

Then, as abruptly as it started, it ended. We had almost become an uptick in the percentage shown on PowerPoint presentations to the generals who gather such numbers. They would pat themselves on the back for how small the percentage was compared to prior conflicts. They would think they were winning the war on fratricide, then they would have to decide between a club sandwich or Caesar salad wrap for lunch – decisions, decisions.

We brushed ourselves off and kept moving forward, if only because it was our one option. The cool dirt of the palm groves had a primordial allure to it. I thought it wouldn't be a horrible place to be buried, beneath the shade of a foreign tree that reminded me of the trees next to the creek in Springdale. I'd be buried six feet deep in the fertile dirt that people had cultivated and fought over since they first decided to give this whole civilization thing a try. I walked past a small crater, created by one of the stranger results of civilization: war.

That would be all our excitement for the day. No one was waiting for us back at the FOB to take statements on the attempted fratricide. We were to make it a fraternal secret, never mentioning the near death we faced at the hands of our sister company to the north. Fine, I figured. We lived, after all, and the palm groves would need to be swept again tomorrow anyway.

**

I can't remember if it was the next day or a week in between, maybe a month. Time has a way of shifting and compressing itself in war. Every day is so similar that only the days of horror or extreme humor stand out and make themselves remembered. Everything else compresses into a homogenous block of scorched memory. I pick at it with my fingernail, trying to get at the edges, hoping I can pop up a corner that will open a memory that I can hold on to. But for the most part it is an exercise in tired futility. My brain has filed and stored the memories as it saw necessary. The only thing I can do is honestly reveal the images that my brain decides to regurgitate.

Eventually, we did find ourselves back in the palm groves. It was Groundhog Day, only Bill Murray wasn't there, and there were more guns. It was another sweep. The command was trying to will a weapons cache into existence, because by God the intel was good and if we just looked harder, we would find it. There was going to be another Echo Company patrol waiting for us at the end of our AO, but this time they knew we were coming, which hopefully meant that they wouldn't try to kill us.

I had gotten complacent staring at the greens and browns, not seeing Iraq but seeing Washington instead, the Evergreen State. I was spotting trees from Spangle and Springdale. Past the trees, I imagined I could see the street corner of Spangle, the two thin roads that were close to my childhood home. I looked to the north and saw Humvees that ruined my illusion and forced me to live in the moment. I looked with contempt at a tan Humvee as its diesel engine purred and knocked. I blinked. The Humvee was suddenly engulfed in sound and dirt.

We were close enough to the explosion to feel the artificial heat and wind from the blast. I didn't know what to do, so I just started sprinting toward it, hoping I could get there in time to make a difference. I thought I saw the rest of my squad flash in my peripheral vision. They all sprinted next to me, probably not knowing what to do either. Conventional wisdom said there was a deadly window of time that existed right after an IED blast. The enemy had taken to setting two charges: one to destroy the

Humvee and a second for the first responders. Though we had this information, we ran straight through it, deciding instead to listen to whatever was moving our feet over the berms and green grass.

The Humvee was a twisted skeleton of its former self. The only thing that told me it was a vehicle was the still-spinning tire that stuck straight up. My eyes moved from the spinning tire to the palm trees. They were painted in varying shades of human. I watched a beige chunk of someone slide off a tree and fall with a wet smack.

Someone's torso had crashed into a yellow Toyota micro truck. The impact had forced both doors open. I thought I saw an infant's footprint tattooed over the heart of the torso. I swallowed vomit.

We formed a defensive perimeter around the explosion, hoping the enemy would send a wave of insurgents at us. That way, we would have something to fight besides the horror that smoldered behind us. We wouldn't be so lucky. The insurgents must have thought we had been through enough for one day, but the day wasn't over. The day would never be over.

We had to pick them up. They deserved to go home as whole as we could make them. They were placed in parts on ponchos. There was a small segment of face that stared at everyone who walked past, the calm eyes not realizing the part they played in this macabre nightmare. I was silent as I watched gloved hands place the head of a drinking buddy into a plastic sack.

***

I blink. Days have passed. A lifetime has passed. The sun shines through the palm groves again. My boots are soaked through with sweat. I'm not far from where the IED was buried. I stand next to the water. It flows past my feet, past the city, away from here, hopefully to somewhere better.

They tell us there is a net stretched across the river at the end of the triad. It's a fishing net that has been thrown across a narrow section of the river to catch bodies. People are being murdered in the city, their often-headless bodies thrown into the river.

I think of the net as I see a small boat in the middle of the river. At first, I think it is a mirage, another fabrication of my deceptive imagination. But the sound of a small boat motor vibrates the image into reality. A man sits at the back of the boat, steering. Another man stands on the front of the boat. That painting of Washington crossing the Delaware comes to mind, the American demi-god who smote a king, unbothered by the arctic chill lashing at his face. But there is no tricorn hat, only a black t-shirt, a mirrored pair of aviator sunglasses, and an AK-47 in his hands. It's strange to actually see a bad guy after fighting his ghost for weeks. I don't wait for permission. I drop instead to my belly, the cool dirt touching bare skin just above my belt line. I pull out the bipods and take proper aim. Huth kneels beside me, not needing to ask what comes next. A deep breath, an exaltation, a seven-round burst of machine gun fire, a man in a black shirt twisting and falling into the water, another trigger pull aimed at the dying air bubbles in dark water, a concerned friend standing in the boat, confused and fearful for a friend, another friend expertly pulling the trigger, a bullet in the heart, more air bubbles, more bullets.

I want it to feel like justice, or a reckoning. But that's only how it happens in stories.

11. Alonzo

A name is more than how we know a person, place, or thing. Names have power. Names carry weight. It's who you are, condensed into a few syllables. To some people, Carl carries the weight of abuse. To others, Carl represents pure love. Mary could be the succubus who stole your life or the saint that saved your soul. A name can change, and its owner might be able to shed the weight of it. But the name always remains, and all who hear its utterance are forced to remember the good and the bad.

Of course, there is always the risk of being branded with a nickname. A name on top of a name. My older brother was the master of demeaning nicknames. He replaced Kacy with Fatty McFatshit; fortunately, the nickname was too complicated to stick, so it quickly faded into the wood paneling of our double-wide trailer. Later, he came up with the name Dually. Initially, I thought it sounded pretty badass. There were worse things than being named after a big truck. Once he saw my pride in the new name, he informed me that "Dually" referred to my two distinct chins. After that, I hated the name. Still, it stuck. My mom called me Kacy; everyone else called me Dually.

In the Marines, your name was immediately reduced to your last name. There were no more Carls, Erics, or Jims. Kacy was nowhere to be found. There were only Smiths, Johnsons, Kowalaskis, Changs, Torreses, and a lone Tellessen.

In Iraq, when I heard someone's first name for the first time, there was a weird ring to it. I knew who the speaker was talking about, but it just sounded wrong. When I met Alonzo, I never bothered to ask his first name. I didn't think we needed them anymore.

Alonzo never really talked to me until we first got shot at. I think he wanted to know if this "Tellessen" was the real thing or another coward who had slipped through the cracks of boot camp. I passed his test; though emotionally immature, I was no coward. After that first firefight, we were as good as brothers. Not brothers in the sense of knowing each other's every secret, but brothers in the sense that we would die a thousand times for one another. Something not quite quantifiable happens between people in combat. There is a kind of invisible chain that connects the two souls. As much as I hated and loved my flesh-and-blood brothers, I hated and loved my combat brothers the same.

About a week into this newfound brotherhood, Alonzo got orders to go to another squad. It was the shits. All of us hated it. We were all just starting to act like a squad. But Alonzo, being the Marine that he was, just smiled and said, "It's all good." The next day, I saw him driving a Humvee outside the wire.

Alonzo refused to change squad bays and kept sleeping in our room. It was about the only thing in the whole situation that made us feel better. The brief moments we had together were nothing but jokes and bitching about how much worse the other guy had it.

The morning of November 20, 2006, my squad was scheduled to move out to a small patrol base. Alonzo had a few hours off and watched us get ready. He made a few jokes about sleeping in and aking the day off. As I was walking out the door, he asked, "Hey man, do you got smokes? I'm out."

I dug through my filthy pockets, moving my toothbrush and half-full bag of Swedish Fish before grabbing an unopened box of cancer sticks. I threw him the red-and-white pack of Marlboros. It was from my private stock of Washington cigarettes with the tax stamp to prove it. He smiled, but there was something behind it, some kind of apprehension or sadness. He looked me in the eyes and shook his head.

"Love you, Kacy."

I didn't know what to say. I didn't know he knew my first name. I just smiled awkwardly back and said, "Love you too, man."

I didn't know his first name.

A couple days later, we were sitting around a small fire at a patrol base on the edge of the city, smoking cigarettes and eating what little junk food we could get our hands on. A porno mag was making its rounds, but I already had it memorized. The copy of *Cherry* magazine reached me. I flipped through the pages and picked out the girl that looked most like the guy sitting next to me. I nudged him in the shoulder and said, "Jesus man, I didn't know times were that tough back home. Your mom has resorted to spreading her butt cheeks in front of the camera for money."

The large Marine next to me reared back. I braced for the punch, hopeful it would be in the arm and not the jaw. I closed my eyes and waited. But the punch never came. Far away, there was an explosion, its sound muffled by our patrol base's thick walls. All we had to do, though, was look up. A black column of smoke reached toward the heavens like an accusatory dark finger pointed at God.

We all ran to the highest point of the patrol base. The explosion was at the far side of the city. I knew it wasn't Alonzo. He couldn't die.

I ran back down to the radio and listened, waiting to hear which one of us was now gone. Through the static and the panicked voices, I pieced together that a Humvee had run over a massive improvised explosive device. It took too long for them to read off the names of the boys that had been hit. I knew of the first Marine Warner. He was dead. The second was Davenport. I never knew Warner well, but I knew Davenport. He was a shy kid. A kid with a huge heart. A kid that I thought didn't belong here. Most of us fit the bill – we were stereotypical ruffians – but not Davenport. He had a legitimately gentle soul; he shouldn't have been behind a machine gun.

The next burst of static cryptically told of a wounded Marine. Severe leg trauma, a medevac had been called. It was Alonzo, I realized. The radio's static turned to white noise.

This wasn't how it was supposed to work. We were supposed to have a few close calls that we would spin into yarns once we were old men. We couldn't tell stories if we were dead. That wasn't how it was supposed to work. But if he lost a leg, he would still be alive. We could still sit on a porch one day and marvel at the badasses we once were.

The radio sat silently as those of us at the patrol base looked at each other. Everyone's faces were filled with rage, sadness, or terror. Some held all three. I don't know what mine looked like.

The radio came back to life. Alonzo was dead. The black smoke still hung heavy in the sky, indifferent and undeniable. They were gone.

Joshua C. Alonzo,

Heath D. Warner,

James R. Davenport.

12. On Creeping Darkness and Candy

It doesn't happen all at once. There is a slow creep to it. First, you hear about a group of snipers found with their throats slit, their gear stripped, and their weapons now in enemy hands. Then you hear about Marines shot by American rifles. You hear about a sniper in the AO that, unlike all his Jihadi counterparts, doesn't miss. Then you start to see the darkness firsthand. You see the Marine carried off post with a hole through his chest, his face such an off-shade that you know he's gone. Maybe you see an IED disintegrate an armored vehicle and its occupants. You might even be tasked with cleaning up pieces of your friends. You can fight the darkness off for a while, just pretend not to notice it, or pretend it doesn't bother you. After a while, the gallows humor begins, and you make jokes that wouldn't have been funny a month ago. That's when the darkness gets your tongue. That's when it becomes a problem.

By then, violence becomes easier. You even see some who enjoy it, almost revel in it. In a world of darkness, why not excel at moving through the void? Others still fight it, but it claws at them under their eyelids, if and when they sleep.

I know for me, the darkness was something I tried preparing for. I thought maybe if I read books chronicling violence and war, I could give myself a small dose of the darkness, like a vaccine. I thought it had worked. For months, the darkness never seemed to bother me. But another thing about the darkness is how it creeps – you don't always know once it reaches you.

We had made it halfway through the deployment when I realized that I wasn't the same Kacy from six months ago. It had been three and a half months of chaos, a dark blur with wet red flashes bursting when we least expected. We had all walked through streets littered with IEDs and soccer fields where children threw grenades. Snipers kept our movements honest, and we moved from place to place with the deliberate violence of action. Even our gait was affected by the dark shroud under which we lived; we walked more like primitive war chimps than homo sapiens, hunched over and weary. And though we were tired, we walked on the balls of our feet like the predatory creatures we had become.

I had lost friends – some dead, some forever changed. I had witnessed the godlike power of the IED up close. Not as close as many, but close enough to feel the brimstone shockwave pass through my body. Close enough to see the Old Testament carnage of military-grade explosives. And honestly, I never felt better. Maybe that should have been my first warning: that I was actually enjoying myself.

Sure, I hated standing post, except for the brief moments when I got shot at or mortared. I yearned to see the enemy. I was learning not only to survive in the darkness, but to crave it, to actively seek it out.

Any day on patrol was better than a day on post. The day I handed out candy was a good day. We walked with our guns at the ready, hoping for a chance to locate and close with the enemy. We walked through alleyways and through houses. We walked through vacant business centers and dead industrial parks. We walked through the marketplace where the children asked for everything we owned.

"Mister, Mister, you give me."

"Please, please. Mister you give me."

"Chocolate, Mister, chocolate please."

Some Marines carried candy in their cargo pockets and handed it out to the city's seemingly endless supply of children. Most days, I only carried cigarettes and Swedish Fish for myself, but on this day I carried Jolly Ranchers and Tootsie Pops that I had grabbed from the MWR. The Morale, Welfare and Recreation center was a living room with four computers that never worked, a foosball table that no one played, and a couch that I occasionally saw tired Marines passed out on. Some unnamed mom had sent an unnamed care package, overflowing with candy and a note: For the kids. There was nothing inside I wanted, so I decided to try and hand out some candy. Why not? I might even make a friend. Maybe, if they saw me again from behind a corner and they had a pineapple grenade in their little hands, they would hesitate. Either way, I didn't think it could hurt anything.

In the market, I handed out candy to the children who weren't too pushy. I tried to make it a point to give the candy to the less fortunate and the shy. When I looked into their eyes, I saw myself reflected back. I was a shy kid too, but I had it better than they did. At least for one day, they would be the ones with candy.

Nearby, a butcher worked on a white goat in his stall. He must have just killed it, because blood still poured from its neck. Strung from its hindlegs, it looked small – springer-spaniel sized. The butcher looked at me with one dead eye as he moved a stainless steel bowl to catch the thin line of blood running from the goat's neck. In the stall next to him, an older man with a dark gray beard and bushy eyebrows fried some kind of meat. It made sense to me that it was goat. The scent of hot oil, seared meat, and sautéed vegetables overpowered the smell of goat blood. The butcher and the cook exchanged a few sentences in a language I knew I would never understand and went back to work, the butcher taking his knife to the goat.

Corporal Gardner was smiling as he exited the shop close by. His green plastic bag was overflowing with glass bottles of orange soda. With an arm signal, he motioned us to leave the marketplace and head north.

The sun filled the marketplace with a heat that radiated off everything, but the alleyway we took was dark and felt ten degrees cooler. The smell of blood and fried meat faded as I walked up the alleyway. A musty mildew smell now permeated every shaded corner. The street was steep enough that at the top I stopped for a moment to catch my breath. Waiting at the top of the alleyway was a beautiful little girl.

The little girl was wearing a pink dress with ruffled shoulders; she looked like an old-fashioned doll. Her copper-colored hair was pulled back in a ponytail, a pink ribbon keeping it all together. Her eyes were a shade of green that I had never seen before. She smiled, and my heart melted. She was adorable.

"Mister, you give me?"

I would have given her my rifle if she asked. She was a bright light in that dark place. I rummaged through my cargo pocket. I was down to my last few Jolly Ranchers: a green, a yellow, and a red. The red was melted and deformed, its wrapper welded to the candy, so I quickly put it back in my pocket. I wished I had more to give her, but green and yellow would have to do. Not exactly the most prized of the Jolly Rancher tribe, but I was sure she wouldn't mind. I handed her the candy.

The girl's smile slowly disappeared. She turned and ran back to two men seated on a step outside of what I assumed was heir house. The older man, probably in his late thirties, had a ive o'clock shadow and hair that was just beginning to gray. He vhispered something into the little girl's ear. I watched the scene vith fascination. I assumed he was telling her to say thank you.

She ran toward me, crow-hopped like a seasoned right fielder, nd threw the candy into my face. I couldn't tell for sure, but I lways imagined it was the yellow Jolly Rancher that hit me in the ip – they were always my least favorite. When I looked back down t the little girl, she was crying on the ground, her pink dress now lirty from the street's filth. I had kicked her.

Fire burned behind my face. I was ashamed and horrified. The irst truly beautiful thing I had seen in the city, and I had kicked 1er. I quickly reached down and picked her up. She recoiled from ny touch, rightfully terrified. With dark intentions, I turned and valked toward the Iraqi men. I projected all my rage onto them. They were what was wrong with this city; they were the darkness. I vanted them to burn.

I grabbed the older man by the shirt and prepared to push his eeth into the back of his skull. I heard the little girl scream even ouder. I pushed him back into the street and walked away. The ittle girl ran to who I presumed was her father. She wrapped her ırms around him, and he quickly stood and whisked her inside. itill hot with rage and shame, I hurried off to find my squad.

My stomach boiled. I had raised my hand against a child. I vas losing control. The dark tendrils of the city had crawled up my pinal column and lodged themselves at the base of my cerebral :ortex. I was becoming what I chased: the bad guy.

I didn't tell my squadmates what happened for a while. I let he incident ferment in my gut for a week or so, turning it over laily. When I finally did talk about it, some of the Marines were lisgusted by what I had done. Others just shrugged it off like it was 10thing. I was them; they were me. We had let the darkness in.

When you read about the horrors of the My Lai Massacre, the Rape of Nanking, or the Nazi concentration camps, it becomes easy to detach yourself from those who committed the atrocities. They were obviously monsters, demons conjured up from the darkness of humanity. It's scarier to think that those monsters were just people capable of both extraordinary kindness and incomprehensible darkness. There are exceptional people who stand firmly against the current of their situation, who never compromise their integrity or moral compass. But it's foolish to presume that you will be one of those heroes. I thought I was one of them, but clearly I wasn't. The monster lives within all of us and only needs a little coaxing before it crawls out of your brain on eight hairy legs.

The shame still comes back to me when I think about that green-eyed girl. Still, I never want to forget her. She reminds me that I'm not as in control as I think I am, that the current of life is powerful, and I have to brace my feet so I don't stumble again. The darkness doesn't come as a tidal wave; it starts as a slow drip, dropping doubts and small pin pricks of pain. You can ignore it, but that doesn't mean it isn't there. The drip, if allowed, will continue until your brain is water damaged, until you look at yourself in the mirror and don't recognize who is looking back.

I carry the little girl's memory with me every day. I see her mostly when I look at my daughter. They both seem to carry that light around with them. The little Iraqi girl reminds me that I am malleable, that I can be bent and twisted with surprising ease. She reminds me that I am the sum of my environment and the inputs I let into my brain. If I could go back, I would smile at her after she threw the candy. Maybe she would smile back. Then maybe I wouldn't have to carry her with me every day. But that's not what happened, and I deserve this extra weight shoved into my pack.

13. Mail Baggage

I tried to act like I didn't care, or that it was just whatever, but I always loved opening letters and packages during deployment, no matter who they were from.

My mom wrote me the most, just like in boot camp. She still managed to find a meaningful quote for the postscript on all her letters: "The object of war is not to die for your country, but to make the other bastard die for his." I smiled when I thought of my mom finding the crazed quote from General Patton and tacking it onto the end of the letter. My mother doesn't make any decision lightly, so I imagined she had a list of quotes to choose from, agonizing over the best quote for the time and clime. I wondered if she thought of her son sticking a bayonet in the belly of an Arab as the quote flashed across my mind, the killing stroke coming with the sanctity of a mother's approval. I loved the quotes, letters, and care packages. I tried desperately to be a hardened Marine, but when I saw my mother's neat handwriting on an envelope, I opened it with a child's excitement and love.

My dad would send letters too. They were always brief and

to the point. He wrote about what construction projects he was working on and what was going on around the community. It was hard to imagine him sitting at a table with pen and paper, but the letters were proof. I always thought I could read "I love you" and "I'm proud of you" in between his lines about road building and BBQ.

My two older brothers sent care packages. My middle brother sent distractions in his boxes: comic books and CDs, things to take me away from where I was. They were things I used to go back home when I closed my eyes. My oldest brother sent me things I could use: flashlights and knives. Ever the pragmatist, my oldest brother knew my job was a trade like any other. I could see both of their personalities in the things they sent. One serious and practical, the other trying everything he could to escape reality.

I didn't respond as much as I should have. I tried to respond to every letter that they sent me, but I would get lazy, deciding to spend my precious downtime with a book or bootleg DVD. But I always responded to the letters Melissa sent.

I had kept writing to her throughout the whole deployment. When I got done with boot camp and could get my hands on a cellphone, I called and texted her, often waiting for the courage provided by heroic doses of alcohol. I would cringe when I checked my phone after a night of heavy drinking, knowing I had called Melissa. I always hoped she had been sleeping and didn't answer my drunken calls.

My first letters to her from the desert were meant to make her miss me, maybe even elicit some sympathy. I just wanted her to think about me, to not forget about me. I was guilty of thinking the world revolved around me, that people just sat around and missed me when I was gone. And yet, people had to be getting on with their lives. I knew Melissa was in college, surrounded by boys who were probably better humans than me: more caring, more compassionate, better educated. I fantasized about her reading my letters in bed, laying her head on a pillow and picturing the desert hell in which I was allegedly thriving.

As per normal, we got into another firefight. Three carelessly sprayed rounds smacked a wall I hid behind, missing my head by a few inches. For the rest of the fighting, I didn't think about it, but when I got back to the FOB, all I thought about were my fundamental beliefs. I tried to distract myself, but the sentences and paragraphs in my book kept rearranging themselves into bullet holes. I thought about what was important to me, I thought about what I wanted when I got out of here. It was a dangerous line of thinking. The future was something that killed Marines. Looking toward what lies ahead, instead of what is directly underfoot, could be as deadly as a sniper's bullet.

When I thought about a future, I thought about a future with Melissa. I was spooked – my I-don't-care-about-death stance faltered. I frantically wrote to Melissa. I told her what an ass I had been for breaking up with her. I asked if she would be careless enough to give me another chance. I told her we could start a romantic relationship through pen and paper. I knew that my predicament held power, that my simple proximity to danger would create in her a certain amount of guilt. Hopefully, that would force her to get back together with me. It was an unfair letter to write.

After a couple weeks, her letter arrived. I was practically floating when Cpl Gardner handed it to me. I decided I would take it on post with me. It would be just the boost I needed to make it through my six painful hours there. By this time, I had learned that the most eventful post duty was Post 6. I mean, the post was nicknamed the Thunder Dome. So, I manipulated my way into changing posts from the ECP to Post 6. The thought of someone else being in the Thunder Dome when the shit hit the fan gave me anxiety. I thought I was designed for it. I slipped the letter into the front of my flak jacket and made my way to the Thunder Dome. I whistled Tina Turner songs all the way to the post.

In the bottom of the building Post 6 sat atop was the detainee watch. A disheveled Iraqi man sat blindfolded and zip-tied on a green military cot, waiting for his ride to the dam for processing. A Marine sat opposite the Iraqi, sharpening his knife as he sat on detainee watch. I whistled past them, waving at the Marine.

I was so happy that I didn't even get annoyed at the douche-bag Marine who I had to do a post turnover with. He was a pathological liar and serial one-upper who always had caught a bigger fish or was in the gnarlier firefight. But I told myself that not even his strain of bullshit could agitate me that day. I had a letter from the woman I loved resting against my heart. The rest of the world could just melt away for all I cared.

By this time, the Iraqis had quit standing post. They couldn't handle the sleep deprivation and had taken to abandoning their posts. I thought it was better to do without them, to drop the act that they were making meaningful contributions to the FOB's defense and let them go back to playing grab-ass and chain smoking cigarettes. I had been involved in a minor incident on post a few weeks prior and felt glad to be rid of the Iraqi post stander.

I had been told by the Marine staff sergeant in charge of the Iraqi post standers that he was sending up a trouble soldier. The staff sergeant swayed and buckled as he spoke. I could smell cheap alcohol on the staff sergeant's breath as he told me that, "This son of a bitch keeps abandoning his post. You don't let the fucker leave until his time is up. I don't give a damn what you have to do." He hiccupped and slapped me on the arm before leaving. Alcohol was strictly forbidden, but different rules apply to different ranks.

The Iraqi showed up minutes after the staff sergeant stumbled down the ladder of Post 6. He seemed like a nice enough guy, rather jolly for the situation we were in. He even had an array of broken

English in his possession that he could use to communicate with. We could actually have something that resembled a conversation.

About forty-five minutes into the post, the Iraqi began to grab his stomach, pleading with me: "Mister shit. Mister shit bad." I laughed at my new name: Mister Shit. "Please Mister Shit." I told him that I couldn't let him leave the post. I tried to apologize, but he just kept getting angrier, cursing this Mister Shit that he had been forced to stand post with. Eventually he got mad enough that he tried to push his way past me. I was thrilled at the chance for excitement on post; it was nighttime and nothing exciting ever really happened at night. I shoved the Iraqi across the post and told him he wasn't leaving. He pushed himself off the back wall of the post and took a swing at me with all his not-so-considerable might. I easily brushed the punch to the side with my left arm before punching the man in the face as hard as I could, immediately dropping him to the floor. I quickly flipped him over onto his belly and zip-tied his hands behind his back, treating him like a captured insurgent. The man began to sob in deep, heaving breaths. The zip ties kept breaking so I called down to the detainee watch, who poked his head through the hole in the roof, laughing out a "Fuuck," before throwing me a zip tie. I radioed the COC, telling them of my predicament. They sent two Marines up to the post to take the beaten man back to his commander.

The Iraqi who replaced him told me that he hated that guy anyways. He told me, "You punch bitch, you number one." We laughed about the punching of bitch. I had to report to the CO after post. He warned me of the international incident that I may have just created. He warned me against peacocking around the FOB like I was a bad ass. He informed me that I was in fact a pussy for getting into a physical altercation. I was to watch my back around the FOB. He envisioned a scene where a vengeful Iraqi would spray me down with AK-47 rounds as I sat on the wooden shitters. I nodded and agreed with him so that I could just get the hell out of his presence. I was able to leave unpunished. But the event was one of the deciding factors that got the Iraqis off our posts, and I was thankful. This meant that I got to be alone with my letter.

After the Marine I relieved left, I did a quick check of the post to make sure everything was in working order. I scanned my sector of fire and found nothing out of the ordinary. After that, I pulled the letter from my flak jacket. I looked at the neatly printed address and thought about Melissa smiling as she put it in the mailbox. I was nervous, but I knew the letter held good news. She had to love me back. I was fighting a war for Chrissake. I opened the letter and took out the folded piece of college-ruled paper. I held it to my nose. She always sprayed her letters with perfume – the scent was intoxicating. When I closed my eyes and breathed deeply, the perfume covered the natural smell of shit and garbage that wafted through the post's tall window slits.

I read the letter, taking each word slowly as if to savor the moment for all time. It was the beginning of the rest of my life. "Dear Kacy," stood at the top of the letter. The letter took a drastic turn for the worse after the first two words. She still had feelings for me, but she said she was with someone else now and it wasn't the right time. She left the door open that maybe when I got out of the Marines, she would be available. I read it once slowly, then again faster and with more anger, and a third time as my eyes welled up. I started to hyperventilate. My fantasy had been taken behind the building and shot in the back of the head. I crumpled up the letter. I couldn't throw it out the tiny window, so instead I stuffed it in a pocket. I tried to mean it when I said aloud that she could go fuck herself. But I was all talk. It was a desperate love.

Now, I can see that I was asking too much, that I was imposing my shitty situation onto her and begging her to carry some of my burden. It was unfair and douchey of me. But it reaffirmed what I already knew in my heart: there was no place for home in this war. My fantasies of a life after Iraq could get me killed. The letter helped me fall back into the mentality that I had carried over there in the first place. I was already dead.

The next day, the FOB was attacked. It was a complex attack, involving rockets and machine gun fire. I was in the Thunder Dome again when bullets began smacking off the post. They made loud slaps as they impacted the sandbags. The fire was coming from my post's blindside. The only way to return fire was from the roof where there was no cover. Corporal Gardner was close by, walking the posts. He informed me over the radio that he was en route to my post.

But I didn't wait for Gardner. I grabbed two hundred rounds of ammo for the 240 and lugged the machine gun to the post's opening. When there was a lull in the shooting, I ran onto the roof. My whole plan was to immediately set up and hide behind my own bullets. It was a stupid and careless risk. I had protection in the post, and the enemy attack would likely lose steam in minutes. But this was a chance, and a chance was more than we were normally offered against this enemy.

I gathered the ammo and pressed it firmly to the underside of the gun. I thought I knew where the shooters were. I knew the direction, at least, which was a good start. The bipods scraped the rooftop as I pressed them into the small eight-inch ledge that surrounded the roof. My finger choked the trigger, and twenty rounds rattled into the city; the bullets made the sounds of a witch's bowl of bones telling a fortune. Whether the noise foretold life or death didn't make much of a difference to me. I felt alive on the roof. In the moment, there was no Melissa and no home – only the rooftop and bullets. It was intimate, a world that only those fighting would ever know. I loved the insurgents in that moment. I felt like only we understood each other. I shifted my hips, squeezed the trigger, calmed my breathing, and felt glad to be practicing my trade.

The insurgents began to lose their courage. A man in a red soccer jersey tried to flee by scaling a wall. Corporal Gardner was now on the roof next to me acting as my spotter. He called out the red soccer jersey: 300 yards, two o'clock. He didn't know what team the jersey represented. I felt like that would have somehow been useful information. My hips shifted, another squeeze, more bullets. A man in black pajamas, another shift of the hips, more bullets. The pattern repeated. The bullets stopped. I was sad when it ended.

I waited for the sniper's bullet that would give me my last tattoo, a crimson cave where my forehead should have been. I waited patiently, but it never came. Gardner moved back to the post and said he had me covered. I grabbed my things and ran back to join him. We laughed hysterically, like we'd gone mad, like we belonged in padded rooms, like we should be sedated before the madness spread to the part of the mind that cannot be medicated. I couldn't breathe. I grabbed my stomach in between chortles, pretending it was from the laughing pain and not from me checking for a bullet hole I might have missed. Gardner leaned against the back wall, laughing tears running down his face. Laughing was better than crying. Laughing *and* crying was better yet.

They sent a patrol across the bridge to count bodies. It took too long for them to leave the wire. It always took too long. By the time they got there, the only things left were spent shell casings, small chunks of flesh, and bloody drag marks. We were fighting ghosts. The enemy's dead vanished. I sometimes thought that maybe the city was insane. That maybe it had lived too long and went mad with dementia. That it wasn't the insurgents fault, and it wasn't ours. It could all be blamed on the city itself.

Once I could breathe again, I looked back onto the roof. Bullet casings and the black metal links that connect the belts of ammo were spread across the rooftop. There were two small oval imprints where I had dug my toes in to steady the gun, just as I had been trained. It's what was left of the witch's fortune, primitive runic symbols thrown onto the roof. I thought I saw death in the random pattern, but maybe it was only madness. I desperately hoped it was freedom. I took out a yellow disposable camera, winding the film into place with a gloved thumb, waiting for the comforting clicks to come to an end. I held down the flash button despite the sun overhead, maybe in spite of it. I looked through the small rectangular aperture at the rooftop. It looked far away; it looked like someone else's life. I pressed the button, hoping the picture would turn out. After the camera flashed, I held down the button for longer, because every Marine worth his salt knows that a good follow-through is paramount to a clean shot.

I had to burn shit after post. I dragged the shit across the motor pool in the familiar grooves that had been used by the poor grunt before me. The barrel sloshed, and some shit splashed onto my gloves. I was thankful I hadn't spilled more. The diesel came out of the jerrican in desperate gulps, splashing and mixing with the liquids and solids. The flames started slowly, crawling across the putrid surface. I pulled the letter from Melissa out of my flak jacket and threw it into the fire, the flame eating away the layers of wadded paper. The letter twisted and convulsed, taking the shape of a disfigured glowing flower before disintegrating into flakes of ash. The boiling shit bubbled and ate the black flakes, pulling my disappointment to the bottom of the barrel. I told myself I was done thinking of home. I told myself I was done thinking of Melissa. My life wasn't written on perfumed college-ruled paper. My life was here in the dancing smoke and flames of burning shit.

14. The Disintegration of Corporal Gardner

The desert has a way of wearing grunts down. The sand that peppers the face of American grunts takes a little something with it as it finds the newly forming lines in young faces, or the deep creases of the experienced. Like the weather-beaten statues that signify Iraq as the genesis of civilization, the weather and war starts to show on the faces of the men and women who spend too long standing against the elements.

When I first met Corporal Gardner, I thought his face already looked weathered, like he had been standing in a storm for most of his life. He kept his head shaved to the skin, taking a razor blade to his scalp every morning. I'm not sure how old he was, but when you're nineteen, someone in their thirties seems ancient. I think he was in his mid-to-late thirties, but that's just speculation. I never sought to verify his stories or ask too many questions when he spoke. It all sounded legit, and without the aid of a google machine, I had no means of looking up the dates and places where he said he served. After the Marines, he had joined the Navy to become a member of the special boat teams. It was the New Orleans Police Department after that. From his time as a cop, he told us stories of shootouts nd face-to-face confrontations with death. All the stories sounded good – damn good. I wanted to believe him because I wanted to believe that I was being led into combat by a 1980s action hero instead of an aging and delusional burnout.

The stories grew in grandeur as the deployment wore on. There began to be stories of espionage and special task units in the police department. Each story began to stray further and further into the realm of action-hero fiction. The retelling of his life began to morph into a Tom Clancy novel. I wanted to believe, but it was getting difficult. Just when I was on the verge of officially calling bullshit, he would go and do something out in the field that seemed to verify his martial prowess.

I watched him throw a knife into a tree from twenty feet away, cutting a rope that was attached to it. He never missed a shot when he took the time to make it. He knew all the lingo when it came to intel and tracking bad guys. He talked about spores when discussing the tracking of humans, and the sci-fi-sounding word instantly gave him credibility.

Corporal Gardner was also a reader. He was a slow reader, one of the most painstakingly slow readers I've ever encountered, but he could often be found trudging his way through a crappy action novel. He read the kind of novels where the lead character would be named Jack Ripper or Mike Strong, books where you could guess the ending after reading the first page: the good guy wins and probably ends up with the girl. I tried to avoid being a book snob, but I gravitated naturally toward obscure books for the sheer sake of obscurity. To me, it meant exclusivity. But Corporal Gardner boldly read his junk fiction for all the world to see. The covers were wallpapered with impossibly attractive men in varying stages of brooding, the whispers of battle on their faces in scars or perfectly streaked soot. They never looked like any of the warfighting faces I knew. There was the occasional model type that existed in the infantry, with the perfect hair and aesthetic jaw line but most of us were ugly. I happily include myself among the dog faced warriors. Anytime I saw an action-hero model on the cove of his books, I looked around the room at our real faces. The one with underbites. The ones with too-pronounced brows. The gian noses. The crooked teeth. I imagined our ugly faces on Gardner' front cover, our expressions dark and mysterious, as dangerous and wiry as a puma's.

Corporal Gardner knew I was a reader. Just as he tried to craf his identity into that of a mysterious shadow warrior's from a bygone age, I was crafting my identity as an intellectual. I think we could smell each other's bullshit. I think this is why he started to offer me his books. I, in turn, felt obliged to read them, so always did. They were awful. I think people find comfort in those kinds of books because there is a formula, and subconsciously they already know the ending. Nothing is certain in life, and sometime it's comforting to engage in a story where the outcome is known.

As the deployment wore on, Gardner's façade began to crack With horror, I began to realize that some of the stories he passed off as his own came directly from the novels he lent me. Three explanations came to mind. The first was that he thought I was too stupid to make the connection. The second was that this was a cry for help, an indirect plea for me to help him with his fracturing reality. The third possibility was that he was losing his mind unknowingly. That explanation scared me the most.

Corporal Gardner now looked tired all the time. His weathered face turned from rugged to worn. Dark bags encircled his eyes a burglar's mask of fatigue and sorrow. He seemed to confide in me for some reason. Maybe it was because I never turned down his book offerings; maybe it was because I was the only one who listened properly.

One night on post, Corporal Gardner came to me. His boots

were untied, and he wore a black fleece instead of his desert blouse. The weather had turned, and now we were no longer under the oppressive rule of the heat but the stifling dictatorship of freezing temperatures. In classic Marine Corps fashion, we weren't issued any cold-weather gear. The squad was initially issued a single black fleece that Corporal Gardner now wore. The rationale was that if the poor grunt was allowed a fleece on post, a fire attack could cause the material to melt to their skin. Of course, none of us cared about that. We were cold. So cold that the risk of a fire bombing almost sounded pleasant. The black fleece became a highly coveted article of clothing, something we all sought to steal for ourselves. Naturally, the officers and staff non-commissioned officers walked around the FOB proudly in their black cold-weather gear, but for the lowly grunt the fleeces were simply a fantasy that we could cling to for warmth when the cold began to crawl up our legs, into our joints and into our minds. The cold hurt. It made everything hurt.

Corporal Gardner took his place beside me on the post, looking out at the dark city. He had a thermos of hot coffee and offered me a cup. I accepted. The rising steam fogged my ballistic glasses. I took a slow sip from the black coffee, which was far too strong, and felt the warmth travel down my throat and into the pit of my stomach. The warmth was almost sensual. Gardner didn't say anything for a while. We were comfortable enough with each other that the silence wasn't awkward. We were happy to be able to hide in the silence with each other, taking comfort in proximity but cherishing the solitude of our own thoughts. Eventually, he began to speak.

For the first time, he told me of his wife and child. I never knew he was married; his stories never involved children. He had kept them to himself until that night. He told me that back before he signed up to return to the desert, his wife had sprung a divorce on him out of nowhere and refused to let him see his child. He responded the only way he knew how. He prepared for war, putting on his tactical gear and loading his weapons. I pictured his face painted black for dramatic effect, but he left that detail out. He told me his plan had been to take his family hostage and kill every police officer that came to try and take his family away from him.

My eyes widened as the story continued. He never outright admitted it, but it was suicide by cop that he was after. I listened to bits and pieces of the story, seeing if I could make a connection to one of the novels he had handed me, but there was nothing this dark in any of the books I'd borrowed. If this was a fiction, it was crafted out of the darkness of his own mind. A wet film slid over his eyes and made them shine in the ambient light of the post. The tears in his eyes made me think that he was finally being honest. He called his wife a whore. His voice shook when he talked about the child. Boy or girl, he never said, just calling the child "my baby." He said his father finally showed up and talked him down. Miraculously, his wife didn't press charges, and he was able to escape his failure by reenlisting in the Marines.

Going to war was an escape for Corporal Gardner. A vacation from the home front. He told me he would stay in Iraq if they let him, and I believed him. It became apparent to me that he was losing his mind. I don't think he told lies intending to deceive. I don't think he believed they were lies. As his mind slipped, it became impossible for him to separate fiction from reality. Reality was horrifying. Reality held his crying child. Reality was where his whore wife lived. Reality was his father pleading with him to put the gun down and let his family go. Reality was chunks of human hanging from palm trees like some hellish fruit crop. Reality was where the responsibility for the squad rested like a crushing anvil, forcing him to live in the present for moments at a time, to make the decision of left or right, up or down, shoot or cease fire. It was easier to live in the pages of his books. This was something I understood. Through Corporal Gardner's trembling lips came a good night. As I watched him leave the post, I wondered if this was where my path led too. Maybe it wasn't death in the actual sense of the word. Maybe it was the death of reality and sanity. The death of a normal life.

We never talked about it again. I told Huth the next morning. We both understood that Gardner's mind had turned to mush, to pliable putty that could easily be molded by praise and reverence. We also knew that Gardner's mind wasn't the exception. Everything – morals, objectives, days themselves – seemed just as fluid, pliable, and confusing.

15. Observation Post

The purpose of the infantry is to locate, close with, and destroy the enemy with fire and maneuver. Sure, there are subtle nuances and specialists within this objective, but at its core, the infantry aims to kill the enemy. Actually, the purpose of the entire military is to support that man on the ground. It takes fifteen personnel per grunt to make sure he is in the fight. Think of all the papers that must be filed, all the shots that must be administered, all the food that must be prepared, and all the training that must be organized to make sure a grunt is ready to stab another military's grunt in the throat with a KA-BAR. It's staggering.

In my Iraq experience, the patrol meant that you walked around trying to get shot at for hours at a time. When our backs would start to give, and our knees began to buckle, we would take an observation post. Observation post is the technical term for home invasion. When we fought in the jungles and in open wilderness, observation posts could be hilltops or some other natural features where the only creatures we displaced were either furry or scaled. In Iraq, we traded wilderness for stucco cities, hilltops for roofs. And instead of evicting squirrels, we rounded up families and took over their habitats for as long as we saw fit.

The protocol was to secure the outside of the house and set up cordon, no one in or out. Then a team of Marines would enter the house and collect all the personnel into one room, then set to clearing and searching the house. Once the house was secure, Marines positioned themselves in the house to provide security while a few Marines would seek the highest point they could find to observe the city. By taking houses throughout the city, we were denying the enemy movement and forcing them to either fight us or go around us.

It sounds a lot better when you use military jargon to describe the "procedure." Cordon and search sound much better than break and enter. It's easier to round up inhabitants or personnel than it is families or toddlers. Securing personnel in a room sounds much, much better than locking a family in their own living room under an armed guard. At the time, I tried not to think about it. But try all I wanted, the stale military terms were never quite strong enough to sterilize words like family and home.

It became impossible for me to take over a house and not picture a foreign soldier kicking in my mom and dad's front door, forcing them into their own living room and posting an armed guard to watch their every move. The thought always made me sick to my stomach, so naturally I tried to avoid it. I always volunteered for the roof. It was the most dangerous job, but it kept me away from the families and their judgmental eyes. I could go to the roof, smoke cigarettes, and look for bad guys. Sure, there was a good chance I would become sniper food, but at least I could breathe and pretend I was fighting a real war.

The houses were all set up the same. Each house had a courtyard surrounded by a high stone-and-stucco fence, normally seven-to-ten feet tall. Some were even topped with shards of sharp, colored glass meant to keep the pigeons and grunts away. Each house was series of beige rectangles. The only color came from the metal door and burglar bars, which were normally bright and vibrant: dark reds, deep purples, and even some soft pinks. Wooden doors were rarity, and a real pleasure to kick open when the opportunity arose They splintered and cracked when you put your boot to them. The sounded more alive and animated than the standard steel doors tha rang and clanked with hollow unsatisfying sounds. Wood mean wealth in the city, so any chance we had to put our boots into th doors of the city's upper echelon, we took with glee. I know I di at least.

But rich or poor, the houses all had the same configuration on the inside. There was a kitchen, bathroom, living room, a few bedrooms, and a single room where they stored stacks and stack of blankets. I'm not sure the significance of these rooms, but ever house seemed to have one. It always looked like generations of blankets had been stacked up, like the strata of an ancient rock formation. Different colors might have represented different eras going all the way back to the nomads that finally decided to settle the area. But of course, that was just a projection; they were probably just stacks of blankets. Most days, I had nothing better to do than daydream about geology when I searched house after house that looked exactly the same. Occasionally, we would find a rifle, bu each house was allowed a single rifle to defend their homes. Some Marines would steal the bolts from these rifles, turning them into ornamental clubs, but I never cared for that. Again, I thought of my own family back home, and the thought of a foreign government disarming my family. It felt un-American, even though some of the rifles were probably used to lob bullets at me on my near-daily strolls through the city. It was one of the many unreconcilable conundrums of our war. I saw it as a violation of one of the core principles of my preschool pedagogy: treat others the way you wish to be treated.

I found it difficult to disarm them, but I never felt the slightest hesitation when it came time to beat them. A large portion of our job was to detain as many suspected and real-deal insurgents as we could. A bound and gagged insurgent was worth more than a dead one. If we could capture them, they could be interrogated. We would never know what they knew if they had a bullet hole in their forehead. As could be expected, some men wouldn't be detained without a fight. I always felt I understood these men, because I always liked to believe that I would never allow myself to be captured alive. To be honest, I enjoyed the fighting.

Catching a man in the act of insurgency was difficult. For the most part, we would find a house that had contraband, whether that be a weapons cache full of grenades and RPGs or an IED factory. The family that lived in the house containing the cache could try to play dumb, like they were as surprised as us, but of course they knew it was there. This didn't mean that they were responsible though. For all we knew, an insurgent could have told the father that if they didn't let them dig up their garden to bury a box of grenades, they would burn his entire family alive while they made him watch. Possession didn't indicate guilt, but there were other factors. If there was a military-aged male in the house, which is anywhere from nineteen to forty-nine years of age, they were under suspicion. If the young or nearly middle-aged man was covered in the bruises of combat, he was guilty. But we didn't have to rely solely on our guts. We were given swabs that could detect gun powder on skin to determine if they had recently fired a weapon. If the swab turned a deep purple, the man was zip-tied, blindfolded, and taken to the dam for processing. After that, they were taken to god knows where.

It was often the case that these weapons caches would turn up in the houses of the elderly and the infirm. A couple in their 70s was powerless to refuse young men with ski masks and AK-47s. It was complicated and practically impossible to act accordingly. We were being asked to do actual police work when all we had been trained to do was kill.

But the majority of observation posts just turned into opportunities to take a load off. To release, for a moment, the pressure of the oppressive weight of a combat load – a weight that dug more than skin deep, that seemed to dig straight into your psyche. The weight from the gear was much more than a physical challenge; it seeped into your thinking. If your footsteps were being lugged down by over a hundred pounds of gear in triple-digit temperatures, then surely the thought process would begin to fall into the rhythmic trudging of the grunt's forced march. Complacency was nearly impossible to avoid after a few hours out on patrol. The moments not filled with insanity-inducing levels of adrenalin and horror all felt like individual lifetimes of boredom. Like a life as an insurance salesman living in quiet desperation, or a housewife that knows she could have done better if only she had looked a little harder, we too were trapped in the monotonous grind of a boring life. But we were uniquely desperate, crushed beneath the horrors of our past and the ever-present violence on the horizon we constantly marched toward.

The observation post could be a reprieve if the conditions were right. If the squad was well-behaved and courteous, there was a good chance that the people of the house would be gracious entertainers, offering homemade flat bread and chai tea that was sweetened to the point of syrup. The bread was always served dry and the tea in small, decorated, shot-glass-sized cups. I'm not sure if it was delicious or simply different, but I always smiled each time I was offered a piece of bread and a cup of tea. I knew that some of these people had very little, and a gesture of food was not as hollow as it would be in the States. A bag of puffed Cheetos doesn't hold the same reverence when it comes from the chubby digits of an

American youth as it does when a piece of handmade flat bread is given to you by the boney fingers of an Iraqi youth that has known nothing but chaos and strife.

We had been walking around nearly all day when we found a nice house to hole up in. It looked like all the others except for the bright rugs in the courtyard. There were deep red circular rugs next to turquois rectangles of handwoven fibers. There were large traditional Persian rugs that took up huge swaths of real estate in the courtyard as we crept toward the house. I imagined they were getting ready for some kind of family get-together. In hindsight, we should have chosen a different house, but maybe not. Maybe that was the exact house we were supposed to be taking as an observation post. Maybe the warm colors from the rugs were supposed to give us a pleasant image to cling to.

I took the roof, finding a nice spot that even offered some shade. I placed an unlit cigarette in my mouth, biting it out of the carton with my teeth, my nose pressed firmly to the other cigarettes that awaited their own pyre funerals. It was my last pack of Marlboro Reds. The last pack in a carton my dad had sent me. My care packages from my dad always had cigarettes and candy in them, both of which I loved. Beyond the scrumptious taste was the fact that the cigarette boxes carried the Washington tax stamp, and there was just something satisfying about knowing that the cigarettes giving me cancer came from home.

It probably wasn't tactically sound to be smoking cigarettes on the roof, but honestly, I had stopped caring. Conventional wisdom said that smoke gave away your position, but I always figured being a behemoth in full body armor gave away my position plenty enough that the smoke would do little harm. With the cigarette clenched between my lips, I took out a red Bic lighter that I had been carrying with me since the beginning of the deployment. I stole the lighter from Melissa the last time I saw her. I wanted something of hers that I could hold onto, some object that I knew she had used. It was creepy, and a little sad, but it was one of my most prized possessions. The ultra-reliable red Bic lit on the first flick. I felt the heat from the lighter as I brought it closer to my lips. The paper around the tip of the cigarette began to retreat from the flame, running toward my lips. I inhaled deeply, and the cigarette smoldered and glowed that happy orange glow, the color of insanity. I smirked at the thought of wearing thousands of dollars' worth of protective equipment to stop bullets and shrapnel, only to be voluntarily poisoning myself. I had taken to all forms of destructive behavior.

I looked past the tip of my cigarette at the city. It sat like it always did, seemingly indifferent to us, but we all knew the truth. The beige of the city was a false layer. Like a tentacled cephalopod that can change colors to confuse prey, the city hid behind the color that is meant to indicate blandness. The true colors of the city were the primal colors of gore and darkness.

The loud familiar crack of a single rifle round materialized out of the beige. There was a stillness that came after. I looked for even an inch of cover to avoid the next rifle shot, but it never came. The screams came, though, just as sudden and profound as the rifle round.

"OH GOD. OH GOD."

There were screams of pain in between the cries to the Oh God. Then the sounds turned for the worse.

"I CAN'T MOVE. OH GOD. OH GOD. MY SPINE. JESUS CHRIST, I CAN'T MOVE. OH GOD."

It was Eastburn, the uglier-than-normal grunt. He screamed outside my field of vision. He was outside the compound, where Corporal Gardner had stationed him to provide security for a blind spot. I didn't even know we had anyone outside of the courtyard. I scanned the rooftops, looking for a shooter, listening to the pleas of Eastburn. He was begging for our help; he didn't understand why we weren't running to his aid yet. But what Eastburn wasn't thinking about, due to being in a state of shock, was that any sniper worth his salt would wound an enemy combatant to draw out his friends. And when the brave souls behind the wall couldn't listen to the screams of their dear friend any longer, they would run straight into the jaws of death. They'd leave their cover, all for the improbable chance to drag their friend to safety without taking a bullet to the spine and collapsing right next to the cross they chose to bear. The sniper would then hope for the pattern to repeat itself, as it had across generations of snipers and grunts. That's why we didn't rush to Eastburn's side. We waited.

We waited while he wailed about the bullet lodged in his spine. He still screamed to god, hoping for some kind of divine intervention, but that's not what he got. Instead, he got two smoke grenades, green and purple, thrown over the top of his body. They landed in the street a good twenty feet from where he lay face down. We waited longer. The smoke built. Finally, the vibrant cinematic smoke made enough of a veil for two Marines to run out and drag Eastburn back to the compound. I watched from the roof as they dragged him. He showed no sign of movement.

The sniper lost his discipline and began firing into the smoke. I watched as bullets hit a pool of Eastburn's blood, sending both dirt and blood high into the air. It looked like the sniper's bullet had wounded the city.

Corporal Gardner yelled for me, so I ran down the stairs. He thought he had the sniper's position down. We were going to assault his position. I ran past Eastburn who was frantically asking if he was going to live. The corpsman, who was not our own Zeb Williams but Doc Lavi, our head corpsman, scolded him for being silly. Doc Lavi had wanted to go on a patrol since his responsibilities as lead corpsman had left him locked behind the walls of the FOB. He was by far the best corpsman we had, and I was thankful Eastburn

had him. As I knelt next to Corporal Gardner, I looked down a
Eastburn and realized that he had not been shot in the spine afte
all. He had been shot in the arm, and the overwhelming electrica
signals from the gaping bullet hole in his arm told his brain that h
was paralyzed. He did have a hole in his body, but that didn't mak
his legs quit working – that was pain and fear. It was no mere flesl
wound though. It looked like the bullet had snapped the arm bon
in half. His muscles contracted, pulling the broken lower arm pas
the broken upper, and wadding his muscles and sinew and flesl
into a tangled mess. It looked awful, and horrendously painful, bu
I believed Doc Lavi when he called him a silly goose and told hin
that he had only been shot in the arm.

Corporal Gardner gave the command, and I moved out th
front gate, running past Eastburn again. Time crawled a little slowe
as I moved past him and stared at the meat that was hemorrhagin
out of the bullet hole. He bled over a Persian rug that was alread
a dark crimson color; the American blood was bright in contrast t
the dark woven fabric. Past the meat and screams, I made it out o
the gateway as the purple and green smoke began to dissipate. /
thick sulfurous scent hung in the air; it invigorated me. My brai
began to dump chemicals into my body, and I felt my heartbea
race as I ran across the alleyway to the far side, where we hoped th
sniper was hiding. As I made it across the alleyway, three round
blasted stucco from the corner of the wall that I was holding ontc
The rest of the Marines that were in the team assaulting the positio
fell in behind me. I told Corporal Gardner I saw the building tha
housed the sniper, and that I would put rounds on the buildin
while the team moved. Once they were set, I would follow whil
they offered the same cover for me. It was classic cover and move.
tried to stop myself from enjoying the moment; after all, my frien
was screaming in agony. But I couldn't help it. I was both terrifie
and unbelievably excited. The two competing emotions turned i

my stomach like an industrial washing machine. I spun to face the corner of the alleyway. The sniper's bullets had put large half-circle holes in the corner. I thought of a large wedge of expensive Swiss cheese as I took a half step and began firing on the building.

I opened with a good twenty-round burst, and bullets spread widely over the building. The burst started in the center of an upper-level window, but then spread in a kaleidoscopic pattern around the whole side of the building. Then I fired controlled bursts, five to seven rounds toward where I thought the sniper was hiding. By now, the rest of the team was set. I waited until I heard their bullets before running to the next position. We kept leapfrogging like that until we finally made it to the building. A woman was screaming from inside. I kicked the front door open just as I had been taught, spinning to the side so that the team could begin clearing the house. I followed the last man in the stack. We spread through the lower level and searched every room, finding nothing but the hysterical woman. We moved her to the living room and left a Marine with her. She was still screaming, holding the side of her head like she was trying to keep out the noise. We had shot out all her windows, and the ghostly silhouettes of the windows could be seen in the rectangular pattern of bullet holes that scarred the walls opposite the windows; it was like a piece of modern art, something about the clash between eastern culture and western civilization, something about the danger of having American neighbors.

We moved slowly up the stairs, careful to keep as much area covered with rifle barrels as we could. There were only a couple rooms upstairs. The door to the roof was barely ajar; a straight line of sunlight beamed through the tiny crack like an invitation, like a taunt. If he had decided to make a stand on the roof and wait for us, the first two Marines through the door would be riddled with bullets before the third man could kill the son of a bitch. I put my hand on Corporal Gardner's back to let him know that I was there behind him, his second man.

Corporal Gardner pulled an M67 fragmentation grenade out of a pouch on the front of his flak jacket. He showed it to me, and I gave him two slaps on the back, telling him that I knew the plan. I focused on my breathing, trying to calm myself down before having to clear the roof. I focused on the sound and speed of my breath, trying to make the breath slow down into a controlled rhythm. I heard my breath in my head. On a deep exhalation, Gardner pushed open the door and threw the grenade. I tried counting to three. The grenades were supposed to be good for a three- to five-second fuse. I had counted too fast. I got to twelve before the explosion shook the house. I followed Gardner out the door and into the harsh sunlight.

Smoke hung heavy on the roof; the sulfur smell now returned. The sniper was gone. All that was on the roof were bullet casings and cigarette butts. He had been smoking on the rooftop just like me. I looked back to the house that had been our observation post. The tall palm tree that I had been using as shade had been blocking me from the sniper's vantage. Long, flat green leaves had stopped the sniper from seeing me. I wonder if he would have taken pity on me because we were sharing a cigarette at the same time. Or if he would have chosen my face as the target because I was in the best position to return fire. But those leaves made it so that I'll never know the answer.

From the roof, we could see the sniper's egress route. There was a series of open gates that were left wide open that created a path leading from the house's roof to deeper into the city. We raced off the roof, hoping we could catch up to him, but I knew that wasn't likely. He was probably dressed in a track suit while we were dressed in full battle rattle. He would move much faster than we could ever hope to, but still we pursued, because that was our job.

I clambered down the stairs, my shoulder sliding down the wall to help me keep my balance. At the bottom of the steps, I turned toward the living room. The woman sat against the wall, rocking back and forth. I wondered if she knew the sniper, or if he took her house like we would have. We burst out the front door, Corporal Gardner pausing long enough to drive the muzzle of his rifle through the rear window of the SUV that was sitting in the driveway. Apparently, the corporal had his own theory about how much the woman knew. I followed close behind Gardner. We were already through three gates before I started to worry about trip wires and ambushes.

It had been an ingenious ploy: Split up the squad with a wounded man, incite rage, and watch as the team followed their maddened Captain Ahab in a charge against you. All it would take is a trip wire across one of the open gates – a grenade with fishing wire wrapped around the spoon, shoved into a soup can – to complete the tragedy. I thought I saw the sun reflect off a string as Corporal Gardner ran through the last open gate.

I was running too fast to turn away, so I simply followed, hoping what I had seen was a spider's web, or that my mind was creating silk threads from the spool of anxiety in my brain. There was no explosion in the courtyard, no grenade, only a large extended family sitting cross-legged in the front yard.

Women, children, and men looked at us as we appeared in the middle of their outdoor picnic. The women and children immediately looked away from us, careful not to lock their gaze with eyes that belonged to the devils from the West. There were rumors spread throughout the city that Marines could only attain the title of Marine by killing their own mother. I thought of my mom as I looked at the women cowering before us. The men stared at us defiantly. They maintained their gazes as I walked toward them, even as I grabbed one of the men by his shoulder. He kept staring, his gaze both accusatory and satisfied, the small hint of a smirk spreading across his face.

The trail from the sniper ended there, in the courtyard, at

the family picnic. All I knew was that the sniper had to have run through here, and they wouldn't tell us anything. He had to have run right past them, if he wasn't sitting in the middle of the family, hiding in plain sight – maybe he was a brother or a cousin. All I knew was that I was going to wipe the satisfied smirk off the man's face. I pushed the man into the house, away from the view of the women and children.

He put his back against the wall in the house. His smirk had turned into a full-fledged smile as I followed him into the room. I smiled back before driving my knee into his stomach. He doubled over, clenching at his stomach and trying to inhale oxygen that wouldn't fill his lungs. I grabbed the back of his head and drove that same knee into his face, the blood from his nose smearing onto the knee of my cammies. Corporal Gardner watched from the doorway. I looked over at him, waiting for approval. He nodded. I pushed the man back against the wall, and he was finally able to breathe again. After he had gulped enough air, I punched him in the stomach. He fell to his knees. I dropped my knee into his back and began to zip-tie his hands.

The rest of our team detained all the men at the family picnic. We would let military intelligence decide what they knew about today. We did a gun powder swab and found purple on the hands of the man who I had beaten, but what the hell does that really mean? Were we using it right? I'm not sure. Was the reaction from one of our own gloves? I did just manhandle the guy, and I was covered in residue. At the time, I didn't care. I wanted to beat him to death. But I don't know if he was guilty. We sent him away in the back of a seven-ton headed for the dam. For all I know, he was questioned and let go once they realized he was actually an out-of-work schoolteacher who had been bloodied and battered by an American savage.

I think about my knee crashing into his face, the blood coming out of his nostrils, deep red strings falling to his chest. His smile transformed to horror as he realized he wasn't safe. I wonder now if he was innocent, if I had beaten a man who was trying to enjoy the afternoon with his family when a crazed sniper ran through his backyard and jumped a fence. If he wasn't a terrorist, I'm sure he was after I got through with him. I think about how my knee crashed into his nose, and the shockwave of the impact that traveled through his face, making his cheeks ripple like a pond that has had a stone thrown in it. Did the violence continue on? Did the ripple effect of violence flow through all of us? Could it have ended with me? Could I have just absorbed it and stopped the cycle? Instead, I kept the wave of violence alive, through that man, through myself, and perhaps through the children who saw their father bloodied, zip-tied, and carried off by foreigners.

One act has the potential to affect multitudes. The violence of that day, both on Eastburn and the Iraqi, could very well have led to another rifle being fired at another Marine. It could have even caused a death. Maybe an Iraqi's, maybe an American's. Maybe that's how violence works. People smarter than me say that energy can neither be created nor destroyed; maybe it's the same with violence. Maybe it just keeps changing forms. Maybe the first chimp to smash another's head in with a rock was living in the same vibration of my knee smashing into that man's face. At the time, I thought it would make me feel better. It didn't then. It doesn't now.

16. Valentine's Day

Valentine's Day. A great Hallmark conspiracy. Growing up, Valentine's Day was an awkward exchange of barely personalized, mass-produced Valentine's Day cards. I remember getting X-Men cards with sayings on them like "You're X-tra special" or "It's you and me bub, side by side." I agonized over who to give what, and with what candy attached. It was a painful process – particularly when choosing combinations for the girls in my grade-school class – that took hours of analysis. Now, when I think about Valentine's Day, I think about grenades.

Travis Dodson and his squad had taken an observation post in the city. He was diligently cleaning his rifle, joking with the Marine next to him, Daniel "Mouse" Morris. Dodson was in my machine gun squad back in Hawaii. He was one of the first boot Marines to make it to the base and had to endure life as one of two boots in the company for a few weeks before we arrived. I'm sure it was terrible. But he had a good sense of humor about it, never taking the punishment too seriously.

One of the things the senior Marines would do is quiz us on

our knowledge of machine gunnery. We were expected to remember definitions and numbers verbatim. Any deviation from the sacred words of the machine gun bible was considered heresy, a high sin that was to be dealt with by the swift arm of hazing justice, normally in the form of PT. In the barracks, among his boot kin, Dodson was perfect in reciting the knowledge. He never missed a question. But when he was confronted by a snarling senior lance corporal, he would lock up; it was a textbook case of the brain farts, and he had it bad. When he came back into our rooms, sweating and out of breath, we would laugh hysterically at his mental flatulence.

We had our spats as friends but all in all we were pretty damn tight. I had met up with him when he was taking trash to the burn pit, a few days before Valentine's Day. We were planning our hazing regimens for the boots that would be waiting for us when we got back from leave. Yes, the cycle would continue, and we would have the responsibility of terrorizing our own boots. We were both giddy, but Travis had a child-like glee. He wanted his turn. I was being groomed to be the number one man when we got back, and I envisioned Travis as my right hand, dealing out punishment and striking the fear of Chesty Puller in the hearts of the boots. We left each other laughing.

On Valentine's Day, Travis sat on the second-story floor of a house in the city, his back to a window with burglar bars. I imagined he had his AP brush in his hand, scrubbing away at the sand that was trying to infest his rifle. As Travis sat cleaning his weapon, his friend Morris stood next to him shooting the shit. Their corpsman, Doc Poquiz, stood in the middle of the room. Meanwhile, a young man was creeping close to the walls that surrounded the house.

If a person clung tightly to the courtyard walls throughout the city, careful to note where observation posts were located, they could move largely unnoticed. That's exactly what this man did, crouching low enough so his head stayed invisible to the sentries on the roof. I imagine once the man got in position, he quickly peeked his head over the wall, locating whichever window was closest to him. Maybe he could see Marines inside, maybe he just knew they were there. The windows of the house had white vertical burglar bars. Throwing any kind of object through the second-story window would take considerable skill or luck, maybe both. The stranger popped his head up again, but this time with purpose; if he had spent years pretending rocks were grenades like I had, this was the culmination of his fantasies. He might have been a paid teenager with a good throwing arm. Maybe he was a true believer, from Iran or homegrown. He may well have been a no-shit insurgent: one of the real-life terrorists who haunted America's collective consciousness since 9/11. It's easier, at least for me, to picture him as a grown terrorist than as a twelve-year-old boy who didn't understand the game he was playing.

The stranger must have felt the deadly weight; maybe he even hefted it in his hand before staring at the pin and knowing what he had to do next. He put a finger through the metal ring, either index or middle would do, then, with a twisting pull, he jerked one arm away, careful to keep a good hold of the spoon. I think afterward, he probably kept the ring that was attached to the pin, a memento of that one time. If he's still alive, he might even wear it as a necklace; I've known Marines who have done the same. But before that – before he made a necklace, or grew old, or fled the courtyard – he first reared back and threw. I like to think that he aimed with precision, that he was just that damn good. It's too painful to think it was blind, stupid luck.

The stranger let the spoon fly off the grenade. The small olive drab orb flew through the air, over the wall, barely missing the burglar bars, thrown with enough force to break through the plate-glass window and fall into the room.

Travis probably heard the glass break. The grenade landed in his lap. I wonder if he had time to look down or not before the grenade did what grenades do. The concussion in the confined room must have been immense; the sounds of the explosion alone enough to give everyone in the room TBIs. But grenades always come equipped with more than noise, with their very own built-in shrapnel. The green metal shell explodes like a dying star, sending fatal elements in any which way the cosmos dictates. The usual kill radius of a frag grenade is five meters, and the casualty radius is fifteen meters. Travis was zero meters away.

The explosion ripped Travis's legs apart. Daniel was blown across the room, his left side absorbing all manner of shrapnel and concussive force. Doc Poquiz was blown backward, like the hero in an action movie, his back slammed against the wall, blood pouring out of his ears, his face covered in soot and blood. Most of the blood was not his own.

Poquiz scrambled to his feet and ran to Travis, who had no business being alive. The rest of the Marines in the squad went into action. Training and love took over. The two wounded Marines were dragged into separate rooms, leaving a trail of themselves along the way. Tourniquets were applied, blouses were ripped off to apply pressure. Everything that could be done was being done.

Travis never lost consciousness, nor did he cry out in pain. He just kept asking his friends to please not let him bleed out. Doc Poquiz, bloodied and bruised, applied tourniquets to Travis's legs. In the next room, Daniel fought to survive. He was given the same treatment, but somehow his injuries were even worse than Travis's. The Marines applied tourniquets and bandages; they applied field dressings and words of encouragement: come on buddy stay with us; you're going to beat this; everything is going to be okay; hey, you're going home, you lucky bastard. Somehow, the words and bandages weren't enough; the hope and love couldn't stop the bleeding. They began to administer CPR to Daniel. They tried to give him their very breath.

They kept splashing water on Travis's face, trying to keep him from slipping away into that sticky darkness. His eyes fluttered, but he stayed conscious. A mounted patrol from the FOB, risking all manner of death by IED, raced to the house, disregarding their own safety for a shot at giving their brothers a fighting chance. They loaded the wounded Marines onto stretchers and put them on Humvees that would take them to a medevac helicopter in the open desert. Daniel had started breathing on his own. They had given him a chance. Travis was still awake and talking, telling his squad leader to stay motivated. The Marines and corpsmen watched as their friends were taken away.

What they don't show in the movies is that the scene doesn't cut away after a tragedy. You can't flash forward to a better time. The ones that lived are stuck there, and I'm certain some of them are still stuck there today. The Marines had to go back into the house and clean up the parts of their friends that were left on the ground. They had to get on their hands and knees and clean, through tears and blind rage. Everything in the room they touched instantly called them back to the jarring explosion and splintered friends. But they had to; we leave nothing for the enemy.

A Marine dipped his knuckles in the blood of his dear friend, vowing to make them pay, to make them all pay. The cycle continued.

The Marines were gathered in the living room when they got the report that Daniel had died. Travis was alive, but his legs couldn't be saved, and there were no guarantees. He had lost so much blood, and the desert cities were filled with infectious bacteria that our western bodies had no immunity for. Infection was a real threat, a silent microscopic killer that was one of military medicine's most nefarious enemies.

Travis would live. Daniel T. Morris would live only in memory, where he still lives today.

I wasn't there. I was in the FOB. When I heard about it, I thought it was another stupid fucking mistake. No way my good friend had lost his legs. No fucking way. I had just talked to him. Besides, he was too good a Marine. I called the Marine who told me a fucking liar and thought about fighting him right there. Maybe if I got angry enough, I could somehow stop it, change reality with my rage. I sat and smoked in silence, knowing everything was different again. Knowing that there wasn't a damn thing I could do about any of it. I smoked until my mouth went numb.

I would get pieces of the story from different Marines and corpsmen, trying to put together a narrative that I could process. I was angry with the Marines standing post. Didn't they see that piece of shit walking down the street, acting like a guy who had a grenade in his waistband? I wanted more people to blame besides the insurgent. But deep down, I knew that shit happened, and in the chaos of war, shit was hiding on every street and down every alleyway in the city.

A reporter from *Stars and Stripes* was there when it happened: Steve Mraz. I got another story from him. Everyone I talked to had a different version, including the reporter. Thirteen people were there; the explosion left twelve different realities. I wasn't there, and now I have my own version. I hope it's close to the truth, if there is such a thing.

17. Sweep and Clear

The battalion command had a grand plan for clearing the city of insurgents. It was the same plan that had worked in Fallujah and Ramadi. Circle the city, control all entry and exit points, and clear every single house.

They brought in the combat engineers with their bulldozers and nail guns. They built an earthen wall around the entire Hadith Triad, using the desert itself to confine the city. Major routes were given entry control points where all traffic could be searched upon entering and exiting the city. Huge x-ray machines were set up to peer through metal and plastic, to see what was really coming in and out. Of course, these checkpoints became targets. But to our relief, all vehicles were to be searched by Iraqis. We were to hide behind Hesco barriers and watch the Iraqis search cars. We'd be behind dirt and bulletproof glass, machine guns at the ready, waiting for the inevitable vehicle-borne IED that would vaporize the poor soul checking trunks. It happened too often, but the checkpoints were effective. We were stopping the flow of munitions into the city.

With the walls built, and entry and exits either under control of surveillance, the entire battalion got on line in their respective cities: Echo Company to the north in Haditha, Fox Company to the east in Barwanah, and Golf Company to the south in Haqlaniyah. We were going to search every house and courtyard, every shop and business, every street and alleyway.

If any insurgents were foolish enough to stand and fight, we brought tanks and all the ammo that we could carry. We were ready to recreate the Battle of Fallujah. We envisioned a last stand. Us versus them. A reckoning where they would stand and fight. But something strange happened.

When we swept the city, not a single shot was fired. The overwhelming firepower we flaunted was enough to dissuade all the fighters in the city. They decided to either flee the city or put down their arms for the foreseeable future. Though we sharpened our KA-BARs and carried extra grenades, the mother of all missions turned into an exhaustive census-taking operation. We still searched houses for contraband, of which we found plenty, but our primary purpose became taking an accurate census of the city's population. Lacking an interpreter, we relied on a member of our squad who had taken a single Arabic class in Hawaii to communicate with the locals. His name was Anthony Vincenty, and he was about as New York as you could possibly get. He was a self-labeled guido who once told me that the Chevy IROC-Z Camaro, which was a popular car in the Italian American community, didn't actually stand for International Race of Champions. Instead, he said it meant Italian Retard out Cruisin'. Vincenty's tactic for communicating with the Iraqis wasn't with actual Arabic words; it was simply saying English words in a Middle Eastern accent. If this didn't work, he would raise the volume of his impersonation. He filled out form after census form, but I always assumed he just made up the information.

The sweep was conducted with almost no incidents. In the weeks that followed, violence tapered off dramatically. There were still plenty of IEDs in the city, some fresh and some just undiscovered, but the actual shooting and indirect fire attacks decreased to almost nothing. Streets we usually ran through to avoid being shot became busy with civilians going about their day. Businesses came back to life while the evil of the city seemed to go back underground, waiting in hibernation until it was jarred back to life.

After the sweep-and-clear mission, fourth platoon was kicked out of the FOB. All the hard-fought territory that we had gained across the bridge was something Golf Company's commanding officer did not want to return to the enemy. So, he decided that we should build a combat outpost, or COP, in the city. This was meant to give us a permanent presence in the city and deny the enemy freedom of movement. It sounded like a swell idea, but the only thing I thought of was the sheer number of sandbags we'd need to fill.

The building selected for the COP was a half-built, two-story house, right across the street from the palm groves. The building sat along Boardwalk, which was once one of the deadliest streets in Iraq. I couldn't argue with them; it was a good location. Combat engineers came and built us a few posts on the upper level of the house, but they certainly didn't bring any sandbags. They brought a few dump-truck loads of sand and a pallet of empty sandbags. For weeks, everything we did was punctuated by filling sandbags. We stood post, and then filled sandbags. We patrolled, and then filled sandbags. We filled sandbags, and then filled more sandbags. Our platoon sergeant developed a kind of sandbag-hoarding syndrome. No matter the abundance of dirt-filled plastic bags, it was never enough. I imagined his parents surviving the depression, then forcing the concept of scarcity down the future gunnery sergeant's throat. We piled sandbag after sandbag onto the building, layer after layer. Each wall in the building had sandbags from floor to ceiling. The entrance to the COP was a serpentine kill zone, created entirely of sandbags. The color of the sandbags was an aberration in our beige world . . . green. Not even an olive drab green, but an artificial light green that was an affront to all of nature's true colors.

The COP required five Marines to be on post at a time. By now, the platoon's numbers were greatly reduced. We were running on life support. Casualties and reassignments had whittled away our numbers; we were barely considered combat effective. Because of this, our patrols became smaller. We would leave the wire in fire teams. Sometimes a corpsman came with us, but often it was just four of us. Thankfully, the violence had dwindled. It didn't take a mathematician to crunch the numbers on what would happen to a four-man team if one of the Marines was seriously wounded and in need of being carried off the street. One wounded, two carrying the casualty, left one Marine to return fire when the bad guys came for us. Running through the scenarios in my head always led to the same conclusion: if our small groups came under any intensive fire, we were screwed.

The IED, paired with sniper and machine gun fire, never came. The complex attack that threatened to consume a fire team remained only a worry. Each day in the city had cost casualties, some not physical, others intensely physical. What the bullets and bombs didn't consume, poor diet and sleep deprivation gnawed away at. A mirror was a luxury we didn't have, but anytime I caught a glimpse of myself in the reflective glass of one of the nicer homes, I was shocked at the feral creature that stared back. Hollow eyes. Sunken cheeks. A jawline that threatened to cut through the skin. My body had aged a decade in seven months, my psyche a few decades more. Though diminished in health, our feral state offered its own protective qualities. We had become wild again, a tribe of early hominids able to communicate without speech, able to sense violence behind the trees before anything sprung out. We had traveled back in time, where social niceties did not exist. We tapped into the memories stored deep in our DNA. I began to fear leaving war more than I feared death.

***

The night was still new, and I was about to get off post. I was standing the south watch. It was a good-sized post, not so small that I felt claustrophobic, but not big enough to let me nervously pace back and forth. But by far the best part about the post was its proximity to the north watch. The posts were close enough to allow for conversations. In south post, you knew that if it was quiet for too long, north watch was either asleep or masturbating.

We talked for hours, mostly about nothing. As the deployment dwindled, it looked like we might actually survive, which was something I hadn't planned on. We talked about the first thing we were going to eat, how much we were going to drink, and what we were going to blow our deployment money on. I had my eye on a new motorcycle, a Victory 8-Ball. I had seen it in a motorcycle magazine that someone had left in the smoke pit and fell in love. I had nothing better to spend the money on – savings were for old people.

I stood opposite Huth most nights. His plans were a lot different than mine. He had gotten married right before we left and had plans of moving his new wife to Hawaii. He was saving his money to start a family, something that he had always wanted. His plans and goals made my motorcycle seem insignificant. I used to make fun of him for being married so young. I would tell him that he had chained himself to one vagina for the rest of his life. He would just smile and say that it was one hell of a vagina.

We were discussing the finer points of eating ass when an explosion rose out of the city, an orange balloon inflated with the hate of man. I gathered my bearings, then yelled to the platoon sergeant who was already at the door, his boots untied and sleep meared over his face. The balloon deflated into itself, bringing the light back to black but leaving a scent we had all come to know.

I waited for rifle fire or rockets. Maybe this was the first stage of an insurgent battle plan to retake the city. But only silence and smoke wafted through the air. The gray smoke that drifted into the COP had a strange undertone to it, both bitter and sweet, like someone grilling porkchops marinated in battery acid. It smelled, in other words, like burning human.

The explosion came out of a building that we called the Saddam Barracks, about a quarter mile from the COP. We knew the place well. It was a series of buildings used by the Iraqi army before the invasion and acted as the garrison for the local military. There was a large stucco billboard of sorts with a mural of Saddam Hussein on it. His lower face had been smashed out with a sledgehammer, leaving a void where his mouth had been. Someone had drawn cartoonish sunglasses over the eyes and written in a dialogue bubble over his head, "Hey, I like you. Do you like me?" I have no idea what the saying was supposed to mean, or who took the time to illustrate the dictator. It was one of the city's anomalies that had become normal to me. The buildings around the friendly Saddam were old and shot to shit. A family had taken to living in the barracks, making the old symbol of oppression into something that they could call a home. I smiled every time I saw the family outside cooking. They seemed content to survive. I knew the feeling.

Staring out from the south watch, I was horrified that the family had been burned alive in some act of retaliation for their friendliness toward us. We gave them MREs, and they gave us fresh-baked bread. We exchanged smiles and waves. I was certain that the wife and small children were burning.

Our relief came, and we quickly grabbed grenades and extra ammunition. We had no idea what to expect, but we wanted to be ready for anything. Corporal Gardner was leading the patrol; it was

going to be just like old times. We put the patrol together as quickl
as possible, then left the COP. We patrolled through the city instea
of right down Boardwalk, hoping that we could use misdirectio
to avoid an ambush. We patrolled to the clearing in the city tha
housed the Saddam Barracks. The smoldering building wasn't th
one the family had made a home. But that didn't mean they weren'
in the building, strung up as a warning to the rest of the city.

The second team in the squad covered our movement, and w
made a run for the building. Smoke wafted out the front door i
lazy billows, turning the night sky gray. The scent became mor
distilled as we entered the front door. The first door to the right o
the front door was blown off its hinges and crumpled against th
opposite wall. Black scorch marks scarred the ceiling and walls.

In the center of the room were the charred remains of a youn
man. His lips were burnt off, exposing his white teeth in a maniac
smile. His track suit was melted into his flesh, some soccer club
deformed seal barely discernable on his chest. The material wa
melted around his penis, informing us that this used to be a man
His hands were twisted and clenched up to his chest like he had
severe bout of osteoarthritis. I was later told that the flames an
heat will cause the tendons to tighten, and the heat will cause
corpse to twist and dance as the fire eats away at the flesh. A charre
propane tank laid on its side next to the man.

We called the Explosive Ordinance Disposal team, or EOD
and waited for two hours for them to arrive. They inspected the sit
and took pictures, documenting the explosion in their extensiv
database. I was standing next to Corporal Gardner when the EOD
tech told him that the man had been trying to set up a boobytra
with the propane tank. He was trying to rig something up so tha
when the door was kicked open, the propane tank would ignite an
consume us. I had cleared that building the day prior, just as I had
been instructed to do on every patrol since we moved into the COI

It could have very well been me, burnt and twisted on the floor.

The protocol for dead bodies was to put them in a body bag and deliver them to the local mosque, where they would be given their proper burial rites. The EOD tech said that the carcass may be boobytrapped, so the plan was to put a couple satchel charges on the burnt body and blow the building along with the corpse: two birds, one explosion. I thought about a mother not being able to bury her son, but it was only for a moment, because the next thought was of me burning into a twisted nightmare. The next thought was of Huth gnarled and burnt, his lips gone, his eyes a matching pair of open sores. I never had a second thought of the grieving mother. I smiled as I waited for the explosion.

We were probably too close to the explosion when it went off. Small chunks of debris rained down on us, but most were only pebble sized. When I popped my head up from the ditch where we'd taken cover, I saw only one corner of the building still standing. The explosion had left the L-shaped corner, exposing the ageless rocks that were hiding behind the stucco veneer of the building. I thought that if I was going to design a piece of war rubble for a movie set, it would look like that L-shaped corner of the building. I wished I had a camera – it would have been a fitting postcard to send home.

We patrolled through the rubble, over burnt rocks and flesh, deeper into the city. The bomb that the young man was placing had been large, and the EOD techs theorized that the man had help. We planned to search houses for the freshly wounded, or the young men that seemed guiltier than usual.

We began by searching the building closest to the explosion, then widened our search in a large circle, careful not to miss a house. At the fifth house, we noticed its inhabitants acting strange. By this time, a mounted patrol from the FOB had come to assist our search. It was my old section leader, the now Staff Sergeant Tardiff's mounted squad. Though I thought the man a supreme dork, I respected him. Staff Sergeant Tardiff was there, at the fifth house, when we found the teenager with a white t-shirt wrapped around his arm, pink stains showing through the makeshift bandage.

The house was well-kept, everything in its place. The smell of their dinner still left a faint aroma of cumin and some other seasoning I couldn't place. The family consisted of an old man who had the milky eyes of the blind, two late-teen boys, and three young women who I assumed were sisters. The mounted patrol had an interpreter with them. He was a skinny man with long greasy hair and a dark five o'clock shadow. He wore a tan flight suit; the tactical onesie was at least three sizes too large for him. He spoke in long streams of Arabic to the family, showing respect to the old man, before turning to us to decipher the family's hysteria. The interpreter would gravely shake his head after finishing an Arabic sentence, as if he was informing them that the test results had come back, the condition was terminal. One of the sisters began to hyperventilate as the 'terp told us that these boys were responsible and that the burnt body was their older brother. I walked toward the unwounded teenager and forced him on his belly. He offered no resistance, the fear of being caught taking the bone and muscle from his frame. I slid the clear plastic zip ties around his thin crossed wrists and pulled, listening to the familiar ratchet of bondage. I thought again about one of us smoldering on the floor, unable to have an open casket funeral, a flag-draped coffin concealing the fire-eaten face of a friend. I pulled the zip ties tighter, the plastic biting into the teenager's wrist.

The old man began to moan like he was in pain, and one of the sisters grabbed me by the leg. From her knees, she looked up at me and we locked eyes. Her brown eyes swam, the light from the ceiling's single bulb reflected off her eyes like a small, tired, yellow sun. She pleaded, "Mister please, please mister." She turned toward the 'terp and said something in Arabic. The 'terp smiled.

She looked back up to me and said, "Sucky," making the hand and mouth motions that transcend language. She wanted to exchange a blowjob for her brother's freedom. She had begun to cry as she pleaded for a chance to atone. She reached up and grabbed my penis through the outside of my trousers. I was ashamed that I was hard as the woman cried on her knees. I found what little self-control I had left and batted her hand away. She fell into a complete state of hysteria and collapsed into her sisters. They clung to each other and cried. All but one of the sisters cried and protested, the oldest sat stone-faced, her eyes cursing all of us. But she was too late; this place had cursed us all a long time ago.

The two boys were taken to the dam, and the one brother was given medical treatment for the burn on his arm. The intel we got back was that the three-brother crew had been placing IEDs in the city for months. We had taken out an entire terrorist cell in one night. It was a good feeling. It was also the last thing of merit any of us accomplished for the rest of the deployment.

The next morning after the explosion, we patrolled the streets, eager to show the city that we were unfazed. We patrolled past the Saddam Barracks. I waved at the woman cooking bread outside her house; she waved back and smiled. I noticed a large white and gray dog trotting over the rubble. His gait was one of smug contentment, prancing like he had just won the Westminster. He trotted past me, not acknowledging the existence of the heavily armed foreign invaders. A burnt hand was clenched carefully in the dog's mouth. The fingers were pressed together, like it was trying to forcefully explain the world to me. The hand shone with the slobber of the canine's happiness. I stopped and watched the dog turn toward the open desert. He never stopped to look back.

18. Cry Havoc and Let Slip the Dogs of War

Packs of mongrel dogs roamed the city streets, taking whatever they could to survive. During the day, many of the dogs stuck to the outskirts, only poking into the city if the opportunity was too good to pass up. But at night, the dogs roamed freely. The people of the city didn't seem to keep any as pets. I always assumed all the dogs were feral; they had the look.

For the most part, the dogs all looked the part of a mutt, with no discernable breed that I could pinpoint. Some were victims of mange, their hair clinging to bony frames in sad clumps. They stayed away for the most part, but some scents were just too much for them to deny. The richness of American trash from the FOB, for example.

Dogs constantly came into the FOB, hoping to have their own taste of western civilization. Some of the Marines fed the dogs, giving them MRE scraps and whatever they could part with. There were certain squads who adopted FOB dogs. The dogs were happy for the attention and the food. When the command found out, they couldn't stand by and allow the Marines to have pets. They thought it was a distraction, though they used words like "infectious diseases" as reasons to ban dogs. We would later find out that the CO had ulterior motives.

The commanding officer was convinced that the dogs had been trained to bring IEDs into the FOB. He had created an elaborate fantasy, in which these mongrels were taken to a secret insurgent canine training facility in the desert and taught to act as hyper-intelligent delivery systems for the enemy's bombs. It was the insurgents' most nefarious plot to date – dog-borne improvised explosive devices. After the dogs had been kicked off the FOB, we were given the order to shoot any and all dogs seen trying to enter the FOB. Some of the Marines looked the other way as the dogs came into the FOB to gorge themselves on garbage. Other Marines were all too happy to follow orders, practicing their marksmanship on the malnourished animals.

A dog never brought a bomb into the FOB, so the CO was content with himself for such forward thinking. But it didn't stop the dogs from hanging around. They always seemed to be there, showing up for the good and the bad, always watching, like they were record keepers, the beasts tasked with archiving the war. We could shoot wave after wave of the mongrel canines, but I don't believe their numbers ever waned. Sometimes I thought they were the immortal spirit of the city. The ones who were always happy when the fire and strife came, knowing that there would always be plenty to eat.

The dogs seemed to follow us to the COP. I used to take pleasure in watching a female dog care for her pups right outside of the COP. We called her momma dog. She had a litter of pups that would play with her outside of the building. It was beautiful to watch. The puppies had a primal joy about them, and the mother's love seemed evident every time she let the puppies feed from her, though maybe it was an anthropomorphized version of reality. I always chose to watch the dogs when they were around my post neglecting my sectors of fire. It was a reprieve. They reminded m of home.

One morning, I woke up and found momma dog dead. Sh lay on her side on the shoulder of Boardwalk. I don't know hov she died. I didn't want to believe that one of us had killed he but you can never tell. Maybe she meant something else to one o the Marines in the COP. Maybe instead of joy, she brought pain and he couldn't bear the sight of the maternal creature for anothe moment. All I knew was that she was dead. I kept waiting for one o us to drag her off and bury her, or at least move her so we wouldn' have to watch as she decomposed, but no one touched her. Th puppies stayed around the FOB. They would occasionally come an nudge the mother, hoping they could revive her with wet prompt from their naked noses. She never responded to their whimpers but they still had to eat. I watched with morbid fascination as th puppies began to cannibalize their own mother. It was the mother' last offering to her children, a final gift of temporary sustenance.

She wasn't the only dog who hung around the COP. There wa another that roamed around our fire pit. He was a huge wolfish dog. His fur was black with subtle streaks of deep red. He possesse huge, golden-flaked eyes that gave him an otherworldly aura. imagined that, like us, he'd come from hell. Marines are know as devil dogs, a name given to us by the German infantry durin the Battle of Belleau Wood. The Germans were in disbelief whe Marines charged through their machine gun fire, leapt over thei potato-masher grenades, overran their position and routed them They had never witnessed such fierce courage on the battlefield They said that the Marines fought like Teufel Hundens: Devil Dog

At the COP, this huge, hellish beast became our mascot. Non of us wanted to get too close to him, but we made sure he had food He wasn't there every day, but when he showed his face, the Marin on post would alert the rest of us so that we could watch him.

My last patrol in the city was early one morning. The sun had begun to return to the desert, and the air was cool but not frigid. We would leave Iraq in the spring with the warmth on our faces. The place had changed, fundamentally. There wasn't the same feel to it. Maybe it was the change in weather, maybe it was because we were getting ready to leave, or maybe it was because our blood had actually made a difference. There was peace in the air. People had returned to the streets in droves, and the sounds of the city returned to normal. The sound of violence had gone, and although I enjoyed the sun on my face, I had already started to miss the terrifying rhythm of the war drum.

We took a few observation posts, trying to be as nice to the families as we could. We patrolled through the market, buying candy and soda, spending what little cash we had. It was a good day. We even took one more stroll through the palm groves, feeling the black dirt under our boots one last time, resting next to the water, listening to the unstoppable trickle of time cutting through the center of the Haditha Triad. I couldn't stop smiling. Sure, I knew it was still dangerous. We hadn't killed all the insurgents and bad men in the city. I'm sure we bumped elbows with them in the market. They were still here, and so were we; all the elements remained to rekindle the fires of war. But against my own beliefs, it looked like I was going to survive. My thoughts began to shift toward what the hell that meant. I knew I would have to go back to war one more time, at least, but for now I could begin to think of what came next. I started thinking about Melissa.

We patrolled back to the COP for the last time, down the center of Boardwalk. Just a few short months ago, doing so would have been unthinkable. Patrolling down the center of Boardwalk was assured death, but now it was just another street. I could still feel the vibrations of violence through the pavement. The street still bore pockmarks from the bombs and bullets. There were fresh patches of new asphalt where the U.S. military had filled in IED craters. The sound of children laughing could be heard from a clearing in the palm groves, where they played soccer. I started to feel like we had made a difference.

A hundred yards from the COP lay our mascot on his side. As I patrolled closer, I saw the blood pooled around his great head. His gold-flaked eyes were closed, and his tongue poked out the front of his mouth, a small puddle of light brown mud at the tip of the still-pink organ. The top of his head had been blown off but still hung on by a small tab of flesh and fur. His brain was exposed, and the sun glistened off the gore that puddled in the open cavity. It was a picture of the war. I walked past him knowing that it would never be over. We would never leave this place.

19. Miles to Go

There was a band waiting for us when we got off the plane in Hawaii. My family was going to be there, and I didn't know what I was going to say to them. But in the fashion of my family tradition, I knew I was probably just never going to talk to them about it. Better to act like I had been away at summer camp.

The plane came to a halt in front of a large crowd. As we pulled closer, I looked out the window at the steps where we were docking. They stood tall and white with aluminum accents on the tarmac. The steps led to nowhere: suicide steps. Trumpets and tubas played a hero's song as we walked down the plane's steps. My face was greasy from traveling. It had been twelve hours of smelling recycled farts and eating prepackaged mashed potatoes and gravy. As I walked down the steps, I searched for my family in the crowd. I couldn't see them anywhere. There was a line of important-looking people there to greet us, collars heavy with brass and silver. I shook their hands and smiled. Many of the men looked guilty as I gripped their hands, like they were embarrassed they weren't with us over there. But really, I couldn't care less about the officers. I wanted to see my family. A good-looking Hawaiian woman put a lei around my neck, and I looked at the pretty pink and blue flowers clashing against the desert camouflage of my uniform. War and peace. An oversimplification of the human condition.

I walked through the center of the crowd and still couldn't find my family. I had talked to them on the phone when we were stuck living out our last week in Iraq on the Al Asad Airbase. The command deemed it a good idea that we had a few weeks of decompression time on the big base before we were sent back to the States. It was a practice run for civilization. We ate Burger King and then went out for ice cream. Many guys hit the gym again, trying to put size back on their withered frames. All the young faces in the company had a wild animal's leanness to them. We contrasted greatly with the base dwellers' soft faces. They looked at us like we were wolves in captivity. We didn't belong on the base; they knew it, and we knew it.

When we first arrived on base, grunts were being accosted at the chow hall for stinking. We hadn't had running water for seven months. I clenched my jaw until it hurt while the well-kept first sergeant of unknown POG origins chastised a 2/3 grunt for having an odor. He stood with his hands on his hips and belittled the grunt, who simply stared back with the dead eyes of a killer. I thought about following him back to his hooch and beating him within an inch of his life. I'm sure I could've gotten help if I needed it. The first sergeant shook his head and walked off, disgusted with the men who fought the war while he tried to have sex with lower-ranking female Marines on a totally secure slice of American real estate. My contempt for non-grunts grew into an inferno of hate. We weren't looked at with awe and respect. We were looked at as an inconvenience, and a grim reminder that while they hid behind walls, there was a real war going on.

I saw POGs trying to sit close to our tables in the chow hall o that they could hear the stories that we told among ourselves. I figured they wanted to regurgitate our tales of war to their families and would-be love interests back home, their faces superimposed over our own. I hated them. I hated that they would be treated with reverence back home. I hated that they wore the same uniform as me. I thought they should wear something different, something to tell the world that they handed out toilet paper while we fought and bled. They were the new enemy, a safe place where I could project my hate for the moment. I yearned for one of them to mouth off to me. I fantasized about fistfights and broken bones. But for the most part, they kept their distance. They knew we would soon be moving on, because that's what grunts do – they just keep moving.

I started to run again, thankful for the burning in my lungs and the pain in my legs. I ran until I felt like I was going to vomit. I ran until my vision narrowed. I tried to read, to lose myself in the pages of books that I loved, but I couldn't stay focused on the words. Sentences would trail off, and I would be back in the Haq on some street or rooftop. The black words turned into shell casings or silent screams. Paragraphs became pools of blood. I watched movies instead. The more violent the better. There was a healthy bootleg DVD industry on base, and I was happy to indulge in the piracy.

300 was in theaters, the movie over-dramatizing the Battle of Thermopylae between the Spartans and the Persians. The video was of poor quality, and the person videotaping the movie in the theater shifted his arm for a good forty-five minutes of the movie, cutting off the top left corner of the film. But I didn't care. I watched the movie over and over again. I thought I saw parallels. I made irrational connections between the battle for western civilization that existed then and the current situation with fundamentalist Islamic terrorism. I mainly watched for the violence, the gore. I thought my appetite for the imagery would have been satiated for a lifetime, but it hadn't. If anything, I had developed more of a taste

for it, like a bear who tastes human garbage and then becomes
serial dumpster diver. I had a real thirst for violence now. As w
were getting ready to leave the country, I looked forward to comin
back within the year. I began to hope that the fragile peace we ha
created would shatter, and we would be forced to plunge ourselve
headlong into the chaos once more.

I was basically all fucked up but unwilling to admit tha
anything was wrong. I thought I had seen the world as it reall
was. I thought blood and fire were truer than everything else, tha
society was just a thin veneer meant to hide that fact. In my heart
I knew everything boiled down to violence. Taxes and laws wer
only followed because there was the hint of violence underneath.
thought I had solved the riddle of the human condition at the ag
of twenty.

But my brooding thoughts evaporated when I saw my parent
in the crowd, smiling at me like I wasn't a monster. I hugge
my mom for a long time, trying not to cry. I felt her warm tear
running down her cheeks, the moisture pressed against the shar
line of my jaw. I dammed my own tears, saving them for when
could be alone. Her hug made me feel like a child again, like mayb
everything was going to be all right if she would just take care o
me. I gave my dad a hug, and the same feeling welled up. My da
was, and still is, the toughest man I know. I thought he would knov
what to do with all this in my brain if I just talked to him. But, o
course, I had vowed to myself that this was mine to carry, and th
last thing I would do was put it in someone else's pack to hump o
my behalf.

Mom and Dad took me and Huth out to dinner that nigh
at the Bubba Gump Shrimp Company. They didn't card us a
the restaurant, so we drank. I was drunk off my third light beer
but I didn't let that stop me. Huth and I both held it together fo
dinner, and my parents were as charmed as I was with the souther

gentleman. They drove us back to the base, and on the way I had to stop three times to piss. The beer ran straight through me.

They dropped us off at the barracks, which were in a state of utter chaos. Music of all sorts exploded from open doors, causing a melodic dissonance that was soothing for no other reason than it sounded like chaos, a whisper from the world we had tried to leave behind. I smiled and thanked my parents for the wonderful evening. As they drove away, I was thankful I could take my mask off and be who I was on the inside. I drank Crown Royal until everything went black. I woke up feeling like death, with dried blood on my knuckles and a pool of vomit on my bed. I had pissed my pants sometime during the night. We all laughed about the debauchery the next morning, because laughter was a proven method for staving off constricting sorrow.

In the morning formation, the Hawaii wind picked up the lid of a trashcan and slammed it into the concrete wall. The entire company of Marines ducked in unison, searching the tropical paradise for the enemy that we were certain had followed us back. We smiled, but there was a collective mental scarring that was easy to see if you were brave enough to look.

My parents left after a few days. It was good to see them, but it was better to be with my tribe. As much as I loved my mom and dad, the men around me felt like my new family. The drinking ramped up to apocalyptic levels. We were trying to burn everything away with hard liquor, to sterilize our memories before we went home on leave. They weren't safe to bring back home.

I got a call from one of my friends in Echo Company. My corpsman, Zeb, was downstairs trying to pick a fight with anyone he could from Echo Company. He was looking for retribution for the time they made us cower in the palm groves, their bullets and bombs almost mistaking us for the wrong killers. They told me to come rescue him before something bad happened. He was accusing them of trying to kill us in the palm groves, saying he would fight any man that called him a liar. I went downstairs and thanked them for calling me instead of just administering a beating. If Zeb had stumbled into the wrong barracks room, I'm sure that's what would have happened.

Zeb smiled when he saw me come through the door, certain that Tellessen "The Mad" was there to fight. He looked betrayed when I shook everyone's hands and thanked them for calling me. I smiled at Zeb and told him I had a bottle with his name on it in my room. He told me to fuck myself, and that while I was at it, the rest of the Marines in the room could go fuck themselves as well. The room erupted in laughter, which only caused Zeb's face to darken.

Zeb is a small man, and he was in a room with the largest breed of grunt in the infantry: machine gunners. He had enough to drink to believe that he was invincible, or maybe he knew I would protect him. I put my arm around his shoulder and told him that these guys were a bunch of fags anyways and that we should get out of there. He frowned before nodding his head in agreement with the homophobic comment. The Echo Company Marines began to dry hump each other and laugh as we walked out. I tried not to laugh as I left the room.

My room was on the second story, so I led Zeb up the stairs. His walk was wobbly and unsure, just like the day he froze in combat. He stopped me on the landing, his back to the wall. A mural was painted on the wall behind him; the mural asked what made the grass grow in bright green letters. The answer was underneath, in red letters, repeated three times: BLOOD, BLOOD, BLOOD. I glanced back down at Zeb who looked betrayed. He swayed a little when he said, "You know what, Tellessen? I think you're a real bitch." He brought his hand up from his side and slapped me across the face. He put his whole body into his right hand and the slap stung my face.

Everything went red, as if rage had slid over my eyes like a visor. When I looked down, Zeb was on his knees, blood pouring from his face. His nose was at an unnatural angle; the blood was pooling on the gray concrete floor beneath the mural's caption. Blood, blood, blood.

I collected my faculties and led him up to my room, knocking on the door of another corpsman's room. The other corpsman immediately opened his door, as if he sensed the blood through the wall. He shook his head and cursed the both of us, grabbing his medical kit and following us to my room. He sat Zeb in a chair in the middle of my room and asked what the fuck happened. I told him everything; he just shook his head. He muttered, "Stupid fucking Marines." Then he looked at Zeb and said, "And what the fuck were you thinking? What the hell did you think was going to happen?" He tilted Zeb's head back to get a better look. The blood that was flowing out of his nose began to drain down the back of his throat, and he vomited a mixture of blood, food, and alcohol on my floor. He wiped his mouth and apologized. By now, I was embarrassed by my loss of self-control. I was supposed to protect Zeb, and I was the one who had smashed his face in.

The corpsman told Zeb that he was going to set his nose for him, on the count of three. He asked Zeb if he was ready. Zeb nodded his head yes and grabbed the side of the chair, bracing for the pain that was about to wash over him. On one, the corpsman slid his nose back to the center of his face. Zeb screamed fuck on repeat, a transcendental mantra that we have all repeated at one time or another. The corpsman told me he was going to take him back to his room. I told Zeb I was sorry, and he said he was too. I told him I loved him, and he said me too.

I spent the rest of the night cleaning the puke off my floor and feeling sorry for myself.

In the morning, Zeb's eyes were black and blue from the broken nose. He never said as much, but I believe his pride hurt worse than his nose. Someone said he looked like the Hamburglar with his new black eyes, and we all tried to laugh away the uncomfortable situation. We never talked about it again. Incidents like this were common in the barracks.

The base all but officially quarantined our barracks. The military police were told to give us a wide berth and to respond only if it was a dire emergency. The command was hoping we would burn out, getting out all our angst in an explosion of alcohol and debauchery that couldn't be sustained. It was sound logic. This type of behavior wasn't sustainable.

We all made plans for leave. We would all be given a month to go home and see the ones we loved. I got drunk and called Melissa. I called her sober sometimes too, but it was easier if I was drunk. It was mostly shallow small talk unless I was drunk enough to tell her I loved her. When it was time to go back home, I was both excited and scared. I wanted to go home, but I wanted to stay in the comfort of the tribe, where I knew I was understood. Where there was no doubt as to what I was: a killer and a degenerate. Back home, I was expected to be a son and a brother, a seasoned veteran who was supposed to somehow be more than when he left, not less. I had performance anxiety. Could I be all those things anymore? Or was I just that one thing now?

I drank heavily the night before the plane ride so that I could sleep for the entire flight. I drank more on the plane, but still couldn't sleep. I looked out the window at nothing for the entire trip. I thought about what was going to happen now. I thought about just exchanging my ticket in Seattle and going back to Hawaii. There were Marines who weren't going home. They had no home, so they opted to save their money and stay in the barracks – a skeleton crew working the debauchery shift late into the evenings. I'm not sure if I lost my courage or found it, but I got on the small ropeller plane in Seattle and once again looked out the window. he sun was up now, and I could see my home state. I searched for ostalgia, for love, but found neither. I hoped they were waiting for 1e in Spangle.

The plane touched down in Spokane and taxied for what seemed ke hours, slowly rolling toward the small terminal. I started to et anxiety the longer we waited on the plane. My throat felt like : was swelling shut, and I had to clench my teeth to keep from creaming. I wanted off the fucking plane. I wanted air. Finally, a londe woman with a prepackaged smile informed us that we could ebark. I hated her for using the word debark. Couldn't we just et off? I thought about a sick pine tree standing naked in a forest, eetle holes pockmarking the pale tree, its brown bark on the forest oor bunched up like a fallen nightgown. I didn't return her plastic mile as I walked past her.

I made my way to the first bathroom I could find. I was ungover and didn't want to smell like booze when I hugged my 1other. I brushed my teeth and splashed water on my face. I shaved vith a disposable razor and stared at myself, hoping the stranger in he mirror would have answers. Sadly, my reflection just mimed the onfusion I felt.

As I walked past the security checkpoint, I saw all of them vaiting for me. My mom and dad, brothers, and people who were •nce my friends. There were cardboard signs, but I can't remember vhat any of them said. The Sharpie lines all morphed and twisted nto, "Welcome to our home, Kacy. Nothing is the same. This place sn't for you." I hugged my mom and dad. I hugged my grandma nd took in her smell. It was age, covered up with perfume, and I ad missed it. I saw her looking at my tattoos, and the feral nature •f my face. I thought she looked like she may have been afraid of 1e. But still she hugged me back, I'm sure thinking of the little •lue-eyed boy whose body she had washed in her kitchen sink.

We ate breakfast, and I listened to everyone's stories about what it was like to be at home missing me. They all waited uncomfortably for my own horror stories, but I wouldn't give them any. I was too sober. There were lunches and dinners planned, people I was supposed to be happy to see, but I was already feeling claustrophobic.

My parents dragged me to a dinner for my grandma's eightieth birthday party. The walls of the restaurant inched closer, the faces of relatives and former acquaintances pressed against mine. I regularly excused myself to the restroom to have conversations with myself. I wondered if I was the crazy one or the one who had seen the truth. I knew what was under the surface, the shit and the fire. I could smell half of the equation in the bathroom. I left the bathroom and made another pass through the smorgasbord, heaping BBQ on my plate, trying to make it back to the white tablecloth where my oversized beer sat.

I smiled and nodded at people, told them I was happy to see them, and that I appreciated their letters and packages. I tried to be genuine, but I felt like a fraud. We left the old BBQ restaurant where we had dinner and drove back to my brother's house. It was the double-wide trailer where I grew up. It was where I learned how to drink in high school. It was the first place I ever masturbated and the first place I had sex. Most of the time, when I thought about home, I thought about that double-wide trailer. The memories weren't how the house stood now; the house was a mixture of aggregate memories that fell into place to make something that seemed whole. I remembered the white carpets and food-themed wallpaper in the kitchen from when I was little. I remembered the house as it slipped into disarray when it sat in limbo after my parents moved. I remembered my brother fixing the place up, only to destroy it himself with the aid of alcohol and good times. When we turned onto Keeney Road, I saw the mailbox. On it was the first address I ever memorized. His driveway was full of cars. It was a surprise party that didn't surprise me at all. The music was muffled from the house, but I could make out the twang of Dwight Yoakam easily enough. I closed my eyes in the passenger seat and told myself that I would have a good time. Not for me, but for the people who wanted to believe that Kacy made it out okay.

I walked inside and smiled. I hoped it didn't look forced. It seemed like everyone wanted a piece of me, like I was supposed to stop and talk to everyone, like they all wanted their own little war token from me. This was to be their closest proximity to the conflict. When their children or grandchildren asked them if they fought in the war on terror, they would say no, maybe even shamefully, but they knew this one guy who did. He came back a little fucked up, but it was hard to tell because he seemed a little off before he left.

I smiled and nodded, pretending to be happy to see these people who I no longer cared about. I cared about the Marines I served with. They were family. These people began to feel like nothing to me, significant only in their proximity.

I headed for the kitchen, hoping to make a drink so stiff that everything would blur. I saw Melissa standing beside the island in the kitchen, a drink in her hand and a smile across her face. We locked eyes, and everything else faded away. There was only her smile. She was no longer an abstraction, an ideal that I elevated to the status of Helen of Troy. She was real and standing in front of me. My smile turned legitimate as I walked toward her. I couldn't believe I was close enough to smell her, close enough to touch her. The noise of the party turned to an insignificant hum. I leaned in and kissed her, half expecting her to recoil from my touch, but she wrapped an arm behind my head and kissed me back. For a moment, there was no Iraq, there were no screams, the blood was all gone; it was only her and me. It was then I realized that nothing else mattered if we could only stay together. She tethered me to the present, even when I felt like drifting off to my old home. We made love that night for the first time.

Two weeks later, I found myself in a jewelry store picking out a ring, not knowing what the hell I was doing. I only knew that this was the only thing that felt right in a long time. I bought the first ring I saw; it seemed like it was waiting there for me. I would ask her to marry me after I got back from a trip to Palo Alto to see an old friend.

I got on a plane in Spokane and departed for Los Angeles. Torres was waiting for me there. We had told each other that we had to go see Dodson at the hospital. He was our friend, our brother, and the thought of him in the hospital alone made us sick. I couldn't help but put myself in that hospital bed. Surrounded by blood family but utterly alone. Away from your Corps family, the ones who came to know you better than anyone. I was certain that if put in the same situation, I would descend into madness.

Torres was waiting at the airport with his wife Nancy. She was beautiful and kind, with a sharp sense of humor. She didn't take any of Torres's shit, which I think is what he liked most about her. He took me to his mother's house. I was the first white person they had ever had in their home. She looked at me like I was a dangerous stranger at first, and she was probably right. But I sat in her kitchen, and she made me feel at home. I didn't feel worthy when she put the home-cooked tamales in front of me. It was one of the best meals I had ever tasted.

After the tamales, Torres took me to the park. He had a handball game at noon that couldn't be missed. I sat on a blue park bench with a garbage can chained to it, but I didn't watch the handball game. There was a homeless man in military fatigues practicing Tai Chi in the park. He moved like he knew what he was doing, but his eyes made him seem lost, like he had ingested something to get away. He moved and exhaled, overemphasizing the exhalation. He looked like a cliché. The broken veteran, disturbed by the war, forced into a life on the streets. I wondered whether a person knew if they were a cliché or not. I wondered if it was comforting to slip into this trope, if there was comfort in knowing how you were supposed to act. I wondered if I would become a cliché. I wondered if I already was one. As I watched him, the man jump-kicked, flicking his right foot in front of him and then came to the position of attention, exhaling a breath that I'm certain smelled of cheap wine or malt liquor. He grabbed his olive drab jacket and pushed his cart away.

Torres's uncle had to rent us a car because we were too young. It was a black Mercedes that neither of us could think of affording in real life. It was comforting, knowing that we could rent luxury when we got older. We drove all day and into the night, chain smoking menthol cigarettes like they were the last ones in existence. Torres's flavor was Newport, and I was happy to indulge. I liked the two-tone turquoise box – I thought it looked medicinal. We stopped only for gas, cigarettes, and Flamin' Hot Cheetos. We tried to talk about everything but Iraq, but everything led us back there. We told each other stories. Neither of us needed to lie or embellish because we each shared almost identical stories. We talked about Dodson. We talked about the unlikeliness of his existence. He shouldn't have been alive; we wondered if he knew that. We were positive he did.

We arrived at Palo Alto with no idea of where in the hell we were supposed to go. Looking for street names, Torres ran a stop sign. I guess you could say that we slowly rolled past a stop sign, but the result was the same. Red and blue lights flashed behind us. The cop asked for identification as he looked into the car, certain that he had stumbled upon some kind of drug deal about to go wrong – a Hispanic man driving a new black Mercedes and a heavily tattooed white male sitting in the passenger seat. Torres tried to explain the situation as the cop wrote the ticket. He said that we were visiting our friend who had lost his legs in Iraq, and that we were lost. The cop told us that we should have told him that before he started writing the ticket; apparently there was no going back once his Bic pen hit his ticket book. He smiled as he handed Torres the ticket and told us to drive safe.

We found the hotel as the sun started to rise above the buildings to the east. We lay down and caught a few hours of sleep before going to see Dodson. It felt like I had just closed my eyes when my alarm went off, informing us that it was time to go see the fate we had avoided by pure chance and happenstance.

Dodson smiled when he saw us come into his room, waving us in with the warmth of a long-lost brother. I tried not to stare at the scarred stumps that jutted from his hips. His mother was there and welcomed us as sons. She looked tired, exhausted from trying to hold it all together. I couldn't imagine what she had gone through. Getting the news that her son had been injured, the cryptic message from a strange telephone number. The updates she received as Dodson made it closer to home. Getting on a plane and losing the ability to communicate. Landing and hoping that when you turned your phone back on there wasn't a message saying that it was all just too much for your son to bear. It was the stuff of nightmares. I hugged her like she was my own mother, because she was. She was a war mom, and the title deserved reverence.

His mother left us, and Dodson asked for details about what had happened after. He wanted to see if he missed anything, if there were battles he missed because he went and got himself blown up. He shook his head with the stories of our inept command and laughed when we told him about having to police call the streets for trash before the arrival of our relieving battalion. Torres and I did our best to act like everything was just as it had been before. But eventually, the talk turned toward his legs, or the lack thereof. He told us they were fitting him for some new legs, and he would be back standing in no time.

I was not expecting his positivity. I pictured a dark, brooding veteran, angry at the world, angry at us because we still had our legs. But I think that was just years of mental conditioning from Hollywood films. Dodson hadn't gone dark at all. I knew he was going to be alright when he told me that since losing the weight of his legs, he could do about fifteen more pull-ups. Dodson was all Marine.

By pure chance, we were there when the Battalion Executive Officer presented him with his Purple Heart. We sat in a crowded room with other wounded veterans; local press had come to document the award ceremony. The XO called attention to orders, and Torres and I shot to attention, our backs straight and hands along the seams of our jeans. I locked eyes with Dodson and saw that he was staring at us, his friends who didn't forget. They pinned the heart-shaped medal on his green skivvy shirt, and the XO shook his hand. The XO noticed us standing at attention during the ceremony and asked who we were with; he had no idea we were in his battalion. We told him we were with him, and he simply nodded his head, awkwardly shaking our hands before disappearing out of the crowded room.

Dodson's parents stood next to his wheelchair, looking both proud and sad. The father's chest was puffed up, and his eyes were reddened by proud tears, but deep lines of fatigue ran through his face too, small fissures of worry and doubt. We hugged them and told them we were in awe of their courage. I gave Dodson a hug, not knowing if I would ever see him again.

***

Melissa was waiting for me at the airport, smiling that smile of hers. I spent the week with her. It was a week of not thinking about Iraq or Dodson or the palm groves. At night, my dreams would betray me. I would go back, then wake not knowing where I was, my heart racing, my hand searching for my rifle. But Melissa was always there. She would put her hand over my heart and hold it there until it slowed back to the normal rhythm, when the leftover adrenaline would drain, and I could remember that I was with her. That weekend, at my going-away party, I asked her to marry me. I didn't get down on one knee, which I regret, but I hugged her and pulled the small leather box out of my pocket, showing her the ring with an arm around her waist. She didn't hesitate, saying yes and pressing her lips to mine. Everyone thought we were crazy. They were probably right.

20. Once More

I was headed back to Iraq. There would be another workup and another leave before deployment. It was the same cycle, only this time I would no longer be a boot. I was tasked with being a machine gun section leader as a Senior Lance Corporal. The command sent me to an advanced machine gun leadership course, where I was supposed to learn everything I needed to lead a section. The school was excellent, but experience is the only true way to learn how to lead.

We received a shipment of fresh boots, directly from SOI. I saw myself in most of them, which made me hate them for their inexperience, just as I had been blamed less than a year ago. We trained hard and regularly crossed the line into the realm of hazing. They all paid a price, and as a result we were the most effective machine gun section in the battalion. They even gave us a piece of paper to prove it.

I tried to be a good leader to the Marines, separate from them, but they lived right next door to me in the barracks, so they got to see me at my worst. That included when the fifth of vodka was almost gone, and I swayed on the catwalk, trying to tell them war stories that could potentially save their lives, but probably sounding braggadocious. I think I had more flaws than strengths as a leader, but I loved those boots and would have done just about anything for them.

Training came and went. Mojave Viper was updated with more realistic training. We stood around a smoke pit, waiting to begin a training exercise when one of the coyotes came running toward a small group of us machine gunners, frantically telling us that he needed our help. The look in his eyes made it seem like something had just gone past the comforts of a training scenario. We followed close behind as he ran into one of the CONEX boxes that the military had transformed into a mock Middle Eastern habitat. Screams echoed off the walls, and blood covered all surfaces. I looked down at the wooden planked floor where an overweight man in digital cammies was writhing on the floor, gore twitching where his legs were supposed to be. A woman on the far side of the room was missing a leg and screaming for help. Two of my Marines went for the woman, and I yelled at them to put on a tourniquet first and then try to apply pressure. I dropped down to my knees next to the overweight man. He had a colonel insignia on his flak jacket. He grabbed me by the sleeve and told me that he had to get to his men, that his men needed him, that I needed to let him up. He called me a fucking idiot as I tried to slide a tourniquet over the bloody stump. He pulled hard on my sleeve, my knees slipped on the blood, and I fell forward, falling back into Iraq, falling back into the blood. I got the tourniquet on and grabbed the man's hand, trying to talk to him, to keep him from slipping away into the shadowlands, the place where people rarely return from. I looked over at my Marines administering first aid and was proud of them. They were handling themselves well in a room that was covered in blood.

The coyote came back in the room with a clipboard and told us that was enough. I tried to hide my shaking hands by gripping onto my flak jacket. He told us we did pretty good, offering a few helpful critiques before dismissing us. The colonel and woman were amputees turned crisis actors. They were good at their jobs. I had gotten lost in the training exercise, lost in the Karo syrup blood, mistaking it for the real thing if only for a moment. The colonel sat up and shook my hand, thanking me for my service. He was still covered in the fake blood, with the trauma appliances still firmly affixed to his legs. He smiled and joked with me, taking one of my cigarettes. I wondered if the shake in my hand was perceptible when I put the cigarette to my lips. It seemed like a dream, the bloody man telling me of his acting career as he sat in a pool of blood. I thought of Dodson. I thought of the palm groves. I thought about my Marines that were going to Iraq with me. I tried to think about Melissa, but I couldn't. There was still too much blood.

***

We got married in December, a month before I flew back to Iraq. The snow was falling outside the Masonic Temple in downtown Spokane. I looked out the window at the large snowflakes; I thought of ash and chaff from a nuclear winter, but I quickly tried to insert an image of happy cotton balls falling from the sky. It was supposed to be a happy day. My eyes were drawn to the contrast of the white snow outside and the red brick interior of the room. The thought of blood came back to me, but I shook it off as the music started playing. I looked down at my uniform one last time. My medals were in their proper place; I had a new chevron on my shoulder and a blood stripe that led down the side of my blue dress pants. I reached down and felt the hilt of the sword that hung on my hip. It was a replica of a civil war cavalry saber that the Marine Corps had adopted as the dress sword for non-commissioned officers. The sword had been my only request for the wedding ceremony.

The room was over-capacity, people crowded into every corner. Most stood because the seats were all taken. I looked out at the coagulated mass of people, their faces blurred. A few stood out – my mother and father – but for the most part they were just bodies. They didn't matter to me.

My eyes stared at her legs when Melissa walked through the doorway. The white gown spread at her feet, but the white fabric clung to her hips as my eyes traveled north. She held a red bouquet of flowers in her hand that my Aunt Marie had made for her. I looked from the flowers to her lips, which were a lighter shade of red than the dark roses, more pink than red. I finally made my way to her eyes, a sharp dark blue that could always look straight through whatever wall I tried to put up. I couldn't stop the smile from spreading across my face. I tried to keep my military bearing, to look like the Marine I wanted to be, but she turned me into a grinning child. The smile was contagious. Everything other than her in that white dress faded as she walked closer. I took her hand, and we were married as the snow fell on a frozen city.

Three weeks after the wedding, I was on a plane going back to Iraq. It was already different. Everything was different this time, though the route and the actors seemed the same. The flight attendants seemed a little more war-weary this time, as if they tired of these overnight military flights. The war ground up all who were involved, including the blonde flight attendants.

We were headed to a small city outside of Fallujah. The town had a name like Shahabe, but it never seemed as important as the Haq – no city ever would. We were staying on a large military base and sleeping in CONEX boxes with air conditioning. It was luxury in comparison to the old FOB. None of us veterans let the boot Marines forget it either. I could see the disappointment on their faces when they realized this deployment would not be what we had gone through the year prior.

By 2008, Iraq had changed fundamentally. The United States had started throwing money at the problem, and not in the form of munitions but actual green stuff. We began financing police forces and army units who I never believed would be competent enough to defend the country from the enemy we fought in the Haq. We didn't get shot at anymore, and most of us suspected we no longer got shot at because we were now paying the former insurgents to be police officers. The type of men we were fighting a year ago were now wearing police uniforms and army fatigues. We stood shoulder to shoulder with the enemy. A fragile peace fell over Iraq.

Envelopes of cash were handed to powerful men, as has been the case since the inception of currency and power. We were informed of IEDs by the police officers, who would regularly place them so that they could receive a reward for finding an IED. We had fallen through the rabbit hole – up was down, down was up. Nothing made sense anymore.

I tried to keep my Marines in the game, to let them know that this could all go to shit overnight, that the men who wanted to kill us were standing right across from us holding rifles. I told them we couldn't trust anyone but ourselves. These weren't our people. But complacency is inevitable when the threat never shows its face. The boogeyman fades from memory if he never sticks a hand out from beneath the bed to grab a foot.

Instead of fighting the enemy, we exercised. The entire squad became obsessed with physical fitness. Hundreds of dollars were spent on supplements and workout literature. Barely legal steroids passed through the ranks, muscles swelled, body fat evaporated in the desert heat. With no enemy to fight, we fought our own bodies, finding weaknesses and destroying them with squats and deadlifts. I did my best to avoid complacency, but I'm human and weak. I became more concerned with documenting my calorie intake and which muscle group I was going to brutalize than I was with a

docile enemy. The problem was battalion-wide. Our bodies ha
hardened while our minds softened.

***

A meeting was scheduled for the region's powerful communit
leaders, the captains of industry the U.S. forces needed in order t
recreate some semblance of normalcy in the country. If we coul
reignite the economy, we could win the war through prosperit
A man with a good job and fat wallet was less likely to pick u
an AK-47 and stuff his pockets full of grenades. The plan wa
to dump money into the local economy and get people back t
work. We were trying to fix what we had ruined. We finance
construction projects that rebuilt schools and dumped money int
local infrastructure in order to repair what our missiles and thei
IEDs had destroyed. It seemed like the strategy was working. Th
accountants had to adjust their figures for standard human greec
but some of the money was actually getting to these projects.

It was about three-quarters of the way through this deploymen
when the meeting was scheduled. I'm not sure what was on th
agenda as I was only a corporal, and for some reason the comman
didn't consult me in their high-level decision making. We ha
heard about the meeting, as the most powerful man in the area wa
supposed to be in attendance. He claimed to be a former genera
and was supposed to act as an intermediary between the U.S. an
whatever shadow forces were still in the area. He was supposed t
be someone who built bridges.

By this time in the deployment, we had been kicked out o
the nice base with all the amenities an airman would take fo
granted. We were forced out to the middle of the desert, to hel
build and fortify a police station that we would ultimately turr
over to the local police. We filled sandbags, and my Marines ha
the opportunity to burn shit. At least they were afforded that smal
rite of passage, so they would have something of significance t

take with them from their seven months of desert purgatory. We fortified the positions and tried to teach the Iraqis how to stand post. They were competent post standers during the daylight hours, but as soon as the sun went down, you couldn't get them to stay awake. We left them the fortified position, fully equipped with radios and bulletproof glass. It was a defensible position that could be held if only they wanted to.

The police station had been turned over to them for twenty-four hours when we took a mounted patrol to go check on them. We pulled through the front gate, which was wide open and unmanned. We looked behind the post to see an Iraqi police officer cuddled up in the sand, using his jacket as a pillow. The diesel engines didn't seem to wake any of them up as we got out of the Humvees. Inside was more of the same. It was like they had all been infected with some viral narcolepsy. All the police officers slept in various states of comfort around the station. The higher-ranking officers, the ones with the most prominent mustaches, slept on couches and large chairs; the lowly patrol men slept on the floors and steps. We walked over them with our flashlights on, not attempting to be quiet. We checked every post, finding each man asleep inside the wooden boxes. We made a report and left the police station. Not a single man woke up while we were there. Maybe they slept so easily because to fear an insurgent was to fear themselves.

We were at the police station when we got the news about the meeting. The local general had never showed – a strange occurrence – but the meeting resumed. The battalion commander, Lieutenant Colonel Max Galeai, was in the room, along with Captain Dykeman of Fox Company, Corporal Marcus Preudhomme, and Battalion Sergeant, Major Wilkinson. The meeting was also meant to address the Iraqis officially taking control of the region's security. No longer would U.S. Forces spearhead security operations in the area.

An Iraqi police officer walked into the room, looking the part of one of the locals. He had the right uniform, the same black hair, and the same five o'clock shadow that spread across most of the younger men's faces. What set him apart was how he accessorized his uniform. Others would try to spruce up their uniforms with random medals found at flea markets and patches sewn on that indicated some form of "special" training they hadn't actually gone through. This police officer chose to accessorize his uniform with a belt full of military-grade explosives and hundreds of ball bearings sewn in front of the explosives. He was going to the dress-up party as a walking claymore mine. I imagined sweat beading on his forehead as he walked into the room, his skin clammy and cold. I imagined his mind struggling with self-doubt. Maybe he fortified his strength with narcotics. I've been told that most suicide bombers are stoned out of their minds when they make the ultimate pledge to the jihad. I like to think that when he pressed the button, he was filled with remorse, the comforting clouds of the opiates parting, for a moment, so that he could see that his death was meaningless, and that he should have tried to go back to school, or maybe help his father on the farm. But regardless, he pressed the button.

An explosion such as that in the open air of the desert would have been devastating, but the amount of pressure involved when he stepped into the closed room was biblical in proportion. The Lieutenant Colonel was killed. The Captain was killed. The Corporal was killed. Against all odds, the Sergeant Major lived. None of us were surprised to find out that he was the lone survivor. His toughness could be heard in his voice and seen in his face. It's rare for a battalion to love their sergeant major. Mostly it's just fear that keeps the checks and balances of military custom in place, but we loved the Sergeant Major. He was with us in the Haq, and he regularly traveled to our FOBs, risking his life each time just to make sure we had what we needed to stay in the fight.

I remember the first machine gun range that I ran as a section leader. I was nervous, trying not to show it, which became more difficult when the Battalion Commander and Sergeant Major showed up to observe the range. But we were hot shit at the time; we all lived and breathed machine guns. This was going to be our day. My Marines shot as well as could be asked of machine gunners; the team leaders directed fire with precision, and the squad leaders kept everything together. I thought it couldn't have gone better, which is why I was surprised when the pissed-off Sergeant Major came walking toward me. I thought we might have unknowingly violated some cardinal range rule. I thought I was screwed. He walked straight up to me, his PPE immaculate and worn with precision. Personal Protective Equipment was one of the Sergeant Major's personal standards that he saw enforced. He had seen it save lives and knew that wearing it incorrectly was an idiotic risk not worth taking. I looked at his eyes through his ballistic glasses as he got closer to me. He yelled my name, "TELLESSEN." I was flattered that he knew my name. He slammed an open hand into my chest and knocked me back a couple of steps, before yelling, "OUTFUCKINGSTANDING." Then he walked off. I always admired the man, but it was at that moment that he became a hero to me.

As others in the battalion became complacent in the AO, deciding that it was okay to take off PPE in certain situations, the Sergeant Major remained unwilling to trust the Iraqis fully. The Sergeant Major refused to take his gear off. He would conduct the meetings in full PPE while the others stripped down to their flight suits for tea and crackers. The Sergeant Major endured the pain of the gear digging into his shoulders because he knew that it was more than just his life that was on the line. He was a symbol of the battalion, and if he showed weakness or a willingness to ease standards, it would infect the other men. Of course, he was badly injured. One leg was reduced to red ribbons of flesh, and his body became riddled with the entry and exit wounds from the surgical ball bearings. But his gear saved his life. His will saved his life. He would make it home to his family.

We had lost our battalion commander and a company commander. The battalion was shaken. We all wanted blood – we wanted to find the men responsible and watch them burn. But we were never given the opportunity. They say we arrested the cell responsible, but it never felt like we got the retribution that was owed to us. It felt like we got our asses kicked and then walked away, limping and embarrassed. Tensions rose between us and the Iraqis, so they kept us on the bases as much as possible. We would still take mounted patrols to monitor the Iraqi checkpoints. Mostly, we verified that they were inept.

My old squad leader was involved in the shooting of an Iraqi police officer. He had his back to a police officer when the police officer raised a pistol to the back of his head. A Marine that I knew well, a Marine that I considered a dear friend, saw the pistol to the back of Gardner's head and raised his rifle. He shot the police officer dead before he could pull the trigger. The insurgents were still here, but now they were wearing police uniforms. We all knew that if these men were asked to truly defend the country against another wave of terrorists, half would defect, and the other half would be killed in their sleep.

21. Getting Out

There is a day that most Marines dream about as soon as they arrive at boot camp. It isn't that first day of leave, or their first chance to prove themselves on the battlefield. What most of us dream about is the day we get our DD-214 and get out. It's the day we can put the uniform in a green canvas sea bag and walk out the front gate, back to where we came from or to a place where we can start over.

I joined the Marines when I was seventeen, so young that I needed to get my reluctant parents to sign a waiver. My brain was still very much malleable when I agreed to join the ranks of America's Spartans. The drill instructors used pain and intimidation to rivet discipline and service onto my spine. I allowed myself to be swept away in the current of Marine Corps tradition and lore. I finally felt like I mattered, like I was part of a greater eternal cause: the very real fight for an American ideology that had cradled my family for over a hundred years. When I looked to my left and right, I saw men just like me, with their shaved heads and a fire burning behind their eyes. We would take that fire into the desert

inferno that burns so hot almost no other flame can withstand th
lack of oxygen. Many fires wouldn't make it out, and the ones tha
did make it out would never be the same.

Most of us took two trips into the desert and then got to g
back home. Others couldn't get enough of the flame. They becam
addicted to the heat, and they would sign the papers that would sen
them back again and again. I did my two trips and then receive
my walking papers. But I wasn't without apprehension. The Marin
Corps couldn't hold onto their infantry non-commissioned officer
especially the ones with combat experience. So, they started offerin
bonuses, sizable ones. On my second trip to Iraq, two gunner
sergeants showed up with nylon briefcases and computers. It was
simple proposition: four more years, two trips to Afghanistan, an
a tax-free lump sum of seventy-two thousand dollars in my ban
account. The money didn't mean much to me, but it added pound
of weight to my decision. My identity was so firmly rooted in bein
an infantry Marine that I didn't know if I could be anything else.
had taken so well to the lifestyle that anyone I told of my EAS (En
of Active Service) would respond with, "Jesus, Tellessen. What th
hell are you going to do as a civilian? You know there aren't an
machine-gunning jobs in Spokane, right?" The officers I talked t
told me I was a born Marine, that guys like me just didn't have
place in the civilian world. But they didn't really know me. The
knew who I wanted them to know. They weren't wrong, but I wa
more than that. Or at least that's what I hoped.

I believed that a person only has so many rolls of the dice whe
it comes to risking their life. I never imagined I would surviv
my first deployment. I was certain I was going to die, which wa
freeing in a way. I ran through the gunfire because I didn't thin
it mattered. If I was going to die anyway, why care if it was from
a bullet or a bomb? I took unnecessary risks because of this belie
and the risks had an exponential quality. Each firefight or IED blas

I survived gave me more confidence, until I was all but certain the enemies bullets were a non-factor. By the end of the deployment, I had a reputation as a crazy fucker, which I relished. But a small whisper in my head told me that I may have used up all my rolls on the first deployment.

The second deployment was nothing like the first. The days weren't filled with bombs and blood, but with humanitarian aid. Though we took the occasional potshot, or found the rare IED, it was barely a combat deployment. I thought I had gotten lucky and shouldn't look the old combat gift horse in the mouth. I would get out, despite the rank of sergeant they offered me and the seventy-two-thousand-dollar reenlistment bonus.

But there was more than that. There was Melissa. She was slowly starting to domesticate me. She had moved to Hawaii to be with me in those final months in the Corps. We got a small two-bedroom apartment on base. There were cockroaches and rats, but we laughed a lot. I started to feel happy, and as combat vets tend to do when they come home from war, I got her pregnant. It wasn't just me anymore. If it was, I think I would have kept rolling the dice, even though I knew that sooner or later the house always wins. I didn't think the military was the best life for a child, and neither did she. We made the decision together that we would try our hand at civilian life. We were getting out of the only world where I ever felt like I belonged.

To say I had mixed feelings would be a severe understatement. I had full-blown decision schizophrenia. Every day, I would view the decision through a different set of eyes. One day, I would be the war-weary veteran who was ready for a chance at peace and an opportunity to see what he could make of himself in the civilian world. Other days, I was the gung-ho Marine who was ready to eat his own guts and ask for seconds. Ultimately, I listened to the war-weary self and kept my hand from picking up the pen. My unit would deploy to Afghanistan while I was in the process of getting out.

I felt like I wasn't pulling my weight for the country. Somehow, two combat deployments seemed like I was getting off easy – like I had more to give but was keeping it for myself. The Marines I had trained were on a plane to Afghanistan, and I was in Hawaii finally enjoying the beach. It felt wrong and right at the same time. As my wife's stomach grew with our new baby, I was able to justify my decision more easily. "See, I'm having a kid. I need to be there for him and her!" The problem was that there were a lot of guys on that plane with kids, both kinds: the running-around type and the expecting type. For the most part, I tried to bottle that voice of dissent and disgust. I figured I had the rest of a lifetime to dwell on my decision; no use in getting started now when I could see the beach from my apartment and I had a beautiful woman sleeping next to me.

Melissa left Hawaii to get our newly purchased Spokane home ready for a new life. It was a small white walk-in-closet-sized home on the South Hill. Melissa was ecstatic, but I couldn't stop thinking of Afghanistan and wondering if this made me a coward. Shortly after Melissa left for Spokane, I got the news that one of my friends, one braver than me who decided to extend for his third deployment, had stepped on a land mine.

Mathew Lembke was a physical specimen, a born athlete and natural hero. If you were to try and build a Marine, you could use Lembke as a blueprint. At over six feet tall with a straight back, broad shoulders, and glacier shards for eyes, he could have been in the movies. But his physical attributes were only a fraction of his worth. He was a mental powerhouse, both intelligent and filled with grit. He was a machine gunner like me; we had gone through boot camp and the school of infantry together. We would always boast of the merits and superiority of the Pacific Northwest to any who would listen to us by shouting "Northwest" in our best Ron Burgundy voice. Lembke was from Tualatin, Oregon, which prompted me to call him the Titan of Tualatin.

After our second deployment, Lembke decided he'd had enough of the world of 650-950 rounds per minute and wanted to become a sniper. He joined the ranks of the 2/3's scout sniper platoon. I was filled with jealousy and admiration. Of course, he was attached to my old company, Golf Company. If I had extended, I might have been right alongside him that day.

The mine took his legs, but his spirit was too strong to die in that godforsaken land of perpetual warfare. He would make it to Germany where the top medical experts could begin to help him recover. If you wanted to find a morbid silver lining in the two wars that America has fought over the decades, you could look to the medical advancements won at the cost of American limbs. We were becoming excellent at saving people who had lost appendages. I was horrified when I heard the news, having to excuse myself so that I could vomit into a bathroom trash can. But I had a vision of Lembke in a wheelchair with arms of banded steel, throwing a shotput in the Olympics. I knew he would come out of this stronger than before. He was literally the best of us. Then we got word that there was an infection.

We were told that to stave off the infection, the surgeons had begun to amputate more of Lembke's legs. It didn't work, but still they kept working on him, and Lembke kept fighting. In the end, the infection gained superiority over my friend and killed him. We lost one of the greatest Marines and humans I have ever had the pleasure of knowing.

There were only a few of us machine gunners left on base. We went to the enlisted club to have a drink in Lembke's honor. We all told stories of the Tualatin Titan, each story ending in a shot of whiskey. We all drank too much. I stumbled back to base housing, drunk and trying not to fall to pieces. We had all kept it together in front of each other, but I had a sneaking suspicion that I wasn't the only one who felt like his guts were being torn out. I made it back to my apartment which was stripped bare. The movers had come so that all our earthly possessions could begin their journey to Washington. The only things left in the house were an inflatable mattress, a lamp, a small box of books, three slices of supreme pizza, and three quarters of a fifth of vodka. I grabbed the vodka and pizza before sitting down on the air mattress.

I stared down at the cold supreme pizza, the same kind I had been eating when I told my parents about my decision to join the Marines. I thought it fitting; the cheese of the pizza no longer oozed off the slice and there were no amoeba-shaped blobs spreading over a blue eggshell pattern of a ceramic plate. I looked at the bright red pepperoni, the red onions that were more purple than red, and the asteroid-shaped sausages that dotted the slice in a random impact pattern, but the image was cold, devoid of that original warmth. I jammed the cold supreme pizza in my mouth, trying to taste the olives and sausages, but being too drunk to appreciate it. I washed the cold pizza down with colder vodka. The glass of the bottle was coated with ice, the clear liquid sloshing as harmlessly as ice water, but I knew that wasn't the case. I knew better, yet I still put the bottle up to my lips and waited for three painful air bubbles. I lay back on the air mattress and stared up at the popcorn ceiling of my apartment. Beige peaks and valleys, just how I imagined Afghanistan to look. I thought of my friend and how maybe, just maybe, I could have made a difference if I had been on that patrol with him. I thought of how I would gladly take his place if only the universe were so accommodating. I sobbed before passing out in a near-dreamless, alcohol-scented slumber.

When I think of getting out, I often go back to that air mattress and my pitiful vodka tears. There's always a "what if" that runs

s simulation between my ears. What if? Could I have done
omething? But when it comes to imagining those scenarios, they
re rather useless. Because I did get out.

The actual process of separating from the military is
raightforward compared to the emotional gymnastics of leaving
behind. The powers that be give you a little slip of paper and
y that you must collect the signatures from just about everyone
n base – from the commanding officer all the way to the dentist.
's the big bureaucratic machine's last chance to give you the run-
round, so they try and make it a literal one. It's annoying, but not
npossible. I got all my signatures in a week, some of which I had
attain with the use of trickery and deception. But by the end, my
aper was filled with the signatures of officers and clerks, each one
cting like individual tumblers in a lock. Everything clicked, and I
w the door crack open.

One of my best friends, Jon Sheldon, gave me an unceremonious
de to the airport on the day I ended my active service. Before I
ent through security, Jon stopped me and put out his hand. He
oked me straight in the eyes and said, "Kacy, you're the best man
ve ever known." I bypassed his hand and gave him a hug. I was
hankful for my sunglasses because my eyes were beginning to leak.
told him the feeling was mutual, and that I loved him. As I walked
way, it didn't feel like a goodbye, though I haven't seen him since.

I took all the end-of-active-service classes they told me to,
ut most of those were on how to fill out a disability claim. My
ompany, Golf Company, had suffered an almost eighty percent
asualty rate in our first deployment, so the information was not
seless to my peers. I had an abundance of blind luck, so I didn't
ave to worry about polishing up a purple heart to pin on my chest.
used to joke with my Marine brothers who weren't as lucky as
was that I was just too fast for the enemy. But truth be told,
here's no running away from combat. You might not carry around

physical scar tissue, but the brain is fully capable of concealing th
deepest lacerations of horror and regret. I got out to be with m
family, and as a result I have two beautiful babies that I'm enjoyin
the hell out of. But my Marine split personality still chimes in fror
time to time to tell me what a coward and fraud I am. He's neve
far away, nor are the faces of the lost. I guess you could say that I'r
always surrounded by Marines.

There's an old bumper sticker that you can see around tow
that says, "Once a Marine, Always a Marine." It's a cliché recruitin
slogan, but like all clichés, the foundation is built on truth. I was
Marine. I am a Marine. You may sign a piece of paper that says yo
can leave the service, but the truth is that you never really get out

22. Kevlar Words

I had been out for a few years, working construction for my dad. I didn't mind the work, but most days when I worked, running a piece of equipment or putting together pipe, I thought about the Marines. I thought about the days when I thought I mattered. When those thoughts came to me, I would press them down as far as I could, hoping that I could just keep moving forward. I put a mask on. A mask that showed a man who had it together, who was better off because of his experiences as a young man. The mask wasn't a complete lie, but it still hid what I needed it to.

Our son, Waylon, was born a month after I got out. He had all the required toes and fingers. He had his mother's eyes and my frown. I wanted better for him than I had, which I think is the standard-issue parental goal. I told myself that this changed everything, that this was my new purpose in life. New marching orders: a life as a husband and father. Most days were better than I thought I deserved. There were moments that made me forget about it all, even if only for a moment. At night when Melissa put our son to bed, when I was truly by myself, I would lose courage. The mask would slide off.

I worked as much as I could, both for the money and to keep my hands busy. There is truth in the old saying that busy hands are happy hands. When I was focused on a task, I could lose myself in it. I longed for the task. I called my Marine friends when I could, trying to keep in contact with as many as possible. The ones that really mattered kept answering the phone; others faded into blurred memories, the final words spoken becoming their only voice in my head. It wasn't rare for a conversation to last over an hour, sometimes two. We poured our frustrations with the civilian world into each other's ears. I paced back and forth during the conversations, filled with an excitement that I don't think many would understand. I didn't have any true friends at home. I had family, which I am eternally grateful for, but all my true friends, the ones that I thought of when I spoke the word, were gone. I could be shoulder to shoulder with people at a concert and still feel helplessly alone. No one knew, and worse, it seemed like no one cared. I tried bringing up the war in conversation with a few people, even my dad and brother, but I always sensed them getting uncomfortable with where the conversation was heading. I chose instead to keep it to myself. All my heroes growing up seemed to always be able to go it alone. I would try.

I self-medicated with alcohol. I knew the trope of the disturbed alcoholic war veteran and found it easy to slide into the well-worn groove of the cliché. People gave me a wide berth. Chasms formed, and for a time I was happy in isolation. I would look out across the distance and be content that others couldn't touch me, that they would never know what I knew. They didn't pay the price for the information like I did, so I felt they didn't deserve a glimpse of the truth. I grew to hate. I hated that people could go on about their days without ever having to look at what was done in their names. I hated that a man living in America could live his entire life without feeling the weight of service. I hated that we shared the same rights and privileges. My thoughts turned bitter and poisonous.

Eventually, I withdrew even from Melissa. I saw her with Waylon and knew that she had found her purpose. I watched as she drifted away, and I never reached out to grab her. We quit talking like we used to. We talked about what needed to get done, bills and chores, and then we went about our duties – Melissa to her life as a new mother, and me to my self-imposed exile. We had always been good at a couple of things that made our relationship work, but the most important was communication. Once I shut that down, everything else began to fail, like the dying organs of a terminal patient. Our history kept us together, our memory of how good it could be.

When Melissa and Waylon went to bed, my drink with dinner turned into half a bottle of vodka by myself. I drank until I was numb, normally until I blacked out. Mostly, I liked to drink so that the swirling, constricting tension I carried around would relax and let me breathe. It worked occasionally, and that's the terrible part. Because that one time it worked, I wanted to go back to it again. Sober, I was in control of myself. I would rarely lose my temper and slide backward into my feral past. But when I was drunk, I found it easy to slide down the hill. Sometimes that slide felt exhilarating; I felt the old rush, the old shot of adrenaline. I would look for violence in those times when I achieved the right levels of drunkenness and nostalgia. I longed for that adrenaline and fear cocktail that used to swell in my youth; occasionally, I found it.

I went to the VA. I lied to Melissa, telling her that I was just going there to see if I could get some of the disability money they were handing out to everyone. My back was a wreck, my knees were shot, and my feet carried the stress fractures of someone who was always trying to prove something to himself. I had a legitimate claim. What I didn't tell her was that I was fucked up. When I was alone, I would cry, careful to wipe my tears before anyone could see. I would pull my hat down low and avoid eye contact so that the pain could remain hidden, right where I liked it. I often felt an irrational rage at the slightest of things. I was ready to burn a building to the ground when things didn't go exactly how I had them preplanned in my head. I went to the VA for help; I was a mess.

I waited for hours in the waiting room to be seen. One waiting room led to another. A series of waiting challenges, where the technique for success involved being able to properly select which magazine to read in which waiting room. After an eight-hour shift of waiting, I was awarded another opportunity to wait in the lobby, after two weeks of practicing at home.

When I finally saw a psychologist, I found it difficult to be honest with him. I was still afraid of showing weakness, afraid of letting anyone know that my façade was just that. I wasn't the invulnerable hero that I had wanted to be. I wasn't a character in a movie or a book. I was human – angry, scared, and flawed.

The psychologist asked me a battery of standardized questions. He didn't try to get to know me, or even get to know what I was involved with in the military. He read his questions off a piece of paper, asking me if I ever thought of hurting myself or someone else. Asking if I had ever blacked out or had a legitimate flashback. Asking if I ever thought about my time over there. Internally, I answered yes to just about every question. I knew what I wanted to tell him, but I kept it to myself. I didn't trust him; I didn't like him. I told him I was angry and that I didn't sleep well. I told him that I was struggling. I was short; he was brief. I walked out of the room after fifteen minutes with prescriptions for four different medications.

I didn't know what they were. I looked a few of them up and realized that I had been prescribed an antipsychotic medication, along with some sleeping pills. I wondered if the man's true rofessional opinion was that I needed a psychopathic blocker, a ill that would curb my appetite for violence. I was scared that he vas right, that maybe I did need the medication. I also wondered this was just his standard prescription to anyone who visited his ffice. The cure-all for what the ex-grunts were bringing back into ie inner cities and suburbs – much easier to medicate than to ommunicate.

I told Melissa the VA was bullshit, and she agreed. The disability noney would have helped, but I didn't want to go back there. I ok the first dose of pills but became paranoid that they would ull my edge, making me a docile lamb, another medicated pack nimal. I threw the pills in the garbage and never went back for iy follow-up. I don't remember getting a phone call to see why I iissed the appointment.

Things got worse. I gained weight – a hundred pounds of veight. My diet was horrible, and my drinking worse. I worked out nnatically but ate and drank my workouts away. I was sliding, and didn't see anything to grab onto.

***

I looked at myself in the mirror, trying to parse out the Marine hat used to look back. I thought those were his eyes, but it was .ard to tell. The rest of him looked like he'd died. The face in the nirror wasn't lean and chiseled by war any longer; it was swollen nd covered in a red beard, some kind of red fungal growth that was ausing the rest of the body to balloon, an allergic reaction to the :ue reality of human nature.

My wife and son slept in the room right next to the bathroom. left the mirror and checked on them. They were just as I had left hem, sleeping peacefully. I remember a small smile on my son's ace, a tiny smirk broadcast from dream world.

I walked back into the bathroom and grabbed my drink off the anity. It was vodka with the tiniest splash of tonic. I had switched from glass fifths to cheap plastic half gallons, and the rubbing alcohol scent from my tumbler reflected this change. I downed my drink, contemplating whether I should make one more, or just get on with it. I decided to stay in front of the mirror. I sat the lowball glass on the faux-marble vanity, startled by how loud it was. I waited, hoping it wasn't loud enough to wake up Melissa. The pause made me think of her. It made me think of what we used to have. The happiness. The passion. It was true love; I was sure of it. And I had fucked it all up. Now we were married strangers. She didn't know who I was anymore, and I didn't care to know who she had become. I thought about my son, about the smile on his face. I thought that maybe the only way he could keep it was if I wasn't around to poison him. I picked up my gun and was comforted by its deadly weight. While everything around me seemed foreign, this felt familiar.

The pistol was a gift from my oldest brother, a Ruger .44 Magnum with a two-and-a-half-inch barrel. It reminded me of the cartoon revolvers from childhood, the ones we watched on VHS tapes. The VHS made me think that old hate was harder to kill than just changing the channel. I thought it was unfortunate that I was using this gun. I worried that my brother would blame himself. But I knew the gun would leave no doubt. I wouldn't be known as someone who had tried and failed. If I was going to do it, I wanted to make people wince when they found out what caliber I used.

I closed my eyes, and the round barrel slid into the indent on my temple. It seemed like the muzzle fit perfectly. I pressed harder, finding a little comfort in the pain. Warm tears ran down my cheeks, a coward's tears, tears that I never once thought I would cry. I had always thought myself the hero, the Odysseus of my own story. But I was just a grunt.

As a child searching for heroic models to aspire to, I never cared about what came after the hero's journey. *The Iliad* ends with warrior's funeral, battle looming on the next day's horizon. Homer never tells us what happens to the lowly grunt who must go home without the adulation of an Odysseus or Diomedes, the warrior who didn't have a kingdom waiting for him, only the monotony of life in the wake of bearing witness to the clash of the gods. This warrior would never have a poet to help him make sense of the sheer dumb luck of survival.

Achilles and Hector died on the field, which in many ways is the easiest way for a warrior to expire. They got to die when they were still the ideal, before age and alcohol could deteriorate them into a faint echo of their armor-clad ferocity. No, Homer gets to skip the afterwards and stay in the throes of us vs them, where life is focused by the will to survive, do or die. But those of us left, who did but didn't die, are waiting for the Homeric spinoff of a peasant spearman who must go back to the fields after turning in his shield, who must raise a family when every thought eventually trails back to the gates of Troy.

I focused on the contrast of my warm tears and the cold barrel pressed into my temple. My finger was straight and off the trigger when I pulled the hammer back. I heard my life's story in that metallic click: here lies yet another victim. I opened my eyes, told myself that if I was going to do it, I was going to force myself to watch. I owed my old self the dignity. I was terrified by the image I saw in the mirror. I was terrified that I was holding the gun, that it wasn't some terrorist in a black ski mask, but me. I had fought so hard to stay alive and now, here I was. I stared past the red-bearded civilian and searched for that Marine. He was a faint outline, but he was there. I focused on the eyes, which was where I could still see him. I picked my finger up, only for a moment, thinking of sliding it to the crescent moon that heralds the long night. I took a breath. Made a decision.

I removed the gun from the groove in my temple and looked at the red ring left there. I pressed the trigger and lowered the hammer, opened the cylinder and unloaded it, placing the hollow point cartridge on the edge of the fake marble. I locked the gun in the safe and stored the ammo.

***

The next morning, I began to put it all down on paper. First, on a yellow legal pad, and then on my computer. I made up the names but told our story. I'm not sure what mechanism was at work, but there was a change. I think just writing the memories down, trying to articulate the feelings, made it somehow more bearable. It gave me the opportunity to put my reality into a digestible narrative that I could make sense out of. I was once told that we all wear packs where we store our stress. Everything gets put in the pack. In the Marine Corps, I had a singular focus – my life – and for the most part, everything fit in the pack manageably. The problem was that I never unloaded it; I kept carrying it around. And when I got out and had to deal with the normal everyday stresses of being a father and a husband, the added weight made my knees buckle. Every page I wrote felt like pounds being lifted from the pack.

I told myself I would write a thousand words a day. I would lock myself in a room and peck at the keyboard until I had my thousand, and when I emerged, I was somehow better for it. Melissa noticed a difference, telling me that she didn't know what I was doing but that I shouldn't ever stop. I began sharing my writing with her. It was easier for me to write than it was to talk. I was insecure when I spoke; I hated my voice, I struggled for words, I shut down. But when I wrote, I felt like I was my best self. When I wrote, I could be who I wanted to be. I could go back and be that Marine who thought he was invincible. I could go back to all my old selves, taking the good and trying my best to understand the bad.

The writing accumulated, and in a couple months I had a

manuscript for a fictional novel about a squad of Marines in Iraq. I knew I wasn't ready to tell the real story, but it felt damn good to get it out in one form or another. After that, I knew I wanted to spend my life with words. Shortly after I finished the book, I enrolled in Eastern Washington University's Creative Writing program where I met a professor who cared. I was still a giant hairy ball of rage, and I found it difficult to sit through the classes where eighteen-year-olds who still lived at home tried to tell me of their struggle. Still, it gave me the opportunity to write. And I found out that those eighteen-year-olds had something to teach me. At first, I thought I had nothing in common with them, that I was their moral superior because of what I had been through. But the more I wrote and the more I thought on it, the more I realized that we were going through the same thing; we were all trying to find out who we wanted to be, and how the written word could help us make sense of that. I was no better than them; I had just made a few different decisions.

I wrote about the palm groves and the IEDs, and I wrote about it in the first-person present tense. I was ready to show the images, but I wasn't ready to try and digest them. The past tense terrified me; the past tense meant that there was space for an attempt at an explanation. My professor noticed this but told me to keep writing. She told me I didn't suck, and that if I worked my ass off, I might have a shot at being a writer. So, I did what I've always done: I threw myself into the work with reckless abandon. She told me that being a good writer meant being a better reader. So, on top of whatever course load she gave me, I forced myself to read two more books a week. I always felt like I had a lot of catching up to do. She saw my earnestness and offered her library to me, letting me borrow books that I should have already read.

Melissa was there the whole time, always my first reader. My writing became a way for us to connect again. A decent story makes a person think about their own, so when Melissa read my work, she felt like she could talk to me about what she had gone through. We had found each other again after years of being lost in the dark. I built a small fire with words and fed it daily with twigs and branches, until the flames were bright and sustainable enough for me to walk away from the fire in search of Melissa.

I hate that this sounds like writing was a cure-all, because it wasn't. I had to take a sabbatical from drinking. I took a year off, cold turkey. I wanted to be able to enjoy a glass of wine with a bloody steak, and after a while that was possible. I dug my running shoes out of storage and began to punish myself on the pavement again. The hours spent on the road gave me time to think; they let me feel the fire in my lungs again. I started looking at my life, not as an affront to my friends who didn't make it home, but as a debt I had to repay by living fully. I owed them that. Melissa and I had another baby, a beautiful redheaded girl named Nora. I owed my kids. I owed my wife. I think it was a combination of all these things that helped me get my shit together. But it was writing that made me realize being a little fucked up is okay, and it's okay to ask for help. I thought I could process all my trauma on my own, that I could carry the weight of it for the rest of my life, but I was wrong. I needed to unload my pack.

It's always filled my heart with grief that I lost my copy of *The Iliad* in Iraq. It was something that I wanted to keep with me forever, a talisman that offered me protection and inspiration. When I lost it, I felt like a small chunk of me was lost. I worried that maybe it was the best of me I'd left in Iraq with the book.

I know that the boy from Spangle who went to Iraq wasn't the same as the man who came home. He died over there in an explosion, or maybe from a sniper's bullet. I tried dragging the boy around with me for a while, a corpse tied to a rope. And the strain almost killed me. But I was able to cut the rope, to turn the body

ver to those who handle and wash such things. With help, I built
funeral pyre made of sentences and paragraphs, ignited it with the
d rage, and felt the fire not as heat that would sear or singe, but as
warmth that I now carry in my bones.

Acknowledgments

First, I would like to thank my wife, who was coerced int reading this thing about ten times. She was always there to kee pushing me forward. Most of what I wrote, I wrote directly to he hoping I could make her smile, laugh, or maybe cry a little.

Thank you to my children, who have put up with having combat grunt as a father for all these years. It's not always easy.

I also want to thank my parents. My mom gave me the gift c reading when I was very young and was always there to help me as struggled my way through high school English class. Also, my da who taught me that the secret to success in life was putting you work boots on every day and getting after it.

Also, to my brothers, who tormented me when I was a chil and helped turn me into the freak that I am today.

I've had a great many teachers in my life, and I owe them all but none more than my first creative writing professor, Rachel Too If not for her pokes and prods, and all-around tough love, I neve would have written this book. Hers is a voice I hear in my hea every time I sit down to write. I am eternally grateful for her takin the time out of her life to give a giant hairy grunt like me a chance.

I also want to thank Latah Books for seeing that I had a story to tell and giving me the space to tell it. Jon Gosch and Kevin Breen have been a joy to work with and gave me enough room to breathe as a writer, but were tough enough to rein me in when I started to go off the rails.

Lastly, I want to thank the immortal American grunt, that filthy bastard who always answers when called. He is the best and worst of us, and we are damn lucky to have him on our side.

About the Author

Kacy was born in Spokane and raised in Spangle, Washington, a small farming community that clings to the edge of the Palouse. Kacy joined the Marine Corps infantry directly out of high school and deployed twice to Iraq as an Infantry machine gunner with Second Battalion, Third Marines from 2005-2009. His work has appeared in *The New York Times*, *Zero-Dark-Thirty* literary journal, as well as the *SOFLETE* website.

Made in the USA
Las Vegas, NV
13 December 2023

82734414R00156